lamingtons and lemongrass

lamingtons and lemongrass

a whole world of food and
recipes from around Australia

Maeve O'Meara & Joanna Savill

ALLEN & UNWIN

The authors would like to thank *New Woman* and Louise
Lister for permission to reproduce photographs on
pp. 133 and 135, and the *Sydney Morning Herald* to
reproduce photographs on pp. 147 and 163.

First published in 1998 by
Allen & Unwin
9 Atchison Street, St Leonards, 1590 Australia
Phone: (61 2) 8425 0100
Fax: (61 2) 9906 2218
E-mail: frontdesk@allen-unwin.com.au
Web: http://www.allen-unwin.com.au

National Library of Australia
Cataloguing-in-Publication entry:

O'Meara, Maeve, 1960–
Lamingtons and lemongrass: a whole world of food and
recipes from around Australia

Includes index.
ISBN 1 86448 332 6

1. Cookery, Australian. I. Savill, Joanna, 1957-.
II. Title.

Designed by Phil Campbell
Set in Bembo 11/14pt by Lynne Hamilton
Printed and bound by MacPhersons Printing Group,
Maryborough

10 9 8 7 6 5 4 3 2 1

Contents

Introduction

Welcome to our first cookbook. *Lamingtons and Lemongrass* — the title says it all — how far we've come and what exotic flavours we've incorporated into our food, while still enjoying the old favourites like lamingtons and home-baked bread and a good old Irish stew.

This book is a collection of favourite recipes from people we've met in the years we have been exploring Australia's culinary horizons, people who may have been born in sixty different countries but who are united in their passion for good food. Through them we take you from East Timor to Eastern Europe, southern China to the southern states of America, North Africa to North Wales, crossing continents and island-hopping too via Mauritius, Singapore and Fiji.

With such a mixture of cuisines, we've tried to make this book as user-friendly as possible. Read it, but above all, use it, mixing and matching in the best Australian multi-culinary tradition! Create a combination of antipasti and mezze from around the world, combine whole fish, barbecued meats or a roast chicken with a Vietnamese dipping sauce, a Persian cucumber dip or a Moroccan salad. Enjoy delectable lamingtons with a perfect cup of tea, instructions courtesy of the Country Women's Association on one hand and someone who grew up amid the tea plantations of Darjeeling on the other!

Herein lie the secrets of today's Australian cuisine — the great melting pot that it is, with our fresh produce and our love of experimenting. These recipes can open some new worlds to you. Most don't need any special equipment, are relatively easy to assemble and are a joy to sit down to.

Happy cooking and happy eating!

Mezze/
antipasti

Mezze/Meza/Antipasti/Tapas

The idea of stimulating the appetite with a selection of small tastes 'before the meal' (the literal translation of 'antipasto') is a particularly Mediterranean phenomenon. At tables and tavernas from Spain to the Middle East you will sit and nibble small tastes of fish, cold cuts, tiny meat balls, creamy hummos, vine-leaf parcels, eggplant in more guises than you ever dreamed of, char-grilled vegetables and fresh or cured cheeses. And where drinking is not out of favour for religious reasons, enjoy a few shots of arak (clear aniseed spirit known as raki in Turkey and not unlike Greek ouzo, French pastis or Spanish chinchon).

The Spanish have turned tapas into a social ritual that can extend into the late hours of the evening. In Italy it's rare to find an eatery that doesn't sport a bright antipasto display of olives, marinated and char-grilled vegetables shiny with olive oil and sweet with garlic, perhaps some smoked meats and chunks of frittata. The antipasto table is a show of abundance, arousing the tastebuds and the eyes. In Turkey you may sit for many hours over little meat or vegetable parcels stuffed with rice and herbs; tangy, refreshing salads in iridescent colours — sunset-orange carrot, emerald-green parsley, neon-pink beetroot, creamy-white cucumber and yoghurt; little zucchini fritters, and eggplant, eggplant and more eggplant. And

that is before you even contemplate moving on to a meat or fish course of finely marinated kebabs and grills.

In the Middle East, however, it is the Lebanese who have the reputation of meza masters. In the best establishments you may be offered a choice of more than one hundred appetisers. There will be much-loved favourites like smoky eggplant baba ghannouj, mashed chickpeas (hummos) and runny sesame paste with a drizzle of oil and lemon (tahina) but they are merely old standards and pale into insignificance beside a variety of kibbe— herbed lamb mince rolls, baked or fried, or even served raw with burghul, onion and chilli. Minty salads, spicy tomato and chilli purees, cured yoghurts and fresh cheeses like labneh and shenklish, little plates of offal, nuts, plates of wild herbs like rocca (a kind of rocket), oregano and thyme … The aim is to showcase the range and breadth of the chef's talent — appetisers as an art form. You could be forgiven for thinking there was no need for a main meal … but then you would not have understood the lingering, palate-teasing culture of the meza.

Turkish Carrot Dip

This is a very simple and brightly coloured dip — healthy too! The recipe comes from our colleague Aynur Acan, who works for SBS Radio in Melbourne. Serve this with a couple of contrasting coloured dips and lots of 'continental' parsley garnish for added effect.

Makes one large bowl

250g carrots, peeled and grated
1 tablespoon vegetable oil
½ cup natural Greek/Bulgarian-style yoghurt
crushed garlic and salt to taste

▮ Fry the carrots in oil for 5 to 10 minutes until tender (keep stirring them and do it on a low heat). Blend the cooled mixture gently with thick natural yoghurt, crushed garlic and a little salt.

Ful (Sudanese Beans)

Made with small brown beans and typically associated with Egypt, ful is a dish popular across the whole of Africa, from North to South. Each country serves it in a slightly different way. This recipe is inspired by a Sudanese version served in Adelaide's Racuba restaurant by its owner/chef, Sam Eltahir. Ful beans are found in any good 'Middle Eastern' grocery — Greek or Lebanese. They are also available in tins — though not quite as nice, they will do as a base. If using tinned beans, omit the soaking and cooking steps and simply crush them with olive oil, etc.

Makes one large bowl

500g dried ful beans (soaked overnight in water to cover)
olive oil
2 cloves garlic, crushed
lemon juice
cumin
salt and pepper to taste
150g fetta cheese, cubed
parsley, finely chopped to garnish

▮ Drain the soaked beans and place in a saucepan with fresh water. Boil them gently until tender (this will take several hours, so don't panic!) When ready, drain and cool. Take half the beans and crush them with olive oil, garlic, lemon juice, cumin, salt and pepper to taste. The mixture should be reasonably sloppy, certainly not dry and pasty. Then gently mix through the remaining beans and cubes of fetta cheese. Drizzle a little extra olive oil on top and sprinkle with parsley.

Baba Ghannouj

Everyone loves this classic eggplant dip, which is enjoyed all over the Middle East — from Lebanon and Israel through to North Africa. The really important thing is to make sure the eggplant is sufficiently blackened, to give this dip its unique smoky taste.

While you can do this on the stove or under the griller, a barbecue is even better for this rather messy task. As Melbourne-based Lebanese cook Abla Amad tells us, back home eggplant were always grilled over little open fires in front of people's homes. She still remembers the wafting smell of charring eggplant and the little gusts of aromatic smoke rising from the fires.

Abla Amad

Makes one large bowl
3 medium-sized eggplant (shiny and firm ones only!)
2 cloves garlic
salt to taste
3–4 tablespoons tahina (sesame paste)
lemon juice (about half a large lemon's worth)
paprika to garnish (optional)

■ Place the eggplant under the griller or blacken them directly in the flames on the top of your stove.
■ Turn them frequently to ensure all the skin burns and the bitter juices inside start dripping out. Don't stop until each eggplant is black and charred. Wash them thoroughly to remove the skin and juices.
■ Pulverise them in a blender with crushed garlic and salt, then gradually add tahina and lemon juice. Keep tasting until you think it's right. It should be smooth and firm enough to sit on a piece of spongy pide bread! Garnish with a little paprika for colour.

Persian Yoghurt and Cucumber Dip

This is the simplest dip in the world to make and one of the freshest tastes you can add to a meal during summertime. This recipe is from Teheran expatriate, chef Jimmy Ghafari. It's not dissimilar to Greek tzadziki although the dried mint gives a special flavour. The texture is also a little different as the yoghurt is not hung and drained overnight.

Makes 3–4 cups
1 litre natural yoghurt
2 Lebanese cucumbers, chopped very fine
2 teaspoons salt
1½ tablespoons dried mint

■ Stir the yoghurt for a minute or two with a wooden spoon. Add other ingredients and mix well. Serve immediately.

Eggplant and Mint Dip

Another Persian recipe from Jimmy Ghafari, who brought all his recipes with him from Iran to Australia twenty years ago. This is served with sprigs of fresh mint, sliced onion and Lebanese or Persian bread. 'With a sip of wine or, even better, arak, it's fantastic,' says Jimmy. The warm mint and garlic topping adds a distinctive flavour that really sets this dip apart and beautifully complements the creamy, smoky eggplant flavours.

Makes 3 cups
4 eggplant, cut lengthwise
1 onion, finely chopped
vegetable oil
½ cup hot water

salt to taste
1 teaspoon ground turmeric
2 tablespoons sour cream
1 tablespoon butter

Topping:
2 tablespoons crushed dried mint
½ tablespoon crushed garlic
4 tablespoons vegetable oil

■ Sprinkle eggplant liberally with salt and stand aside for an hour.
■ Pat dry and grill both sides until the skin blackens. Once they cool slightly, remove the skin and process pulp in a blender.
■ Fry the onion in a little oil until it turns golden and add to the pureed eggplant. Add the hot water, salt to taste and turmeric. Pour into a saucepan with the sour cream and butter and cook over a low heat for 1 hour, stirring occasionally.

To serve:
■ Fry the mint and garlic in oil for 10 to 15 seconds then drizzle over the top of eggplant mixture. Serve with fresh mint, sliced onion and rounds of Lebanese or Persian bread. This can be served hot or cold.

Mrs Vatsikopoulos's Tzadziki (Yoghurt and Cucumber Dip)

Victoria Vatsikopoulos was born in north-western Greece and now lives in Adelaide. From an early age she learned to prepare dishes in the simple peasant-style of her native region. This is a family recipe that is delicious and easy to make.

Makes 3 cups
1 200g tub natural yoghurt
1 large cucumber, peeled and grated
4 cloves garlic, crushed
½ tablespoon olive oil
1 teaspoon white vinegar
salt to taste
white pepper

■ Take yoghurt and strain overnight in cheesecloth. This is to make sure all the water is removed. Squeeze out the moisture from the cucumber in cheesecloth and then again in the palm of your hand. Mix garlic with the yoghurt and cucumber. Add olive oil, white vinegar and a pinch of salt. Mix the ingredients well with a large spoon until all the lumps have gone. Add a spray of white pepper and taste.
■ You may want to add some more vinegar or salt to taste but don't overdo it. It's ready to eat with crusty bread or pita or as a nice accompaniment to lamb.

Rattlesnake's Black Bean and Roasted Garlic Dip

American-born Victor Pisapia is a chef who specialises in the hot wild flavours of South Western American cuisine, perfecting his repertoire through a string of restaurants he set up back home in Delaware and cooking across the States from Key West, Florida to New York City. This dip, says Victor, is great for a light and tasty snack or a perfect lead-in to dinner served with a margarita!
Note: Chipotle chilli is a smoked jalapeno and is found in tins at any gourmet specialist store.

Serves 4 to 6 (Makes 3 cups)

2 cups black beans

½ cup white onion, diced

1 fresh jalapeno chilli, seeded and diced

½ red capsicum

½ bay leaf

½ teaspoon ground cumin

3 litres water

salt to taste

1 whole garlic bulb, roasted

50g cream cheese

1 1/2 tablespoons chipotle chilli puree

◾ Sort the beans by hand to remove small stones, then clean under running water.

◾ Combine the black beans, onion, jalapeno, red capsicum, bay leaf and cumin in water in a stockpot and bring to boil. Reduce heat to low and simmer uncovered for about 1½ hours until beans are soft. Add water to beans while cooking to keep beans immersed. Season with salt when done.

◾ To prepare the garlic bulb for roasting, remove the excess papery skin but leave the bulb whole. Cut off the top 0.5cm of each bulb, exposing the tops of the individual garlic cloves. Place the garlic bulb in aluminium foil and drizzle olive oil on top. Wrap tightly and bake in 180°C oven for 1 hour or until soft. Allow to cool slightly, then squeeze out the buttery cooked garlic.

◾ Drain the cooked beans in a colander. To make the puree, combine the cooked beans, roasted garlic, cream cheese and chipotle puree in a processor and blend until smooth. You can serve this with corn tortilla chips or fresh vegetables as a dip. You can also refrigerate it for up to 2 days. Serve chilled.

Auntie Koula's Skordalia (Garlic and Potato Dip)

Auntie Koula is known among the Greek community of Adelaide for her delicious garlic and potato dip. It goes beautifully with any lamb dish, works as a starter with a selection of crunchy vegetables or can be simply dolloped onto crusty bread. With the power of all that garlic, it's guaranteed to ward off any ills. Skordalia keeps well in the refrigerator for up to a week.

Makes 2–3 cups

12 cloves garlic, crushed

salt

500g potatoes

½ espresso cup olive oil

¼ cup white vinegar

◾ Combine garlic and salt. Boil potatoes. Gradually mix them in a blender with a mixture of olive oil and white vinegar, as well as the garlic.

Elizabeth Marchand's Cheese Dip

Elizabeth Marchand grew up in a small country town in Bern, Switzerland, working on a local farm during her school holidays and cooking from an early age, before completing an apprenticeship and working in Switzerland, London and Germany. She and husband Frank came to Australia where he took up a job as master cheesemaker in Tasmania. 'We came for two years and we're still here after twenty,' she laughs. Frank and Elizabeth have a large dairy farm in the rolling green hills outside Launceston and make a range of award-winning authentic Swiss-style cheeses. True to the couple's origins, they've called their business Heidi Farm Cheese.

Makes 2 cups

Low-fat cottage cheese
1 clove garlic
½ finely sliced red onion
8 anchovy fillets
2 shallots, finely sliced
freshly ground black pepper
crusty loaf of bread

■ Gently mix together cheese, garlic, onion, anchovies, shallots and pepper. Spread on crusty bread and enjoy!

Labneh (Lebanese Fresh Cheese Dip)

Labneh is an integral part of Lebanese eating— a breakfast food usually made with yoghurt or fresh cheese. 'But what's to stop you using something else, like goat's cheese?' asks George Haddad, a former restaurateur from Tasmania who takes great delight in playing with the culinary customs of his native Lebanon. A firm believer that the cuisines of Australia belong to all of us, and that they are ours to adopt and adapt, George and his wife Anne Ripper are legendary for their amazing Sunday lunches. These feasts that go on for many hours and feature up to twenty different dishes, all Middle Eastern in name and flavour, but with variations and twists. This labneh is one of those — perfect as a dip or as an accompaniment to fish, meat or vegetables.

Makes one large bowl

5g fresh thyme
5g fresh oregano
500g fresh chevre, cut into 1cm cubes
50ml olive oil
freshly ground black pepper and salt to taste

■ Grind herbs in the food processor. Add chevre slowly while drizzling in the olive oil. Season with pepper and salt. Take care not to overbeat the mixture or it will become too runny.

Mary's Tarama (Fish Roe Dip)

Whenever there's a family gathering, newsreader Mary Kostakidis is in charge of the tarama—or taramosalata as most of us know it. The trick, Mary says, is in choosing the right ingredients. These are a day-old Vienna loaf, salt-preserved fish roe ('not the canned variety') and olive oil and lemon to the right consistency. It's not a quick and easy task, there is lots of soaking and squeezing and patient beating involved—and 'never use a blender', Mary warns. 'A friend of mine lent me one once and it completely ruined the tarama. The texture of the fish eggs was completely destroyed and the whole thing was full of air.' It's back to the hand-held beater from now on.

Makes one large bowl

1 day-old Vienna loaf
a 'handful' of tarama (not the canned type, but a scoop from the salt barrel — any Greek delicatessen will know how much!)
1 glass of olive oil
juice of 4–5 lemons

■ Grate the crust of the Vienna loaf to a fine powder (on the finest setting on your grater). 'This is the most moreish part,' says Mary, 'and you can't have tarama without it!' Cut the rest of the loaf into slices and soak quickly in water, by running under a tap. Squeeze out the moisture. Leave the finely grated crust meanwhile in a bowl with a little water for about 5 to 8 minutes, mixing it around so that it absorbs the water and does not form clumps. Then squeeze it free of as much liquid as possible.

■ Place the damp bread and roe in a bowl along with most of the oil and lemon. Mix gently, then begin beating with an electric beater. The object is to break up the clumps of bread and produce a smooth consistency without losing the texture of the fish roe. Taste and add oil and lemon to suit. 'The idea is to get it to the point where you want to keep on eating it!' says Mary.

Eggplant and Peanut Dip

This very simple and yummy dip comes from the Sudanese idea of simple food and an economy of flavours in one dish. Its creator Tahir Malik was born in Sudan, in the capital Khartoum. An engineer by training, Tahir co-founded Adelaide's Racuba eatery in 1984, then went on to open Babanusa — an airy, modern restaurant serving a variety of Sudanese and other African dishes. 'It's not too hard,' says Tahir modestly. 'After all, when you cook in Sudan you always cook for lots of people because you don't know who might be coming to visit you. The same principle applies in a restaurant.'

Makes one generous bowl
½ cup raw peanuts
salt, pepper and a dash of cumin

2 large eggplant, sliced in rounds
1 clove fresh garlic, diced finely
chilli, lemon juice to taste

■ Roast the peanuts in their skins until the skins loosen and come away. Remove the skins and grind the nuts in a blender or mortar and pestle. Season with a little salt and pepper, a dash of cumin, and if dry, a little ghee (clarified butter).

■ Salt and drain eggplant for around 1 hour. Rinse and dry, then fry in oil until soft. While it is still hot, add fresh garlic 'so that the garlic cooks a little into the eggplant', says Tahir. Season with chilli, salt and pepper and lemon juice. Add the peanut paste and serve with Lebanese-style bread.

■ The same dip can be made using zucchini — peeled and cut lengthwise before frying, or steamed sweet potato or pumpkin. And don't tell Tahir, but you can use ready-made peanut butter!

Pumpkin and Sesame Dip

'Why make your stomach confused?' says Tahir Malik, stressing the importance of using just a few simple flavours at a time. 'If you put too many different things in one recipe, it won't know what to do and it will give you a pain.'

Makes one generous bowl
½ cup of sesame seeds, roasted
1 teaspoon freshly grated ginger, or fresh ground ginger (it must be fresh though, says Tahir)
300g pumpkin, peeled and steamed until soft (boiling adds too much extra water)

■ Roast and crush the sesame seeds to a paste, adding the ginger at the end. Mash pumpkin and mix in the sesame paste.

■ This can also be made with tahini — ready-made sesame paste. You will only need about 1 tablespoonful.

Aynur's Turkish Chicken Liver

Aynur Acan, Melbourne-based broadcaster originally from Turkey, is responsible for this 'mezze' recipe. A clever alternative to pate, with a Middle Eastern bite (thanks to the sumac spice — a reddish-brown pepper with an agreeable lemony taste).

Makes one medium bowl
2 handfuls of chicken livers
seasoned flour for dusting
vegetable oil
1 onion, sliced finely
sumac spice

Cut the chicken livers into small pieces and wash well in hot water. Pat dry. Roll in a little salted flour, one by one, then fry them in vegetable oil. Serve them with finely sliced onion and sumac.

Abla's Marinated Eggplants

Pickles are an integral part of any mezze plate — with dips, olives, bread and salads. Abla Amad, originally from Lebanon, makes these tasty little eggplants for her special customers and her family. The trick is waiting until they are ready before devouring them. They are great with Lebanese or Mediterranean dips, or even a simple salad of tomatoes and olive oil, or perhaps a little fetta or goat's cheese.

Makes about 15 pickles
1kg baby eggplants
1 cup walnuts, finely chopped
2 cloves garlic, crushed and diced
green and red chilli to taste
salt
400ml white wine vinegar
400ml water
1½ tablespoons salt

■ Cut the stalk end of the eggplants, but without cutting right through so that it remains attached. Place in boiling water for a couple of minutes. Drain and cool immediately in cold water. Strain. Cut an incision down the middle of each eggplant without slicing them through. Leave them to drain for a day.

■ Make a paste of walnuts, garlic, green and red chilli and a pinch of salt. Fill the opening in each eggplant with mixture.

■ Place eggplants firmly in a preserve jar and leave for a day to drain. Pour off any liquid that is formed in the bottom of the jar. Then, for a 1-litre jar, mix equal parts water and white vinegar with 1½ tablespoons salt, cover the eggplant, then seal with about 2cm of oil.

■ Ready to enjoy after 2 to 3 weeks.

An Antipasto Platter

While the recipes in this chapter have been chosen as perfect bites for getting a meal started, we have plenty of other suggestions for putting together a mouth-watering selection of 'pre-dinner' tastes.

Try serving chunks of Victoria's frittata or some Polish stuffed eggs. Char-grilled vegetables like escalivada or pickles like Abla's baby eggplant make a nice contrast to small squares of bush tomato tart, a selection of salads or even some sushi rolls and oysters with barbecue sauce. And salsas and sauces of all descriptions will add a whole new dimension to freshly sliced raw vegetables like cucumber and carrot, or even a few perfect slices of cos lettuce or Chinese cabbage.

Gabrielle Kervella's Marinated Cheeselets

This tempting idea comes from the award-winning cheese craftswoman Gabrielle Kervella, of Gidgegannup in Western Australia.

Quantity as desired
a quantity of small goat's cheese rounds (preferably Kervella's of course!)
olive oil
1 bay leaf
a few sprigs of fresh thyme
a few sprigs of rosemary
¼ clove garlic
a handful of juniper berries
a handful of black peppercorns
whole chillies to taste

■ The cheeses must be dry, not moist — at least a week old. Leave them for 2 weeks uncovered in the fridge, then scrape or wipe off any mould. Place the cheeses in a jar and cover with olive oil. Add to the oil a bay leaf, fresh thyme, a little rosemary and a quarter clove of garlic, plus a handful of juniper berries, peppercorns and chilli.

■ The jar should be covered with breathing papers, not tightly sealed.

■ Resist trying the cheeses for at least 2 to 3 weeks. The oil is wonderful for cooking or in salads and the cheeses themselves can be enjoyed as they emerge from the marinade, or grilled. They puff up beautifully thanks to their new oily coat.

■ The cheeses are also good spread on fresh country bread, sprinkled with lemon juice and cracked pepper and grilled until really warm.

Soup

Stock

There is chicken stock and chicken stock. While the principle remains clear — simmering chicken or chicken bones in water with a selection of herbs, spices and vegetables, — what you put into it can determine how you end up using it.

For Chinese and Asian-inspired recipes, try Sydney chef Kylie Kwong's method — covering a 1.2kg corn-fed chicken with about 2 litres of water, adding a bruised 8cm knob of ginger, 1 medium Spanish onion and 4 or 5 shallot stems.

An Italian-style stock can be made by simmering a few chicken carcasses, with one peeled onion, two celery sticks, a couple of carrots, a potato, a little parsley and salt. Allow it to cool, pour through a colander to remove the bones and vegetables, refrigerate it overnight and you'll find the fat solidifies on the top for easy skimming.

Vietnamese chicken stock always has plenty of ginger in the base, a pinch of all-spice and a fragrant clove of star anise while the Thais add lemongrass and lime leaves. Better still, try one of the prepacked stock mixes sold in Asian grocery stores. They are full of all sorts of herbs, spices, roots and interesting bits and will give your broth all the flavour it needs and perhaps surprise you into the bargain.

The French cook a classic bouillon with plenty of extra giblets and vegetables such as leeks and potatoes — and let it bubble away for several hours. But for the mother of all chicken soups, check out our recipe for Jewish 'penicillin'.

Lemon Consomme

'This mightn't sound much but it's an amazingly refreshing and invigorating start to a meal,' says translator/editor Kate Johnson, who learned this from a friend during her years studying languages at Cambridge. Kate's languages are Spanish and French but the origins of this recipe are Portuguese — ever since she discovered Spanish and French food, Kate has run a pretty multicultural kitchen.

■ Use a good, strong consomme of beef, veal or chicken. (You can make your own by simmering meat and vegetables, reducing it considerably and clarifying by straining and adding egg whites. Alternatively, try a can of Campbell's beef consomme!) When almost ready to serve, heat the strained, de-glazed consomme and add two to three finely sliced rounds of lemon (with the peel still on) into the soup. One good-sized lemon is about enough for four bowls. Gently poach the slices in the broth for a few minutes, then serve. Dust soup with a garnish of finely chopped parsley if you like. Don't use the chunky ends of the lemons, and don't let the consomme simmer for too long after adding the lemon slices as it can get bitter.

Cambodian Samlor Mchou Youn (Spicy Sour Soup)

This recipe is from Kim Ley Chau, chef and owner of Sydney's Angkor Wat restaurant. He came to Australia sixteen years ago, after surviving the horrors of Pol Pot's 'killing fields'. He lost two brothers and a sister and almost died of starvation during that terrible time.

While he'd trained and worked as an electrician, Kim had always remembered watching his grandfather cooking. 'He cooked for the love of it and I suppose some of that love lives on in me,' he says. 'We lived with my grandparents so it's something I remember very well.' Since opening his restaurant, Kim has introduced the delicious fresh tastes of his homeland to many Sydney diners. Samlor mchou is one of the most popular Cambodian dishes, fragrant with fresh herbs and with a delicious sweet and sour flavour.

Serves 4

1.5 litres chicken stock
8 slices galangal
8 kaffir lime leaves
1 stem lemongrass, cut into half and crushed
4 tablespoons lemon juice
2 tablespoons fish sauce
1 tablespoon sugar
1 tablespoon chilli paste (or a fresh chilli cut into halves)
4 king prawns, peeled and deveined with tails intact
4 green mussels, meat only
4 good-sized scallops
100g calamari pieces
100g good-sized fish steak
2 tomatoes, cut into cubes
½ pineapple, cut into cubes

Garnishes:
1 fresh chilli, finely sliced
fresh coriander leaves
shallots
sweet basil leaves
fried slices garlic

■ Bring chicken stock to boil and add galangal, kaffir lime leaves and lemongrass and boil rapidly for several minutes.

Dur-é Dara

■ Turn down heat to low and add lemon juice, fish sauce, sugar and chilli paste. Stir and simmer for another minute.

■ Add seafood, tomato and pineapple and cook another 3 minutes, being careful not to overcook. Taste to see if you need extra lemon juice, fish sauce or chilli paste. Serve garnished with chilli, coriander, shallots, sweet basil leaves and fried garlic.

Laksa Lemak

This recipe was given to us by Melbourne restaurateur and culinary legend Dur-é Dara who developed it with her friend Honey Koh. Honey comes from the Malaysian city of Ipoh and has worked as a cook in a number of eateries around Melbourne. These days, however, the recipe is in the hands of chef John Mackay at Dur-é's Nudel restaurant in the city.

While every Malaysian state has its own style of laksa, Dur-é tells us, 'this particular dish is exactly right, because it's Ipoh-style — which is where I am from, too!' The flavours of laksa, a fierce, aromatic broth eaten with noodles, can vary from the tamarind-tangy Assam laksa to the dense, coconut-creamy laksa lemak. ('Lemak' signifies a rich, coconut flavour — common to the southern states of Malaysia and the Straits-born Chinese population, known as Nonyas.)

'Basically,' says Dur-é, 'the beauty of this dish is that it has two bases, a curry base and a chicken stock base. That's what gives it its "high and low tones". It's also hawker food and recipes go down from family to family.'

Serves 8
Curry Laksa:
6 onions

7 cloves garlic

1 thumb-sized piece ginger, sliced finely

4 stalks lemongrass, chopped finely

½ cup Malaysian curry powder (mild)

2 tablespoons belachan powder (dried shrimp paste)

2 tablespoons paprika

¾ tablespoon chilli powder

1 cup vegetable oil

5.5 litres of good chicken stock

4 x 60g packets dried coconut powder

2 400ml cans coconut cream

1 tablespoon sugar

¼ cup salt

■ Slowly puree the onion, garlic, ginger and lemongrass in a food processor, starting with the onions as they are the wettest and help in pureeing the rest. Be sure the mixture is finely broken down and that there is no trace of lemongrass fibre.

■ Combine the curry powder, belachan, paprika and chilli powder and add to the pureed onion and garlic mix. Heat the oil in a large pot and add the paste, cooking until the paste separates from the oil and it becomes fragrant. This can take about 25 minutes.

■ When the paste is cooked, add chicken stock and simmer gently for 1 hour.

■ Mix 2 packets of coconut powder to 1 can of coconut cream. Add the liquid to the laksa stock and bring it to the boil to thicken the broth. Reduce heat to a simmer and add the remaining 2 packets of coconut powder and second can of coconut cream. Do not reboil the mix as it will curdle. Season with sugar and salt.

Suggested additions:

2 500g bags of hokkien noodles

1 100g packet rice vermicelli, soaked and drained

4 handfuls bean shoots

½ packet pre-fried tofu (you can fry your own in hot oil, tofu will crisp quite quickly)

250g green beans, sliced and blanched

Garnish:

½ cup crispy fried shallots

½ cup sliced spring onions

1 bunch spicy Asian mint

Seafood:

8 prawns, cooked and peeled

16 scallops

16 clams

½ loaf of prepackaged fishcake, sliced

1kg mussels, steamed open and removed from their shells

Meat:

8 slices of steamed chicken breast

16 small pieces of barbecue pork

1 cup green Chinese vegetable, blanched

■ Reheat noodles and bean shoots for a few seconds in boiling water and add to bowls. Reheat other selected ingredients, once more by plunging them briefly into boiling water. Arrange in bowls.

■ When everything has been placed in the bowls, pour over boiling broth. Garnish with crispy shallots, spring onion and mint leaves.

Tom Yum Goong (Hot Sour Prawn Soup)

There's a perception that all fast food is not quite as fabulous or nutritious as something that takes much longer to prepare, but in the case of spice mixtures and pastes that are the basis for many Asian recipes, the prepackaged versions are often just as good as you'd make yourself, if not better. And it's refreshing to know that this 'short cut' recipe for tom yum goong comes direct from two Thai home cooks — you still get the authentic flavour without all the work. Thanks to our Thai friends Maow Krungvong and Chris Panasbodi.

Serves 4

prepackaged tom yum paste (or make a broth by boiling prawn heads in 1.5 litres of water for 20 minutes and add to a spice paste of garlic, coriander and ginger)

2 whole fresh chillies (if you like it hot!)

a stick of lemongrass, chopped

a handful of chopped, fresh coriander leaves

4 kaffir lime leaves

8–12 green prawns, shelled and deveined (leave heads on)

2 tablespoons lemon juice or tamarind

1 tablespoon fish sauce

few drops nam prik

■ Using any good prepackaged tom yum paste as a base (see, even the Thais cheat!), add hot water, fresh whole chillies, lemongrass, coriander and kaffir lime leaves. Boil for 10 minutes, drop in prawns and, when cooked (after a couple of minutes only) add lemon juice or tamarind, fish sauce (nam pla — also available commercially) and a few drops of nam prik.

Greek Egg and Lemon Soup

If you've been brought up in a Greek family or nursed while sick by a Greek friend, you'll know the ultimate pick-me-up is tangy avgolemono or egg and lemon soup. The good news is that it's easy to make too — this recipe is from Greek-born Helen Manikakis who brought up three children with it and now has a new generation coming through ready to appreciate her culinary flair.

Serves 4–6
1 whole fresh chicken
1 teaspoon salt
coarsely ground pepper
8 tablespoons rice
1½ to 2 lemons, freshly squeezed
2 eggs

■ Place chicken in a large pot and cover with water. Bring to boil and skim froth from surface water as it simmers. (If you don't spoon it out, the stock will have to be strained, either with a fine sieve or cheesecloth.)
■ The chicken is ready when it's pierced easily by a fork. Remove the chicken from the water, cut into serving pieces, place on a platter and season with salt and coarsely ground pepper. Put aside and serve with the soup.
■ Pour out 3 cups of the stock and set aside to cool. Put rice into the remaining stock and boil. Either with a hand-held mixer or blender, mix the eggs until very frothy. Pour in the lemon juice and continue to mix. While still mixing, gently pour the cooled stock into the egg and lemon mixture (slowly — about half a cup at a time).
■ Finally pour the blended mixture into the stock and rice and mix thoroughly.
■ Serve the soup separately in bowls, with a platter of the chicken that can be cut up and put into the soup if desired. Add cracked pepper, and serve with a basketful of crusty bread and some extra lemon wedges for those who want a more tangy soup.

Chicken Soup with Matzo Balls

Some call this sort of chicken soup 'Jewish penicillin', others the 'wonder drug'. This recipe is guaranteed to cure everything from the flu to a broken heart — well, that's what we're told. It has been handed down the generations to Danielle Charak, head of the SBS's Yiddish radio broadcasting team in Melbourne.
For the chicken stock cubes, the chicken fat substitute (Jenny's Schmalz brand) and the matzo meal in the recipe, Danielle suggests trying kosher supermarkets. The chicken and chicken bits are available from kosher butchers — the extra 'bits' are the difference between a good chicken soup and a sublime experience. Matzo balls, incidentally, are especially eaten during Pesach or Passover.

Danielle says that when this is well prepared it's a delicious and satisfying soup for cold days or when you're feeling weary. 'Perfect the recipe through experience,' she advises. 'The more you make it, the better you will get at it. Do not lose heart if your first attempt fails and the balls fall apart. Try again. It is not difficult. Good luck — the soup turns out differently in the hands of each cook!'

Serves 4–6

Soup:

½ boiler chicken
6 giblets, cleaned
small piece of top rib
3 pairs of chicken feet
3 large bunches celery, including leaves, washed
1 medium parsnip, peeled
2 medium carrots, peeled
1 large leek, washed and trimmed thoroughly
few sprigs dill
3 large chicken stock cubes
salt to taste

Matzo Balls:

2 eggs
½ teaspoon salt
a dash freshly ground black pepper
4 tablespoons melted chicken fat (a substitute product called Jenny's Schmalz is available in Jewish stores)
1 cup coarse matzo meal

To prepare the soup:

■ In a large stockpot place the chicken, giblets, top rib, chicken feet and 3.5 litres of water, and bring to boil slowly. Skim carefully and thoroughly. Boil for 45 to 60 minutes on low heat. Add the celery, parsnip, carrots, leek, dill and chicken stock cubes. Bring to boil, reduce heat and cook on low heat for 2 to 2½ hours until

chicken is soft and soup has good colour and the tantalising aroma of vegetables. Adjust quantity of water if necessary. Season to taste with salt.

■ Serve with piping hot matzo balls — two, three or four depending on your appetite — and with soup vegetables if desired. Danielle loves the carrot and the leek and tosses out the parsnip and celery.

Matzo balls (kneidlach):

Beat the eggs and add salt to taste, along with pepper, chicken fat, ½ cup cold water and matzo meal, and make a stiff batter. Let stand in refrigerator for 1 hour or more. Using your hands, roll the mixture into smooth balls the size of large marbles. Boil in salted water for 20 minutes until the balls are soft but still a little firm. Serve with chicken soup.

Melokhia Soup

You can smell this soup every Friday all over Cairo, wherever you go in the old town. Or so says Egyptian Mohammed Elfakahani who gave us this recipe for what is considered his country's national dish. The important part about melokhia (which are slippery, glutinous vegetable greens you can buy frozen or dried in Middle Eastern grocery stores) is to add that 'shhhuuussh' at the end — the sizzle made by the hot butter and flour as you add it at the last minute.

Serves 6

1 litre good stock, meat or chicken
500g bag of frozen melokhia leaves
1 clove garlic, crushed with a little salt
1½ tablespoons butter
ground coriander
pepper

■ Boil the stock and meanwhile chop the leaves finely. When stock is bubbling, drop in the melokhia. Boil for 5 minutes. Fry the garlic in the butter until it starts to sizzle then add the coriander and pepper. Pour the paste into the soup, making sure it sizzles and allow to simmer for a couple more minutes. You've got your melokhia!

■ Many Egyptians like to eat this with the boiled chicken used to make their stock. It's also good with rice on the side.

Minestra Paradiso (Italian Paradise Soup)

This incredibly simple dish falls into the category of comfort food. It's certainly top on the menu whenever 'Nonni' Ilma Dambelli comes to stay with her Italian–Australian granddaughters Lily Rose and Milena (daughters of Giuliano Dambelli and co-author Joanna Savill). A good chicken stock is the base (see stock box p. 14)

Serves 2
2 cups chicken stock
½ cup grated parmesan cheese
½ cup fine breadcrumbs
2 eggs
salt to taste

■ Bring the chicken stock to the boil while mixing the cheese, breadcrumbs, eggs and salt in a separate bowl. When the stock is bubbling, pour in the cheese, egg and breadcrumb mix and stir. It will cook almost instantly and form a nice eggy layer on top of the broth. Serve and feel comforted.

Masha and Avram Zelesnikov, owners of the Scheherazade Coffee Lounge

Cold Borscht

This is just one way of serving that spectacular bright-pink soup known as borscht in Russian or barszcz in Polish. It's certainly one of the least complicated recipes. Remember to serve it with dill potatoes or freshly fried latkes (potato cakes). The recipe comes from that Melbourne institution, Scheherazade Coffee Lounge on Acland Street, St Kilda.

Serves 4
5 medium-sized peeled beetroot
2 litres cold water
tablespoon of salt
½ cup sugar, or less if you prefer
½ cup lemon juice or vinegar
1 cup yoghurt or sour cream

■ Cut the beetroot into quarters and place them in a saucepan with cold water. Allow to boil. While boiling add salt and sugar. Continue cooking until the beetroot is soft. Let the borscht cool to room temperature. Add vinegar or lemon juice.

■ Strain the mixture and then fold in sour cream or yoghurt. Do this very gently or the mixture will curdle. Serve in a glass, chilled. The leftover beetroot can be used for a salad.

Barszcz (Polish Beetroot Soup)

Katrina Karon, who was born in Krakow and emigrated to Australia eleven years ago, was surprised that beetroot, such a staple at home, was virtually unknown here. For Katrina it's the ultimate vegetable — delicious steamed, grated and served with cream and butter — used in a number of dishes, the most famous being barszcz. This is one of many Polish versions which Katrina has added her own special stamp to. (Canned beetroot can be used for this recipe)

Serves 6
5 medium beetroot
500g beef brisket
mixed fresh vegetables, peeled and chopped (carrots, celery, onion)
5 whole allspice (pimento)
pepper to taste
2 bay leaves
1 cup beet juice (reserved cooking liquid or from can of sliced beetroot)
salt to taste
sugar to taste
2 cloves garlic
sprigs fresh parsley

■ Wash beets under running water, peel and cut into small pieces. Place in a saucepan and cover with boiling water. Cook until tender then drain, keeping liquid aside.

■ Rinse meat and bones then cover with water and cook on medium heat. Before meat is fully cooked, add vegetables and allspice, pepper and bay leaves. When cooked, drain, and add liquid to beet juice.

■ Add beet liquid, salt and sugar to taste. Add minced garlic, bring to the boil, skimming fat off the top of the soup.

■ Serve in soup plates and garnish with fresh parsley.

■ Variations: Can be garnished with fresh cream and served with boiled potatoes sprinkled with freshly chopped dill. Some people enjoy a little of the stock meat and vegetables in the soup.

Cawl Soup

For many years Alice and Geraint Rees ran the Welsh language broadcasting group at SBS Radio. They were a familiar sight in the studios, usually in the company of fellow broadcaster Owen Ellis. As is often the case, the mere mention of the word 'food' was enough to trigger a conversation that could last for hours as the three of them endeavoured to enlighten their colleagues to the meaning and significance of such delicacies as 'mushy peas' and 'faggots' (pig's liver to the rest of us). Although we decided to pass on the faggots, we do have this recipe from Alice for a very Welsh soup — containing a leek, of course. It's the sort of home-style broth we've somehow forgotten how to make, and yet it takes very little effort to prepare and is easy to freeze for future nourishment. St David (the patron saint of Wales) would approve.

Serves 4

neck of lamb or 4 stewing chops (as needed per person)
a selection of vegetables, including parsnips, swedes, carrots and soup bits
1 leek
chopped parsley to garnish

◼ Boil the meat the day before until tender, in salted water to cover. Remove the meat and, when cool, skim fat from the stock. The following day, add your vegetables, diced, and simmer in stock until cooked. Return meat to the stock, heat and, just a couple of minutes before serving, toss in finely sliced leek. Garnish with parsley.

◼ 'This is the type of dish,' Alice says, 'that's always best the following day.'

Agnes Oltvay's Authentic Hungarian Gulyas (Goulash Soup)

Agnes Oltvay was administrator with the Hungarian Radio Symphony Orchestra before coming to Australia from her native Budapest with her musician husband. Once we worked out that what we think of as 'goulash' is what the Hungarians call 'short goulash' or 'porkolt' (see Kate Johnson's recipe pp. 81–2) we were ready to tackle this delicious soup, known as 'gulyas'. Made with beef and potatoes — and paprika, of course.

Serves 4

1 large onion
vegetable oil

1 tablespoon red Hungarian paprika
600g beef (osso buco, the meat only, or gravy beef is best), cut into cubes
salt to taste
hot chilli if desired
1kg cubed potato (and 1 carrot, diced, and 1 turnip, diced, if you like)

◼ Fry the diced onion in a little vegetable oil until soft. Remove from heat, add paprika, return to heat and cook for a moment only. Add the meat, stir it into the paprika and onion mixture and cook until browned. Add water (around 2 litres), salt and hot chilli. Finally tip in potatoes, carrot and turnip, cover and allow to cook for around 1½ hours or until meat is tender.

◼ Serve with noodles (any kind of pasta will do) cooked al dente, then baked for a few minutes in the oven, mixed with sour cream and topped with bacon and cottage cheese!

West African Groundnut Soup

Kay Lanceley (nee Blackley) comes from a large and adventurous family. 'My mother was the first person I ever knew who put garlic in salad dressing,' Kay recalls. 'And I nearly died of embarrassment!' The Blackleys were travellers too. Aunt Dorothy, for example, married a mining engineer and went to live in Ghana, West Africa, where she learned to prepare this dish. While Kay remembers how exotic they all found it the first time the family tried it, it became something of a Blackley tradition and over the last fifty years has become a festive dish for family functions. The original recipe was typed by Kay's mother Margaret and kept in a volume that is 'more

Kay Lanceley and her mother Margaret

like a history book', Kay says. This is Kay's version — altered slightly to suit contemporary tastes.

Serves 4–6

2 teaspoons minced onion

2 tablespoons butter

½ cup peanut butter

4 tablespoons flour

6 cups chicken stock (in Margaret's recipe part of this can be scalded milk)

red chillies to taste

salt and pepper to taste

1 chicken, cut in pieces or 2 rabbits

hard-boiled eggs (one per person)

rice and accompaniments (see below)

■ Cook onion in butter and peanut butter for 5 minutes, add flour and stir until smooth. Add stock or milk slowly, cook for 20 minutes over very low heat, then season to taste. (If using milk, Margaret suggests it's 'best to cook this on a heat-diffusing mat as the milk is inclined to burn if you are not very clever at stirring all the time'.)

■ Divide the soup into two portions. To one half, add meat — chicken or rabbit — on the bone. Cover and cook until tender. Remove the bones and return the meat to the soup. ('Much better if left standing in the soup all night', says Margaret, 'then you only have to put the large pots on about an hour before your dinner party and let cook very slowly — on your heat-diffusing mat'.)

■ The other portion is served with hard-boiled egg halves.

■ Serve the two soups in tureens, next to a bowl of steamed rice and side dishes as desired. Margaret suggests taking a little of each in order, starting with cayenne pepper (or sliced chillies), rice, then the meat soup. Follow that with the egg soup, and then a selection of:

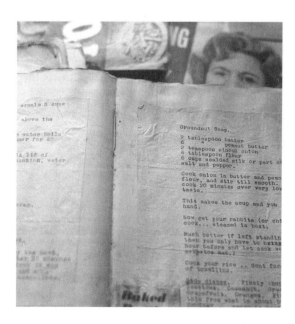

finely chopped onion in vinegar

sliced tomatoes

coconut toasted in oven until pale brown

green capsicums cut up

diced bananas in lemon juice

sliced grapefruit

oranges and pineapple

chutney ('mango is best')

■ Kay adds: 'In Ghana the peanuts were ground by hand. But Dorothy soon discovered peanut butter was a much less time-consuming substitute and tasted just as good.'

■ Note: Chicken and groundnut stews are found all over Africa — usually with tomatoes and several spices in the base, not to mention traditional vegetables like okra, sweet potato or yam, carrots and corn. They are usually served with grain dumplings. This is clearly a more 'tropical' version!

Moshe's Two Minute Lentil Soup

('Well, two minutes to prepare … Twenty minutes to cook.')

Moshe Rosenzweig comes from Tel Aviv and is very fond of good food. He also knows lots of quick and easy things to make the way all good Israeli men do (see recipe for Shakshooka pp. 31–2.) This is his idea of a quick, easy and nourishing soup.

Serves 2

½ onion, chopped

1 clove garlic, diced

olive oil for frying

1 cup red lentils, washed and well rinsed

■ Fry the onion and garlic in the olive oil.

When soft, add red lentils and cover with 2 cups of water. 'Be prepared to add a little more water as it goes,' says Moshe. The result should be a thickish, mushy soup. His tip, don't add salt until the very end, when the lentils are soft, otherwise they take too long to cook.

Zucchini Soup

A favourite Italian vegetable, zucchini seem to go beautifully with parmesan cheese, garlic, basil, parsley — all those very Italian ingredients. This recipe for a creamy zucchini soup comes from accomplished Italian cook, Victoria Cosford. Remember to select zucchini that are crisp and firm, not rubbery to the touch.

Serves 6

1kg medium-sized zucchini

25ml olive oil

2 cloves garlic, chopped

salt and pepper to taste

500ml chicken stock

140ml cream

1 small bunch basil

1 small bunch parsley

120g parmesan cheese, grated fine

■ Cut zucchini lengthwise into quarters, then into 3cm pieces. Heat the olive oil in a heavy-based saucepan, add chopped garlic and zucchini. Cook gently for about 25 minutes until soft and well browned. Add salt and pepper to taste, then chicken stock and simmer for several minutes. Pour into a food processor or mouli and reduce to a puree. Return the mix to the saucepan and add cream, herbs and parmesan.

■ Serve with crostini (toasted rounds of bread) spread with black olive and chilli paste.

Shanghai Wintermelon Soup

This is a real show-off dish as the thick, flavoursome soup is actually served in a large hollowed-out melon. It's great if someone in the family has a flair for carving as the most beautiful pictures can be made with a sharp knife on the outer flesh. We have enjoyed this soup made by Shanghainese chef Qi Sheng Zhu who goes to great trouble to carve the outside of the melon into pictures of dragons and warriors.

Other than finding the right sort of melon, the only problem you might face is finding a saucepan large enough to accommodate it for steaming. You'll notice that like many recipes from China, this includes the lucky number eight in its list of ingredients.

Jing-haur ham is top-of-the-range ham named after a small village in China where it originated. You can buy it in dried form from selected Asian grocery stores.

Serves 8

4kg melon (Chinese melon or East melon recommended but a round-shaped watermelon is fine)
200g Chinese Jing-haur leg ham
1 225g can wild mushrooms
8 dried scallops
1 225g can sliced bamboo
8 fresh prawns, peeled with tail left on
100g sliced fresh chicken
100g finely diced pork
a few beans
salt to taste
a decent slurp of rice wine
clear chicken broth
1 knob fresh ginger, finely chopped
handful of shallots, finely chopped
vegetable oil

■ First wash the outside of the melon and dry it. If you are going to carve the melon, now is the time. Then cut just the top of the melon off so you have a deep bowl shape. With a spoon, dig all the flesh and seeds of the melon out and put aside (you may want to use in other recipes). Keep the 'hat' and hollow it out to make a lid for the melon.

■ Put half the ham, wild mushroom, dried scallops, bamboo, prawns, chicken, pork, beans, salt, rice wine, chicken broth, ginger and shallots into the inside of the melon. Add a little cooking oil.

■ In a large saucepan filled with cold water, steam the melon (its lid on) for 2 hours. Dress with the remaining Jing-haur Chinese leg ham, cut into small precise pieces.

Thai Duck Soup

Anne Sanpasiri really knows her way around a kitchen. The Bangkok-born chef was taught by her mother who is, in fact, a cooking teacher. And it's no surprise that Anne's sisters and brother also own restaurants — in fact, they've all ended up in Australia and have all opened restaurants in the same city though all operate in different areas so there are never disputes about who may be stealing whose customers. This duck soup is a favourite that her devoted customers keep flocking back for.

Serves 10

3 roast ducks (buy already cooked from a Chinese barbecue shop)
5 litres water
3 cloves garlic
1 teaspoon pepper

1 teaspoon ground coriander

2 sprigs coriander

1 stick cinnamon

3 soup spoons soy sauce

3 soup spoons double-strength soy sauce

1 soup spoon fish sauce

1 soup spoon chillies in vinegar

½ teaspoon sugar

1 400g packet Thai rice noodles

couple handfuls mung bean shoots

chopped shallots, coriander and pepper to garnish

■ Remove meat from ducks so you are left with bones. Place these in pot with the water, garlic, pepper, coriander and cinnamon. Bring to the boil and simmer for 1 hour.

■ Prepare sauce mixture by combining two types soy sauce, fish sauce, chillies and sugar.

■ If you've bought thin rice noodles, you'll need to soak them for 10 minutes in warm water before cooking. Boil a separate pan of water and add noodles. Cook according to instructions, adding bean shoots to pot 2 minutes before the noodles are ready. Strain the noodles and bean shoots. Place in a bowl and ladle on duck broth, soy and chilli mixture to taste then arrange slices of the roast duck on top. Garnish with shallots, coriander and pepper and serve immediately.

Brodo di Pesce (Fish Stock)

There is nothing like a good fish stock in which to simmer a little seafood and a few tomatoes for a simple fish soup. Star chef and multi-restaurateur, the ebullient Bill Marchetti, gave us his recipe for a fragrant broth — useful for seafood sauces (like his accompaniment for squid ink linguine on p. 137) and for poaching a couple of fish fillets for a light, tasty dinner. When selecting the fish bones for this recipe, Bill says, take those from large-boned, deep-sea fish for preference (including the heads). For example, large snapper, blue eye, hapuka or tuna. Avoid oily fish such as the mackerel family or rockling, which make the stock cloudy. Have your fishmonger remove the eyes, gills and intestines and cut the fish bones into 5cm square pieces.

Makes about 1.5 litres

2kg fish bones

100ml olive oil

200g butter

500g (total) diced onion, carrot, celery and leek

350ml dry white wine

2 bay leaves

½ bunch parsley stalks

10 peppercorns

1 cup fresh fennel sprigs, in season

cold water to cover, about 1.5 litres

■ Soak the fish bones in a large bowl, regularly changing the water over at least 2 hours. Remove all the blood clots and fat pieces. Then take a large, heavy-based stainless steel stockpot and heat the oil and butter without browning the butter.

■ Add the diced vegetables and saute for about 15 minutes or until they are tender. Add the fish bones and saute until all the bones have whitened, but avoid browning them.

■ Add the white wine and over a very high heat evaporate some of the alcohol. This should take no more than 10 minutes.

■ Add the bay leaves, parsley stalks and peppercorns and, in season, fennel sprigs. Just cover the bones with cold water.

■ Bring the stock to a boil, turn down the

heat to a simmer and continue skimming constantly. After 35 minutes take the stock off the heat, set it aside and let it infuse for another 35 minutes. Ladle the stock out of the pot when straining. Great care must be taken at this stage not to break up the bones and make the stock cloudy. Strain it through muslin or a very fine strainer.

■ Let it rest and cool for an hour, then remove the excess fat floating on top, then decant the stock.

Eggs

Beid Hamine (Moroccan-style Eggs)

Sydney restaurateur Hugh Foster was so entranced by his travels in North Africa that he decided to come back to Australia and open a restaurant. His recipe for Moroccan-style eggs takes only a few minutes' preparation the night before and makes for an instant breakfast.

Serves 8

8 large eggs
2 cups onion peel (just the dry papery peel) from brown or red onions
vegetable oil (optional)

■ Place onion peel in a large pot, place whole eggs on top and cover with water at least 3cm above the eggs. Pour on a layer of oil to prevent evaporation or cover with a lid. Cook for six hours or overnight on the lowest possible heat on your stove top — a heat-dispersing mat is strongly recommended. The water should be moving not boiling.
■ Serve with toasted pide, cacik (Turkish garlic yoghurt dip) and maldon or sea salt flavoured with equal parts of paprika and cumin.
■ Whole eggs may be added to slow-cooked meat dishes such as cholent (see Meat chapter).

Kai Yang Nam Pla Wan (Eggs with Sweet Fish Sauce)

David Thompson's love affair with Thai cuisine began in the late 1980s. But it was his meeting with an elderly woman called Khun Sombat Janphetchara, whose mother was attached to one of the palaces of Bangkok, that set him on his path to learning the fundamentals of Thai cuisine. 'Thai food has three levels or tiers,' he explains, 'There is the flavour of the ingredients but also their textural components and finally the contrasts of seasoning — sweet, sour, salty and hot.' The perfect Thai meal strikes a balance of all three — flavour, texture and seasoning.

As one of Australia's foremost restaurateurs (with Darley Street Thai and Sailor's Thai, both in central Sydney) David has continued his voyage of discovery into the secrets of Thai cuisine and returns to Thailand regularly. He has even begun to collect old cookery books — not only repositories for recipes but records of the life and interests of their owners. This dish, in its simplicity, embodies all the principles of Thai cuisine. And what a great thing to do with a couple of luscious, fresh, free-range eggs!

250g palm sugar
100ml fish sauce
15ml tamarind water
1 egg per person, steamed, poached or fried
5 red shallots, finely sliced lengthways and deep-fried
3 cloves garlic, finely sliced lengthways and deep-fried
6 dried small red chillies, roasted or deep-fried
4 tablespoons coriander leaves, chopped

■ In a small pan combine the palm sugar, fish sauce and tamarind water, and simmer until the sugar has dissolved, skimming if necessary. It will taste sweet, salty and slightly sour. Steam, poach or fry one egg per person.
■ To serve, place the eggs on a serving plate, cover with the warm sauce and sprinkle with the shallots, garlic, chillies and coriander.

Champ
(Potato and Scrambled Eggs)

In 1585 Sir Walter Raleigh planted a potato in Ireland. 'The poor man had no idea of what he was unleashing on an unsuspecting world,' says SBS Television's flamboyant Irishman Austin Steele. However, he points out that without the Irish potato and nature's cruel nineteenth-century blight, we would not have had the Irish exodus. And without that, says Austin, just think — no police force in New York, no motorways in England and no right wing of the Labor Party in NSW!

Serves 4–6
a bunch of spring onions or a couple of leeks
½ cup milk
a couple of cups of hot mashed potato, just boiled
salt and pepper to taste
a few caraway seeds
¼ cup of melted butter
scrambled eggs — your own recipe

■ Chop the spring onions or leeks and simmer in the milk until soft. Drain them but keep the milk. Add the onions to the mashed potatoes, season with salt, pepper and caraway seeds and pour on the warm milk. Mix to a creamy dish. Make a well in the middle, pour in a little melted butter and fill the space with freshly made fluffy scrambled eggs. Sprinkle with chopped parsley and serve.

Hungarian Scrambled Eggs

This dish is a firm favourite amongst the brunch crowd at Bondi Beach who flock to one of the older European-style cafes on the beachfront for this family recipe from Peter Berger of the Gelato Bar. It's just the thing to fuel up after a big morning riding the waves at Australia's most famous beach.

Serves 2
½ onion, chopped
½ red or yellow capsicum, chopped
4 medium mushrooms, chopped
10 slices csabai (Hungarian salami), chopped
3 eggs, well beaten
salt and pepper to taste
paprika
cooking oil

■ The vegetables should all be chopped fairly coarsely. Heat oil and saute vegetables until they are well coated and are just starting to soften. Add csabai and cook for another minute or two.
■ Add the eggs and scramble quickly. Don't overcook. Season to taste with salt and pepper and sprinkle generously with paprika. Serve with toasted sour dough bread.

Shakshooka
(Israeli Eggs — 'the Definitive Version')

'This is the meal every Israeli man knows how to do,' says TV producer Moshe Rosenzweig. Being an Israeli man himself, he is to be trusted, although he admits everyone has a slightly different method. His, of course, is the best. It's certainly yummy.

Serves 1 hungry Israeli man ... or woman
1 onion, chopped
1 green capsicum, diced in 8 x 8mm squares

2 tomatoes, diced

2 eggs

Salt and black pepper to taste

You will need a medium-sized frypan with a lid. Fry the chopped onion in a little olive oil in a frypan. Add the diced capsicum and cook until soft. Add the diced tomatoes and cook for a further 5 to 8 minutes. When it is soft and quite 'juicy', Moshe says, make two wells in the pan mix and break an egg into each one. Cover the pan and allow it to cook for another 5 minutes or so until the eggs are just hard. Season with salt and black pepper.

This is the sort of dish you'd get in a workers' eatery, Moshe says. It has to be eaten with a good bread — preferably a seeded rye — and in Moshe's case, plenty of continental butter.

Victoria's Frittata

Victoria Cosford is an accomplished Italian cook, who has certainly done her time in Italian restaurant kitchens, over several years in various parts of Tuscany. One dish automatically associated with Victoria's abundant antipasto platters, her fabulous frittata, was not gleaned from a Florentine friend or Chianti-based colleague. She developed it back home in Australia, with the very un-Italian addition of 600ml of cream. Having said that, she tells us it was a great hit last time she was working in Italy (in a picturesque country restaurant in the Chianti hills). With some trepidation she whipped up a creamy frittata, perfumed with some local truffles. Waiting for universal disapproval, she was gratified to find the Tuscans loved her Aussie innovation.

Victoria Cosford

This is a party-sized recipe and makes about 80 generous pieces — divide for smaller gatherings! It does make a great entree too.

olive oil

1 large onion, sliced thinly

3 large potatoes, thinly sliced

a sprig of rosemary

1 large red capsicum, sliced and cut into strips

3 cups washed and shredded silverbeet

24 eggs

salt and pepper to taste

100g ricotta

a good handful of freshly grated parmesan

600ml cream

■ Heat the oil in a medium-sized saucepan, fry the onion, potato and rosemary for about 5 minutes until soft, add the capsicum strips and fry for a further few minutes. Add silverbeet and allow to wilt. Set aside to cool.

■ Break the eggs into a large bowl, season with salt and pepper and beat lightly. Add the mashed ricotta, parmesan cheese and cream and beat further until smooth. Fold in the cooled vegetables and pour mixture into a greased oven dish, about 50cm square and at least 5cm deep. (Victoria uses a canola spray but also suggests greased baking paper or simply, olive oil, to ensure the frittata does not stick).

■ Bake in a moderate 180°C oven for about 1 hour. You will know when it is cooked when it is firm to the touch and golden brown on top. It is important to make it in a deep dish so that the finished squares (you cut the whole pie into squares) reveal several layers of colour — the red capsicum and the green silverbeet.

Katrina Karon's Jajka Z Pieczarkami (Polish Stuffed Eggs)

These rich eggs are a perfect starter for a meal and also make good party finger food. 'They're very simple,' says Katrina, 'But every time I make them people are impressed and ask for the recipe.' One word of warning though — seek out the sweetish German brand of mayonnaise — Thomy. 'It just doesn't taste right otherwise,' says Katrina.

Serves 4
8 eggs
½ onion

Jerzy and Katrina Karon

300g mushrooms
1 tablespoon butter
Thomy mayonnaise
lettuce leaves
dill for garnish

■ Hard-boil eggs, cut in half lengthways and remove yolk. Grate onion and mushroom very finely and sauté in butter until liquid evaporates. Place mixture in egg cavities and spoon 1 teaspoon of mayonnaise on top of each egg. Grate yolk over mayonnaise and arrange on bed of lettuce with sprigs of dill.

Rattlesnake Eggs (Huevos Motulenos)

On the first Sunday of every month, Sydney's Santa Fe-style restaurant, the Rattlesnake Grill, comes alive to the uplifting sounds of gospel music while those in the know feast on brunch dishes such as these amazing eggs. The recipe originates from the village of Motul on

Mexico's Yucatan Peninsula. According to Rattlesnake's well-travelled owner/chef Victor Pisapia, the key to this combination of delicious flavours is the fried bananas.

Serves 4
2 cups black beans
3 litres water
salt to taste
¼ cup clarified butter
4 bananas, peeled and split in half lengthwise
2 tablespoons clarified butter, extra
8 eggs
8 regular flour tortillas
8 fresh coriander sprigs to garnish
1 cup crumbled fetta cheese

Salsa:
5 tomatoes, diced
¼ red onion, diced
¼ cup chopped coriander
1 tablespoon chipotle chilli puree (chipotle chilli is a smoked jalapeno and is found in tins at gourmet specialist stores)
2 tablespoons fresh lime juice

■ Sort the beans by hand to remove small stones and straw, then clean under running water. Combine the black beans and water in a stockpot and bring to boil. Reduce heat to low and simmer uncovered for about 1½ hours until beans are soft. Add water to beans while cooking to keep beans immersed. Season with salt when done.
■ Make the salsa by combining the tomatoes, red onion, chopped coriander, chipotle chilli, lime juice and salt and stir well.
■ In a saucepan, melt a quarter cup of butter over a medium-high heat. When butter sizzles, add banana halves and cook turning once, until golden brown on both sides. Set aside.

■ In another saucepan, melt 2 tablespoons butter and cook the eggs any style you like: scrambled, sunny-side-up or over easy. Take the flour tortillas and warm them on a flat grill or in a warm pan until soft. This takes only seconds.
■ To assemble the motulenos, place 2 flour tortillas side-by-side on each serving plate. Spoon ½ cup of the beans onto the centre of each tortilla and place the cooked eggs on top of the beans. Ladle the salsa around the eggs, covering the beans. Scatter ¼ of the fetta cheese over each serving. Place two fried banana halves along either side. Garnish with coriander sprigs and serve immediately.

Elizabeth's Tilsit Eggs

From Tasmanian-based Swiss cook Elizabeth Marchand — and yes, it calls for cheese. Elizabeth and husband Frank run the well-known Heidi cheese farm in the north of the island.

Serves 4 as an entree
250g Tilsit cheese, grated
2 egg yolks
50ml cream
pepper to taste
6 slices thick bread

■ Mix cheese, egg yolks, cream and pepper together in a bowl.
■ Toast one side of the bread under the griller, remove and spread mixture over untoasted side and grill for 5 minutes under medium hot grill.
■ Serve immediately with a garden salad.

Preserved Eggs

If you ever get lost browsing among the many delicacies to be found in an Asian emporium, no doubt you've come across a range of unusual eggs. Some are coated with what looks like a thick coating of straw and mud. Crack through the outside covering and the shell to find a rich deep brown-coloured egg inside. The aroma is strong and eggy. Slice it in half and you can see the yolk is a deep grey-black, the centre slightly jellied. Preserved eggs or thousand-year eggs are traditionally made using duck eggs.

So how old is a thousand-year-old egg? Not quite a thousand years, but at least a month old. Only the freshest eggs are chosen, coated with a paste of lime, wood ash and salt and then rolled in straw. They're then packed into an earthenware jar with a lid. The method is beautifully described in Amy Tan's novel *The Hundred Secret Senses*. 'After many weeks the lime and salt soaked through the eggshells. The whites of the egg became firm green, the yellow yolks hard black. I knew this because I sometimes ate one to be certain the others were ready to go into their mud coats.' The eggs were coated in mud, wrapped in paper then put once more in the earthenware curing jar and the storyteller dreamed of one day tasting them when they were perfectly cured.

Preserved eggs generally have a creamy taste and texture. Eat them cut in quarters and served with slivers of fresh ginger and wedges of lime.

Savoury tarts
and breads

Korean Mung Bean Pancake

Doo-Young Lee is a young Korean who came to Australia in search of adventure. A professional photographer, the last thing he thought he'd do would be to set up a restaurant — let alone two! In Sydney's inner-city suburb of Glebe, Lee and his wife have set up an elegant Western-style cafe and in the garden they've installed a pond and a series of tables with traditional Korean barbecue plates built-in. Upstairs there's also a more formal Korean restaurant where dishes such as these mung bean pancakes are served. This is a traditional dish, eaten on special occasions in Korea.

Serves 4
4 cups dried mung beans, prepared by crushing to split the skins
salt to taste
water
450g shredded pork, fried in a small amount of oil until nicely browned
2 leeks, chopped finely
1 clove garlic, finely chopped
1 tablespoon sesame salt
1 teaspoon finely chopped fresh ginger root
½ cup kimchi, chopped

■ Soak the beans in water overnight, for 10 to 12 hours.
■ Cover the beans in fresh water and rub between the hands to remove the skins, which will float to the top of the water. Repeat this process until all the skins are removed; skim off and drain well.
■ Grind the beans in a blender or with a mortar and pestle. Add enough water to make a thick paste. Season with a little salt — do not make the batter too salty as the finished

product is usually dipped in soy sauce at the table. Add the pork, leeks, garlic, sesame salt, ginger and kimchi.
■ Drop the batter by the tablespoonful onto a heated greased pan or griddle and cook like pancakes, browning lightly on both sides. Serve with soy sauce for dipping.

Anne Sanpasiri

Thai Pastries

Anne Sanpasiri goes home to Bangkok every year to search for new recipes for her tiny Bondi Junction restaurant. This is an unusual starter made with garlic chives which give a fresh taste and texture — and you have the choice of steaming or frying the pastries. Rice flour and tapioca flour can be found in most Asian grocery stores.

Serves 6 as a starter
500g rice flour
200g tapioca flour
1kg garlic chives, washed and chopped
1 small clove garlic
½ teaspoon salt
½ teaspoon sugar

Sauce:

1 teaspoon soy sauce

1 teaspoon vinegar

1 teaspoon chilli sauce

½ teaspoon sugar

◼ Chop the clove of garlic into fine pieces. Put salt, sugar, garlic and chives into large bowl and mix together.

◼ In a separate bowl mix rice and tapioca flour. Slowly add 1 tablespoon of warm water. Start to knead the dough on a chopping board and consistently add more tablespoons of water for about half an hour.

◼ When ready, take small amounts of dough and shape them into round flat pieces about 7.5cm wide. Put about 1½ tablespoons of the garlic vegetable mixture on the centre of the pastry and wrap the corners to the middle. Put the wrapped pastries in a steamer and steam for 15 minutes. They are now ready to eat. Serve with a sauce made by combining the soy, vinegar, chilli sauce and sugar.

◼ For another version of the pastries, wait until they have cooled and deep-fry them for 5 minutes until they are crispy. Serve with the dipping sauce.

Ajoy's Samosas

Ajoy Joshi is passionate about good, authentic Indian food. He trained at the Taj group of hotels in India before coming to Australia where he specialises in South Indian cuisine. As well as cooking in his own restaurant, he's now teaching groups interested in learning to prepare typical snacks like the popular samosa. These are made throughout India and are a common teatime (tiffin) treat. This recipe will take you about an hour to prepare and around 20 minutes to cook.

Makes 10–12
Pastry:

500g plain flour

salt to taste

50ml vegetable oil

Filling:

30ml vegetable oil

10g cumin seeds

10g ground chilli powder

25g fresh ginger, chopped

1kg potatoes, boiled, peeled and mashed

250g fresh green peas, shelled and blanched

10 fresh chillies, chopped

20g chat masala (available in Indian grocery stores)

salt to taste

1 bunch fresh coriander leaves, chopped

vegetable oil to deep-fry

To prepare pastry:

◼ Sift the flour with the salt. Pour in the oil and mix gradually (as you would for shortcrust pastry). Add warm water and make a semi-hard dough and cover with a moist cloth and keep aside for 20 minutes.

To prepare filling:

◼ Heat oil in a pan and crackle cumin seeds, then add the chopped ginger. Add the mashed potatoes and the green peas with the ground chilli powder and the chopped chillies; cook for a few minutes. Reduce heat and cover, stirring occasionally.

◼ Sprinkle chat masala, salt and fresh coriander into the mix and stir through. Put aside to cool. Divide into 10 to 12 equal portions.

Smorgasbord and Smorrebrod

As Danish radio broadcaster and TV subtitler Zanne Mallett relates, most people approach a typical Scandinavian smorgasbord with great trepidation. Where to begin? What to eat next? How to end? Smorgasbord, literally 'bread and butter table', is a carefully organised and arranged feast of cold smoked fish, cold cuts and a variety of little hot dishes. 'Start with the herring' is our expert's advice. 'Don't hang back. Try four or five varieties. Then go to the fish, after a change of plate. Smoked salmon, eel or jellied salmon and a cold, vinegar-sharp cucumber salad stimulate the palate. Change plates again and on to the meat — ham, roast beef, calf's liver pate and cold cuts, for example. Now you're ready for the hot dishes. Some meatballs, a mushroom omelette or the like precede a variety of cheeses and fresh fruit.'

Smorrebrod on the other hand, is all about open sandwiches on fresh rye, wholemeal or even crusty white bread. And they all have names, Zanne says, like the 'vet's breakfast', concocted for a hungry medico who's been up all night bringing a calf or two into the world — bread is spread with dripping, covered with liver pate and topped with aspic and thin slices of salami.

The 'Hans Christian Andersen' is liver pate with bacon, onion and mushroom. The 'rush hour' is shrimps with remoulade sauce (which Zanne makes with mayonnaise, mustard, finely chopped capers, gherkin and tarragon). The 'politician's promise' is sliced bologna sausage, cheese and sour pickles and the 'honeymoon' a raw oyster with horseradish and bacon. See if you can invent some combinations of your own and create your own Scandinavian spread. Don't forget the rye bread.

To prepare samosas:

■ Divide the dough into 6 equal parts. Lightly flatten and roll over a floured table into an oval shape and cut into two parts. Place one half on your palm, and with a finger of the other hand, apply water all along the cut edges of the pastry and fold to form a three-dimensional triangle.

■ Fill with approximately one tablespoon of the spiced potato mixture and firmly press with fingers to seal the pastry in the form of a cone. Arrange on a lightly floured tray and keep aside.

■ Heat the oil in a pan and fry the samosas over medium heat until crisp and golden brown.

Snobrod (Traditional Midsummer's Twisted Damper)

It's somewhere between a sausage roll and a battered sausage on a stick — the kind you get on Show day. The result is certainly special — great for kids. Snags in their own individual baked-on bun.

The recipe comes from Danish-born Zanne Mallett, translator, broadcaster and tireless ambassador for things Danish. Especially important to many of her recipes is the ambience in which they are consumed — preferably a party atmosphere.

Serves 6

a fine evening
copious amounts of liquid refreshments and good company
2 teaspoons of salt
25g dried yeast
500g flour
200ml warm water
15 frankfurt sausages, preferably Houlberg's Danish hot dogs

■ Mix the flour with salt and add the yeast which has previously been mixed with a little warm water. When mixed well add 200ml of warm water. Keep mixing until you end up with a reasonably pliable dough.

■ Roll dough into oblong, thin sticks and twist them around some long, not too thick sausages. Grill your finished creation on a barbecue and, if you survive all that, 'Velbekommen,' Zanne says. 'May the food become you well.'

Bush Tomato and Chilli Tart

Passionate advocates of the indigenous flavours of Australia, Juleigh and Ian Robins run a condiments/catering business in Melbourne. Since 1987, Robins Bush Foods has been finding new and creative ways to incorporate the tastes of native plants, spices and herbs into everything from chutneys to cakes, pies and pasta. Bush tomatoes or 'desert raisins' — known in the Northern Territory region around Alice Springs as akadjura — are a wonderful ingredient for adding a little piquancy and sweetness to any dish where you would normally use European tomatoes. They are usually available in the sun-dried, raisin-like form and in most cases, are best used that way. If you have found them whole, make sure they are well dried and grind them to a coarse consistency. The recipe for this tart comes from the Robins's *Wild Lime: cooking from a bushfood garden* (Allen & Unwin 1996).

500g puff pastry

1 x 55g egg, beaten with a little water for egg wash

1 medium onion, finely chopped

3 cloves garlic, minced

¼ cup olive oil

10 large ripe red tomatoes, coarsely chopped

½ cup ground bush tomatoes

3 native pepperleaves, left whole

½ teaspoon dried wild thyme or common thyme

salt to taste

½ tablespoon tomato paste

1 large capsicum

pitted black olives and a little extra olive oil

■ Carefully roll out the puff pastry to fit a 23cm pizza tray. From what is left over, cut several 2–3cm wide strips. (These will be placed around the edge of the pastry base to form a wide border — you will need to go twice around the circumference of the pizza tray.)

■ With a pastry brush, paint a strip of egg wash around the perimeter of the base and place the pastry strips flat along this strip to make a border. Continue placing the strips until you have a border around the perimeter of the tart that is two strips high. Rest this pastry tart case for at least 20 minutes in the refrigerator.

■ In a large saucepan, sauté the onion and garlic in the olive oil until tender. Watch the heat so the garlic doesn't burn.

■ Add the fresh tomatoes and cook for 20 minutes. Then add the bush tomatoes, native pepperleaves, thyme, a little salt and tomato paste. Cook to reduce for a further 30 minutes or until the volume of the filling has halved, and the texture is almost jam-like.

■ Puree the filling in a food processor until smooth. Refrigerate until cool. Spoon into the chilled pastry case, spreading almost to the edges but heaping it in the centre so that it does not spill over when cooking. You can spread the filling out further once the pastry starts to rise.

■ Cook in a preheated oven (190°C) for approximately 40 minutes.

■ While it is cooking, roast the capsicum directly over a gas flame or under a char-griller until blackened all over. Wrap in a clean tea towel until cool enough to handle. Peel the skins, rinse them in cool water and cut into long, thin strips. When the tart is cooled to room temperature, form a lattice pattern on it with the capsicum, placing a whole olive in each lattice square. Gently brush the surface with a little extra olive oil.

Timpana (Maltese Macaroni in Shortcrust Pastry)

If you ever saw the charming Italo–American movie *Big Night*, about a passionate and perfectionist Italian chef, you'll have come away longing to try the dish that stole the show. Timpano is a pastry drum filled with rich pasta, sauce and cheese — a Sicilian specialty baked as the finale of the film. Well, the Maltese do it too, as former SBS broadcaster Edith Lanzon tells us. In Malta, timpana, as it is known, is regarded as a real showpiece of island flavours. It makes a spectacular entree, but is certainly filling enough for a main course. The chicken livers in the sauce give it extra flavour and richness.

Serves 8 – 10

1 onion, chopped

1 clove garlic

oil for frying

500g mince (Edith combines veal, pork and beef)

150g chicken livers, chopped

1 x 425g can tomatoes

¼ cup tomato paste

salt and pepper to taste

750g shortcrust pastry

2 hard-boiled eggs

grated parmesan cheese to taste

750g pasta (the penne tube-type is best), well cooked or it will soak up all the sauce

beaten egg for pastry top

To prepare filling:

■ Fry onion and garlic in oil until soft, add mince and chopped livers and continue frying until cooked. Add tomatoes and paste and a little water if needed. Simmer, covered, for about 30 minutes. Season.

To prepare pastry:

■ Roll out thinly and line an oven dish or spring-form pan. Keep some for covering the dish when filled.

To assemble:

■ Mix meat sauce with chopped hard-boiled eggs, parmesan cheese and cooked pasta. Spoon into pastry lining and cover with remaining pastry. Pinch the edges together to seal and brush with a little beaten egg. Cook for about 40 minutes in a hot 220°C oven or until the pastry has turned golden brown. Serve. Can also be eaten later cold.

Elizabeth's Quiche Lorraine

Swiss-born cheesemaker Frank Marchand and his wife Elizabeth live in the idyllic green hills outside Launceston in Tasmania, a world away

Frank and Elizabeth Marchand

from their small villages in the Bernese Oberland area of the Alps. Both grew up being able to milk cows almost as soon as they could walk — 'when we were not at school we had to help on the farm', Frank remembers.

On their own farm, the couple once knew the names of all their 60 cows, until the popularity of Frank's Swiss-style cheeses meant the herd grew to 200. 'Too many to name,' Elizabeth laughs. The product of all those cows is put to good use in the family kitchen where many a meal is cooked using the luscious cheeses produced in the small factory down the back (under the award-winning Heidi cheese brand).

Serves 4 (for a 29cm flan tray)
Pastry:

250g plain flour

125g butter

1 teaspoon salt

5-6 tablespoons water

Filling:
2 onions, sliced
3 rashers bacon, cut into large squares
150g Gruyére cheese, grated

Batter:
1 cup milk
¼ cup flour
2 eggs
parsley, chopped
salt and pepper to taste

To prepare pastry:
◼ Rub the softened butter into the flour and salt until it resembles fine breadcrumbs. Moisten with water and form into a pastry. Set aside for 1 hour. Then roll out with a rolling pin.

To prepare filling:
◼ Gently cook the onions and bacon in a pan with a little butter until onions are soft and transparent.
◼ Line a flan tin with the pastry, pierce a few times with a fork and put into the fridge for a while.
Distribute onion, bacon and cheese on the pastry shell, pour over the batter and bake in a moderately hot 190°C oven for 30 to 40 minutes until golden brown. Serve immediately with a tossed salad.

Torta tal-bajd u L-Gobon (Maltese Ricotta Pie)

This typically Maltese pie comes from Edith Lanzon, a Maltese broadcaster of many, many years, who, with her husband Mike, was the backbone of SBS Radio's Maltese language program in Sydney. Ever an enthusiastic promoter of the traditional dishes of her native land, Edith brought in pages of tempting ideas for us to study — in an attempt to capture the essence of a cuisine influenced by Italian, North African and British gastronomy. This 'rikotta' pie was adapted from a recipe published by the godmother of Maltese cooking, Carmen Carbonaro, whose *Recipes of Maltese Dishes* was published in 1958 by Empire Press.

Serves 4
250g ricotta
a splash of milk
2 eggs
salt to taste
pepper to taste
1 tablespoon finely chopped parsley
½ cup peas (tinned or fresh)
grated parmesan cheese for top
puff or shortcrust pastry

◼ Mix the ricotta with milk, add beaten eggs, salt, pepper, parsley and peas. Mix thoroughly, then top with grated cheese.
◼ Line a small greased Pyrex dish with puff pastry, fill with ricotta mixture and cover with a layer of pastry. Decorate the top of the pie with leftover pastry. Brush with milk or beaten egg. Bake in a moderately hot 190°C oven until pie is a pale golden colour.
◼ As Carmen Carbonaro says, 'the ricotta can either be home-made or bought from any grocery or hawker'.

Lakror (Albanian Pizza)

This unusual but very clever pizza recipe comes from Edi Kane, Albanian-born but now living in Melbourne. It's the original pizza pie!

Serves 4

pizza dough (made from scratch — see Joanna's recipe below or try a packet version)
2 medium onions
4 medium tomatoes
2 Balkan long chillies (peppers)
2 tablespoons butter
1 teaspoon cooking salt
1 teaspoon red pepper (paprika)

▨ Roll out two pizza dough bits, each to the size of a normal pizza. Lay one out on the bottom of a round tray. Eventually you will place the other one on top of it and pinch down the sides. But first chop the onions, tomatoes and chillies and fry them in the butter for about 15 minutes on medium heat. While they are frying add the salt and stir, then add red pepper. Pour the mixture over the first layer of dough and spread it out evenly. Cover with second piece of dough and pinch the two layers together around the sides. Bake in a hot 220°C oven for about 15 minutes or until it is golden brown.
▨ Serve like pizza.

Joanna's Pizza Dough

This dough is fun to make and not at all hard. Kids love playing with pizza dough and little rounds made with biscuit cutters topped with a little tinned tomato and mozzarella or galbanino cheese only take about ten minutes to cook. This tried and true recipe comes from co-author Joanna.

Makes 2 large rounds

30g dried yeast or 50g fresh yeast
pinch of salt
1 teaspoon sugar
250ml just warm water
500g strong baker's flour
2 teaspoons dried herbs, rosemary, oregano, or mixed
4 tablespoons olive oil
extra flour for rolling

Dissolve the yeast, salt and sugar in warm water and beat thoroughly. Allow to stand for a few minutes. Place the sifted flour and herbs in a bowl, make a well in the centre and pour in the yeast mixture and the oil. Mix to a dough, adding more flour if necessary. The dough should be smooth, coolish and a little shiny. Remove from the bowl, flour the ball and the inside of the bowl, return the ball of dough to the bowl and leave to rise in a warm place for a couple of hours, covered with a damp tea towel. It should double in size. You can tell by making a cross in the top. When it has risen the cross will have widened. Knead it thoroughly again, making sure you punch out all the air. Form a couple of balls, roll out the dough onto oiled pizza trays and leave for another 30 minutes to rise. Place in a moderate oven for about 20 minutes to cook blind, or about 30 minutes with the toppings of your choice (but not too many things at once!).

Irish Soda Bread

Round Irish soda bread loaves with a cross marked in the top are sold the length and breadth of Ireland, the crumbly chewy texture unlike any other commercial bread. Despite the ease with which it can be bought over the counter, many Irish people still make their bread, including Melbourne-based expat Jean Tongs, who swears her recipe is 'eejit-proof'. A busy mother of four, Jean still finds time to make a loaf every day.

Makes 1 large loaf (serves 6)

500g coarse wholemeal flour (as coarse as you can get)
250g unbleached white flour
2 teaspoons baking soda
1 generous pinch salt
450ml buttermilk (available in supermarkets) or full-cream milk soured with juice of half a lemon or yoghurt or any mix of the above.

■ Mix dry ingredients thoroughly. Make a well in the centre and pour in the buttermilk all at once. Mix with a knife so you handle the dough as little as possible. Turn onto a floured baking tray — the dough should be in a rough circular shape. Make a deep cross in the dough with a floured knife.

■ Bake in a hot 220°C oven for 25 minutes, then reduce heat to 180°C for 15 minutes. Test bread with a skewer — it should be dry to the touch and make a hollow sound when thumped underneath. Cool on a tray. It's best eaten cold and set. Bread can be frozen.

Christos' Greek Fennel Bread

Christos Sorilos was born in Athens under Lykavatos, the little white church on top of the mountain opposite the Acropolis. In Australia he owns and runs a taverna-style Greek restaurant in which he cooks, plays

bouzouki and sings traditional Greek songs. His fragrant bread has drawn such accolades that we couldn't resist getting the recipe which comes from his grandmother. 'From a young age, I was the breadmaker in the family — my mother told me I couldn't go outside to play soccer until the bread was done,' he says. All these years later, Christos says he's too old for soccer but still makes lovely bread.

Makes 36 rolls

2.2kg plain flour
a generous handful of fennel seeds
200g compressed yeast
1.5 litres water (tepid, about baby-bottle temperature)
pinch salt
sprinkling of freshly ground black pepper

■ Sift flour and add fennel seeds. Crumble yeast into water and mix well, then add to flour mixture. Knead on a floured board — it's hard work, says Christos, and will take you a good 15 minutes. The result should be light, fluffy and not sticky. Leave aside in a warm place to rise until double in size, then knead again for 15 minutes. Let it rise again then divide and form 36 individual rolls.

■ Bake in a 300°C oven until tops are golden brown. Turn them over quickly and return to oven — the whole process takes about 10 to 12 minutes.

■ Note: With a fair degree of yeast used, these rolls are best the day they are made — we defy you not to pig out on them!

Meat

Chicken

Mauritian Chicken Fricassee

Chinese, French and African … They're the combined flavours of Creole cuisine, as found in the island paradise of Mauritius where the legacy of British and French colonisation rubs shoulders with the African, Chinese and Indian populations. This interesting combination is responsible for the fascinating flavours in this dish, a recipe given to us by former schoolteacher and now restaurateur Alain Albert. Alain is quite an ambassador for his native cuisine and passionate about the rich heritage of his homeland. He points out the French notes (thyme, red wine and tomatoes), the African spices like cloves and cinnamon and the Chinese touch — shiitake mushrooms.

Serves 4

16 dried shiitake mushrooms (soaked for about 1 hour)
1 whole chicken, cut into pieces
salt and pepper to taste
2 tablespoons vegetable oil
1 large onion, thinly sliced
1 teaspoon fresh thyme
3 cloves garlic crushed
5 fresh Roma tomatoes, finely chopped
¼ teaspoon ground cinnamon
¼ teaspoon ground cloves
1 glass of red wine
parsley to garnish

■ Wash the mushrooms carefully to remove the grit and cut off the stems. Season the chicken pieces with the salt and pepper and fry gently in the hot oil, in a heavy-based pan. When well sealed and golden, remove the chicken and set aside.

■ In the same oil, lightly brown the onions, thyme and some salt. Add the crushed garlic and stir for approximately 1 minute. Then add the tomatoes, cinnamon and cloves and simmer until the tomatoes have released their juices.

■ Return the chicken pieces to the pan. Add the mushrooms, cover and cook over a gentle heat until the chicken is tender and the sauce juicy. A little stock or water may be added if too dry.

■ Approximately 5 minutes before serving, add the wine and cook uncovered. Sprinkle with fresh parsley and serve.

Inder's Chicken Tikka

Delhi-born restaurateur Inder Mehandiratta actually came to the food industry via a science degree and several years' working and training in hospitality in Switzerland. All that snow and ice must seem very far away these days — Inder now lives in tropical Noosaville just north of Brisbane! It's the perfect climate for Inder's luscious tandoor dishes, like chicken tikka, which he and his tandoor chef Brij Sharma have down to a fine art. But if your kitchen doesn't happen to feature a tandoori oven (and let's face it, whose does?), Inder has come up with the perfect way to recreate that smoky, dry-roasted flavour in a domestic cooker. An important part of the process is to have a couple of white-hot pieces of charcoal handy — you could grab a couple from your barbecue. Inder adds, 'This marinated chicken can also be cooked on a charcoal barbecue with spectacular results.' By the way, the name 'tikka' comes from the Persian word 'tikeh' meaning 'little piece'.

Serves 6

1kg chicken fillets, cut into pieces

Marinade:

¼ cup natural set yoghurt
2½ teaspoons minced fresh ginger
2½ teaspoons crushed fresh garlic
50ml vegetable oil
2½ teaspoons salt
1½ teaspoons ground cumin
3 teaspoons garam masala (Indian spice mix sold under this name)
½ teaspoon hot chilli powder (optional)
4 teaspoons lemon juice
2–3 pinches of tandoori colour or turmeric powder or
5 teaspoons sweet paprika powder (this step is for the colour)

Garnish:

1½ teaspoons chat masala (tangy, slightly pungent spice mix sold under this name)
3 teaspoons lemon juice
sliced onion
fresh coriander

■ Blend the yoghurt with a whisk then add all the other marinade ingredients. Mix well. Add the chicken fillets and ensure that they get well covered with the marinade. Cover the bowl and refrigerate overnight (or for at least 8 hours).
■ Preheat a normal convection oven to 180°C (fan forced to 160°C). Place a couple of smouldering charcoal pieces on a metal plate at the bottom of the oven (to give the right smoky flavour!). Place the chicken fillets on a

rack with drip tray underneath and slide onto the middle shelf of the oven. Cook for 15 minutes, then brown them at top heat for 5 minutes on either side. Place chicken tikkas in a bowl and sprinkle with chat masala and lemon juice. Serve on a warm plate, garnished with sliced onions and fresh coriander.

Estofado De Pollo (Peruvian Chicken Rice)

This is a little like a paella in a pot, enhanced by the musky flavour of coriander. The recipe comes from former colleague Flor Reyna, who was born in Lima, Peru.

Serves 6–8

1 whole chicken, cut into 8 or 10 pieces
2 onions
1 teaspoon crushed or minced garlic
1 teaspoon salt
1 chicken stock cube and water to cover, or ½ litre chicken stock
1kg rice
1 cup peas
6 potatoes
2 red capsicums
1 bunch coriander

■ Fry chicken pieces in a little oil with the chopped onions, garlic and salt until golden. Cover with water, add stock cube or stock and bring to the boil for 20 minutes on a high heat.
■ Add rice, peas, potatoes cut in half and capsicum cut in long, thin strips. Blend coriander with some water and add to the pot. Lower the heat and leave to simmer for a further 20 minutes. When it's ready you'll have an entire meal in itself.

Great Things to do With a Whole Chicken

Thirty years ago, roast chicken was a real treat in this country. Now it's a staple and with the availability of the sorts of spices and herbs we could only dream about three decades ago, it's become gourmet fare. Take Stephanie Alexander's 'Chicken Dionysus' — a Greek-inspired dish inherited from her well-travelled mother.

For experienced chefs, there is Cheong Liew's chicken, baked in a pastry crust, and Shanghai-style Eight Treasures chicken which requires a completely deboned bird. Or pack a thick crust of rock salt and pepper around the chook and let it roast in its own juices — the secret of Max Pantacchini's whole chicken in rock salt. Pria's 'home alone' Tamil-style chicken curry on the other hand, is a great example of how whole chicken pieces, complete with bones and skin, can greatly enhance the flavours of a sauce.

If you're tight for time (although chopping a chicken into sections using a Chinese cleaver is tremendously stress-relieving and not at all difficult), use chicken thigh fillets which are easy to handle and provide a good texture to casserole-style dishes.

If you're really tight for time, buy a ready-roasted chicken and try the following sauces and relishes to accompany it:

■ Fiery piri-piri sauce — ideally your takeaway chook would be Portuguese-style, flattened and cooked over charcoal.

■ Tomato chermoula — North African salsa-style accompaniment or bush tomato and chilli salsa.

■ A sweet, spicy accompaniment such as Byron Bay Nectarine Chutney. Add a simple green salad, some crusty bread and you have a meal!

■ Satay sauce is marvellous — so is zhug, a Middle-Eastern paste fragrant with cardamom, coriander, caraway seeds and cashew nuts.

■ Make a salad — Vivien's potato salad, Israeli avocado salad with some of Susie's brilliant pink raspberry vinaigrette on the side or settle for the wonderful textures and tastes of a couscous salad.

■ Instead of a sauce, why not try a dip — luscious potato and garlic skordalia, Rattlesnake's black beans and roasted garlic or minty Persian yoghurt and cucumber dip.

■ Rice goes really well with roast or barbecued chicken — if you have time, try rice Iranian-style or spicy Fijian-Indian tamarind rice spiked with fresh curry leaves, mustard, fenugreek and cumin. Combine the textures of barley and rice in a Greek pilaf or enjoy the typically Sicilian flavours of anchovies, tiny black olives and finely diced tomato in Sicilian summer rice.

Virginia Richardson

1 tomato, seeded and chopped into chunks
1 stalk lemongrass, chopped
1 teaspoon salt
1 can coconut milk

■ Place vegetables, lemongrass and salt and half the coconut milk in a saucepan over medium heat and cook for 3 minutes. Add the chicken, stir well and cover until cooked. Add the rest of the coconut milk and serve with steamed rice.

Virginia's Chicken La-Oya (Chicken with Ginger and Lemongrass)

Virginia Richardson is from the village of Lazi on the Philippine island of Siquijon, famous for its faith-healing and witchcraft. When she came to live in the heart of Australia — Alice Springs — she brought many of her family recipes with her, including this favourite for chicken which features the fresh tastes of ginger and lemongrass. This is perfect for busy people, taking at the very most 20 minutes to prepare and cook.

Serves 6
1.5kg chicken thighs, fat and skin removed
1 red capsicum, seeded and chopped into strips
1 good-sized knob of ginger, peeled and sliced into fine discs
1 onion, peeled and finely chopped

Chicken Chettinad (Indian Pepper Chicken)

One of Taj-trained chef (see pp. 162–3) Ajoy Joshi's signature dishes, this 'devilled chicken' will take you roughly 45 minutes to prepare and 45 minutes to cook.

Serves 4–6
1kg chicken thigh fillets, cut into 2.5cm pieces
250g onions, chopped
150ml vegetable oil
1 cinnamon stick
4 whole cardamom pods
4 whole cloves
1 teaspoon asafoetida powder
1 tablespoon ginger paste
1 tablespoon garlic paste
salt to taste
1 heaped teaspoon ground turmeric powder
1 tablespoon ground chilli powder
1 heaped tablespoon ground coriander powder
200g tomato puree
2 heaped teaspoons crushed pepper
2 sprigs fresh curry leaves
1 bunch fresh coriander leaves, chopped

■ Note: Asafoetida powder, often used as a subsitute for onion and garlic, can be found at Middle Eastern and Asian grocery stores. Beware, it has a powerful odour so store in a well-sealed jar!

■ In a pan, heat vegetable oil, then crackle the whole cinnamon, cardamom and cloves. Add asafoetida powder, immediately followed by the chopped onion. Saute onion over low heat until golden brown, then add the ginger and garlic pastes and cook a few minutes. Add salt, ground turmeric, chilli and coriander powders and saute over a low heat. When the oil leaves the sides of the pan, add the tomato puree, stir for a while, then add the chicken.

■ When chicken is cooked, add the crushed pepper, fresh curry leaves and the fresh coriander and serve hot with steamed plain or pilau rice.

Oiy's Green Chicken Curry

Oiy Arthur lives in Humpty Doo in the Northern Territory and spends her days hard at work in her enormous Eden-like garden, filled with lush tropical plants and herbs, trees and shrubs. She sells many varieties of chilli, turmeric, basil, eggplant and other vegetables and spices to restaurants in the Top End. From the village of Chun in Northern Thailand, Oiy has worked as a chef and revels in being able to cook with produce straight from her garden. She believes most Australians overcook their curries. This should take no more than 10 minutes. The other interesting thing about watching this Thai chef at work is that Oiy doesn't bother to de-seed the chillies that finish off the dish.

Oiy Arthur

The recipe features two interesting types of eggplant which you will probably only find in a good Asian greengrocers or a specialised fruiterer.

Serves 4

vegetable oil
1 can green curry paste
2 cans coconut milk
1 whole chicken, chopped into small serving pieces or 1kg chicken meat, chopped
2 tablespoons sugar
2-3 tablespoons fish sauce
1 cup sliced eggplant (try to find yellow golf-ball sized variety)
1 cup cherry eggplant, (these are tiny green ones, the size of a large pea)
1 handful sweet basil
4 kaffir lime leaves
6 large red and green chillies, sliced

■ In a large saucepan over medium flame heat a generous tablespoon of vegetable oil. Add curry paste. Stir and fry until, says Oiy, it 'smells right'. Add coconut milk, continue stirring and bring to boil. When oil starts to appear on coconut milk, add the chicken. Boil for about 5 minutes, add the sugar, fish sauce, eggplant, basil, kaffir lime leaves and chilli. Continue cooking (boiling) for 2 to 3 minutes. Serve immediately with steamed rice.

Hassan's Chicken Tajine

Hassan M'Souli comes from a large family in Casablanca, Morocco. His mother Barka (of the preserved lemons recipe, pp. 181–2) was brought up in Marrakech — the home, says Hassan, of great cuisine. It's no surprise her son has gone on to open two successful North African restaurants in Sydney. This recipe is served almost every day in Morocco. Tip: Get the best quality preserved lemons and olives you can find.

Serves 4

1 quantity of chermoula marinade (see pp.xx, in the marinades section)
1 whole chicken
15 marinated green olives
2 large potatoes, (preferably old) chopped into wedges
½ bunch shallots, finely chopped
1 preserved lemon, cut into fine wedges
freshly chopped coriander for garnish

■ Cut the whole chicken into large serving pieces. Wash and dry it using paper towel. With a sharp knife, make small slits along flesh, especially the breast area and rub in the chermoula marinade. Cover with plastic and refrigerate overnight. The next day, transfer the chicken to a saucepan with the marinade. Add 1 cup of water, cover and allow to steam for 45 minutes. When almost cooked, remove from the sauce

and roast in a separate pan for 10 to 15 minutes to brown the outside. Add olives to sauce mixture in the pot, then add potato wedges and let them seal in the sauce for 5 minutes. Cover the lot with cold water, add finely chopped shallots and leave until cooked.

■ Place chicken on a serving platter and surround with potato, pour sauce on top. Garnish with preserved lemon wedges, olives and freshly chopped coriander.

■ Note: Like curries, the flavour of this dish improves overnight — it can be cooked ahead and reheated the next day.

Chicken Tinola (Chicken with Green Papaya)

Versions of tinola are eaten throughout the Philippines every day. The special taste comes from the addition of green papaya, which you can find in almost any Asian food store. This is from Melbourne-based Filipino, Roland Pintay.

Serves 4

1 onion, chopped finely
1 clove garlic, crushed
1 tablespoon grated fresh ginger
oil for frying
1 chicken, cut into pieces
1 cup water
salt
1 green papaya, peeled and sliced just prior to cooking

■ Fry the onion, garlic and ginger in oil until soft. Add the chicken pieces and fry until browned a little. Add water and a little salt and allow to boil. Cover and simmer until chicken is cooked in its broth. Add the sliced papaya and continue cooking until tender. Serve.

Pria's Tamil-style Chicken Curry

Pria Viswalingam knows a good curry. Growing up in Kuala Lumpur, his earliest memories are of food, of the grilling of satay sticks, the hiss of spices hitting the woks at the hawker stalls and the delicious food his Colombo-born mother would prepare.

This recipe is for a Tamil-style curry which means, says Pria, that there is a lot of gravy for fluffy white rice to absorb. It has an extended name which proves that Pria really does have a special relationship with food: 'Saturday Night Home Alone Chicken Curry (So You Can Eat Obscene Amounts with Your Fingers and Suck Slowly On the Bones in Peace)'.

Serves 4

1 decent corn-fed/free-range chook
1 large onion
lots of garlic
lots of ginger
1 teaspoon black mustard seeds
ghee
3 green or red chillies, (about finger-length)
2 ripe sweet tomatoes
large dollop tamarind paste
1 tablespoon ground chilli powder
½ teaspoon turmeric
¼ teaspoon cumin
¼ teaspoon cloves
1 cinnamon stick
1 tablespoon dried coriander
4 curry leaves
salt and pepper to taste
1 potato, cubed
fresh coriander leaves

■ Joint chicken, keeping meat on the bone. Fry onion, garlic, ginger, mustard seeds in hot ghee. Add chillies, tomatoes and tamarind and fry. Add all the powdered spices, cinnamon stick, dried coriander and a little water to make a paste and fry until the oil separates.
■ Throw in the chook, a couple of cups of water along with the curry leaves, season, cover and cook on low heat. Add potatoes halfway through. A few minutes before finishing, add coriander leaves. Serve with white rice, dry-fried long beans and coconut sambol (see p. 185), with some good quality yoghurt on the side.

Mediterranean Chicken and Fennel Sausages

Claire de Lune is larger than life, probably due to her 18cm-high platform shoes, her lolly pink mini-length vinyl apron and, not least,

Claire de Lune

her flair in the kitchen. She's the alter ego of chef Marc Kuzma (French-born of an Ukrainian father and Italian mother) … in drag. And yes, says Marc, clothes do help to put you in the right mood — both Marc and Claire love to cook. Claire is just the more flamboyant of the two!

'It's like travelling,' she says, 'no need to leave my kitchen. With the right ingredients and flavours you can transport your tastebuds anywhere in the world! I just have to close my eyes for a few seconds — or is it that my false eyelashes are too long? Wonderful Mediterranean products are easy to find here, so as my grandmama always said, "Choose the best in season" and enjoy!'

The pork casing for these Mediterranean sausages you can get from a butcher's. As Claire says, 'It's not hard to use it. It's a bit like putting on a very long condom. Good practice and not so silly when you consider that the first condoms were made with pork casing. What a thought!'

Makes about 20 sausages
1kg chicken thigh fillet
1 egg
salt and pepper to taste
1 teaspoon paprika
small chopped red onion
little chopped fennel top
2 cloves garlic, crushed
2–3 tablespoons yoghurt
about 2 metres of pork casing (sausage skin)
large piping bag with a long nozzle

■ Place the chicken with the egg, salt, pepper, paprika, onion, fennel and garlic into a food processor. Using the pulse button, process until the mixture is coarsely chopped. At the last minute add the yoghurt to blend with the mixture, but do not over process. Soak the pork casing in warm water, place around the tube at the end of the piping bag and fill the bag with the sausage mix, twisting the top of the bag and pushing gently until the sausage mix fills the casing. Tie a knot at the end of your sausage and there we go.

■ It takes a little practice but what fun. Before barbecuing, prick them all over. Serve with a simple salad of sliced ripe tomato, thinly sliced raw fennel and red onion, a little crushed garlic, dressed with a little olive oil and a few drops of red wine vinegar. 'Simple, fresh, homemade and trust me', says Claire, 'nearly as good as a trip overseas. Bon appetit.'

Jewish Stuffed Chicken Legs

Edytta Super, from Israel, but now living in Sydney, subtitles Hebrew and Yiddish language films, works as a government interpreter, has two grown children and a dog and can be inspired on special occasions to put on a display of her culinary proficiency. You can use chicken drumsticks (2–3 per person) or make parcels with chicken thigh fillets (roll them around the mixture and secure with toothpicks).

Serves 6
12–18 chicken drumsticks

Stuffing:
400g chicken livers
2 medium-sized onions, sliced
2 cloves garlic, crushed
4-6 tablespoons olive oil
2 hard-boiled eggs, grated
1 small onion, extra, grated

■ Bone the drumsticks so that you have a pocket-shaped piece with two openings. ('If you can't do it yourself, ask your butcher,' says Edytta. 'It will take him half a second. And then tell all your friends you did it yourself.') Leave the skin on.

To make the stuffing:

■ Clean and wash the livers, 'cut off all the bits that look irrelevant' (Edytta again) and fry the sliced onions and the garlic in oil. When the onions are nice and brown, toss in the livers and fry quickly until almost dark-brown. Allow to cool, grate the livers (don't mince them) and add the eggs and grated onion. Fill the drumsticks with the stuffing, bake in a medium 180°C oven for a good hour and enjoy.

Stephanie Alexander with Joanna Savill

Mum's Chicken or 'Chicken Dionysus'

Stephanie Alexander is one of Australia's best-known cooks and cooking writers. Her mother, Mary Burchett, was the one who introduced Stephanie to the joys of preparing food and Stephanie still remembers 'Mum bent in front of the Aga oven scooping baked potatoes into her apron, shaping bread rolls for dinner, forking rough troughs in the mashed potato on top of the shepherd's pie' ... (*The Cooks Companion* by Stephanie Alexander, Viking, 1996). Mary Burchett was also an avid traveller. Born in 1916 she took her first trip to Japan in 1936, and never stopped from then on, documenting her travels in diaries and journals — under the title, 'The Cook Packed a Suitcase'. She also loved to re-create the food she had enjoyed and would often cross-examine waiters and other locals on the ingredients and methods of preparation used in the dishes she tasted. Mary Burchett did publish one cookbook, *Through the Kitchen Door*, but typed up many more recipes for her own reference, and that of her family — a wonderful record of a pioneering Australian cook in her own right. This dish was originally made with the family's own chickens and cumquats from a large tree in their abundant garden and was inspired by travels in Greece (hence the very classical name!) This recipe is reprinted here with Stephanie's kind permission.

Serves 4

■ Note: Maggie Beer's verjus is a tangy juice distilled from unripened grapes and used to deglaze and marinate a variety of foods — as a superior substitute for lemon juice or vinegar.

2kg roasting chicken, preferably free range
salt and pepper to taste
1 lemon
4 cumquats
4 cloves garlic

several sprigs of sweet marjoram

2 tablespoons of olive oil

2 tablespoons Maggie Beer's verjus (See Note)

12 baby turnips, peeled

12 small carrots, peeled

8 flat mushrooms

8 small potatoes, scrubbed but unpeeled

½ cup well-reduced chicken stock

Carrot pudding:

1 cup grated carrot

1 cup fresh breadcrumbs

½ cup celery, finely chopped

1 small onion, finely diced

2 cloves garlic, finely chopped

½ cup currants or seeded raisins

1 teaspoon fresh marjoram leaves

¼ cup toasted pinenuts

1 egg

salt and freshly ground pepper

½ cup well-reduced chicken stock

■ Season chicken with salt and pepper inside and out. Cut lemon in half and squeeze juice of one half inside and over the chicken. Place the spent lemon half in the chicken cavity. Do the same with 2 of the cumquats. Place the garlic and marjoram inside the chicken. Rub outside with the olive oil and place on its side in a baking dish into a preheated oven at 200°C for 20 minutes.

■ Baste with juices. Lower oven to 180°C. Turn chicken to other side for a further 20 minutes. Remove from oven, baste with juices, squeeze over juice of remaining half lemon and remaining cumquats and drop the rinds into the baking dish. Pour over the verjus.

■ Turn the chicken breast uppermost and scatter prepared vegetables around the bird. Place the prepared carrot pudding in the oven

at this time and cook the entire meal for a further 45 minutes.

■ At the end of the cooking time, remove chicken and vegetables to a warm place. Spoon off any fat in the baking dish, add chicken stock and bubble up the juices. Carve chicken, surround with the vegetables, spoon over the juices and serve with the carrot pudding alongside.

Carrot pudding:

■ Mix carrot and breadcrumbs in a bowl. Saute the celery, onion and garlic in a little oil for a few minutes until the vegetables have softened. Add to the mixing bowl. Stir in the currants or raisins, marjoram and pinenuts. Mix in the egg. Taste for seasoning and adjust. Add sufficient of the reduced stock to make a soft but not runny mixture. Pack into an oiled ovenproof dish and bake approximately 40 minutes until well browned.

Cheong Liew's Whole Chicken Baked in Salt Dough

Cheong Liew is a legend. He's credited with inspiring the 'fusionist' or 'East meets West' approach to modern Australian cooking — the marriage of Asian and European techniques and ingredients in creating new dishes and taste sensations. He is also widely respected as a lecturer on food. He grew up in Kuala Lumpur and has always been adventurous when it comes to cooking. He's currently head chef at The Grange Restaurant in the Adelaide Hilton where he prepares this knockout dish using plump organic chicken (from Kangaroo Island, off the South Australian coast).

Tandoor/Tandir/Tanoor

A tandoor is a cylindrical oven built around a clay or pottery sphere ('like a big bottle', says Indian restaurateur Inder Mehandiratta). And although the tandoor is automatically associated with India, the idea of baking one's food in a drum-shaped oven, originally made of baked earth, is one that is common to many countries across what was once known as Asia Minor. The technology is simple — a clay drum encased in an insulated box. Charcoal is allowed to burn in the bottom of the drum, with the help of an air vent let into the rear or side of the oven. It must be white-hot to send the right amount of heat along and up the oven walls. Marinated meat is threaded on skewers and placed vertically in the oven so that the metal skewers help conduct the heat through the centre of the meat.

Once upon a time this type of oven was built into the ground, and still is in some villages. In restaurants however it is housed in a series of casings and bricks for insulation, often with tiles on top around the opening. A Middle Eastern tanoor·can be quite sumptuously decorated with blue, yellow and white tiles although the simple roadside versions are often merely old petrol drums! No matter how basic or fancy, like its Indian counterpart the tanoor is a great spot for sticking flat rounds of uncooked dough! They turn into aromatic slabs of fresh-from-the-oven bread, some parts crisper than others, all with that toasted just-baked taste that makes you want to eat nothing else.

Most of the Indian restaurateurs in Australia have bought their tandoors here — there are a couple of enterprising people making them. And if you are such a tandoori fan, you could even get a little one for domestic use! They certainly give a flavour you would find hard to replicate, although our friend Inder Mehandiratta does have a suggestion (see recipe for Inder's chicken tikka on pp. 48–9).

1.8kg whole chicken

30g salt and pepper for seasoning

60mls cognac

60ml madeira

40ml truffle juice

50g butter

4 shallots

2 cloves garlic, crushed and chopped

300g fresh chicken livers, cleaned with white tissues removed

8 cepes, cut into halves

8 mushrooms, cut into quarters

6 cloud ear fungus

1 tablespoon tarragon

1 tablespoon thyme

1 tablespoon rosemary

150ml creme fraiche

100g beef bone marrow

Salt dough:

1kg salt

500ml water

1kg plain flour

1kg salt

For the salt dough:

◾ Mix salt and flour together, then add enough water to form a soft dough. Allow to rest for 2 hours.

For the chicken:

◾ Season chicken by rubbing salt and pepper, 20ml of cognac, 20ml of madeira and 20 ml of truffle juice inside the cavity thoroughly, and on the outside of the chicken. Set aside and let marinate for 30 minutes.

◾ In a large heavy frying pan, heat butter and saute shallots and garlic.

◾ Add chicken liver and saute until lightly brown. Add the remainder of the cognac, madeira and truffle juice. Remove chicken liver from the frying pan.

◾ Add cepes, mushrooms, cloud ear fungus and herbs to the frying pan and cook for 30 seconds, remove from heat, mix in chicken liver and fold in the beef bone marrow. Fill the cavity of the chicken with the chicken liver mixture, season with salt and pepper and seal the chicken on all sides in a hot frying pan with butter. Whip creme fraiche until light and brush onto chicken. Using butcher's twine, truss chicken firmly. Roll out salt dough large enough to wrap the whole chicken. Place chicken in the centre, fold all sides together and invert onto a baking tray. Bake chicken at 180°C for 1½ hours. Allow to rest for 10 minutes, then discard dough and carve chicken.

Eight Treasures Chicken

This is a traditional Shanghainese dish eaten at Chinese New Year or for a special birthday. In China, it is more common to eat Eight Treasures Duck but in Australia, master chef Qi Sheng Zhu finds chicken works best. Once you've perfected the fine art of deboning the chicken (a good boning knife is a must), the rest is easy and the result is absolutely delicious. You could also get your butcher to debone for you. Alternatively, this will work with an un-deboned chicken. You could also experiment with the stuffing in a chicken breast fillet, which you can slice into with a sharp knife to make a pocket. Eight is a lucky number in China, hence the eight treasures — all easy to find in Asian food stores. If you use a deboned chicken, the shape made once you've trussed the chicken is — you guessed it — a number eight!

Qi Sheng Zhui and his wife Ba Boa Ji

Serves 4

1 whole chicken, preferably with feet and head still attached

handful green peas, shelled and blanched

handful diced carrots, blanched

3 slices ham, diced

5 king prawns, shelled and sliced

8 scallops

8 dried mushrooms (soaked in water for 20 minutes)

handful peanuts, fried

8 lotus seeds

1 cup glutinous rice, soaked in water for 20 minutes

2 tablespoons oyster sauce

pinch salt

1 small knob ginger, finely chopped

¼ cup Chinese wine

2 tablespoons sesame oil

2 star anise

1 tablespoon Thai fish sauce

⅓ cup soy sauce

3 tablespoons potato starch

vegetable oil for frying

■ Debone the chicken, using a sharp boning knife (or ask your butcher to debone). Cut the bone carefully away from flesh. It's important not to break the skin as it must form a seal to keep flavour intact.

■ In a large bowl, mix the green peas, carrots, ham, king prawns, scallops, dried mushrooms, peanuts and lotus seeds with soaked rice, oyster sauce, salt, Chinese wine and Thai fish sauce. Stuff into the cavity of the chicken and place one of the chicken wings in the opening.

■ Secure the chicken with twine. Move stuffing through chicken using your hands so it's distributed evenly. Tie another string about ⅔ down the length of the chicken so there's a smaller bulge sitting on top of a large bulge — it should have the shape of a figure eight.

■ Rub skin with sesame oil, place two large ovals of ginger and star anise on top of chicken. Wrap completely in foil and place in a large steamer with a plate under the chicken. Steam for 2 hours.

■ Wearing rubber gloves to protect your hands, remove chicken from steamer, pouring away the liquid on the plate.

■ Rub chicken all over with soy sauce for flavour and colour. Pat on a light, even coating of potato starch so the entire chicken is covered.

■ Heat enough vegetable oil in wok to completely immerse the chicken. Deep-fry for 2 minutes. Check every 10 seconds until skin is golden brown. Use a long-handled sieve to remove and set aside.

■ Cut the twine and place on a serving platter. Garnish with steamed green vegetables.

Slice into thick slices. Serve with low-salt soy sauce and finely sliced chilli.

Max Pantacchini's Whole Chicken in Rock Salt and Black Peppercorn Crust

This recipe comes from Max Pantacchini, a classically trained chef who grew up in Cannes, worked for a swag of international hotels and settled with his wife Francoise in Cairns, Far North Queensland. The couple run a hugely successful gourmet food company, specialising in smoked fish, particularly salmon and barramundi. The recipe can also be used for a whole fish.

Serves 6

1kg rock salt
2 teaspoons whole black peppercorns
4 egg whites
Size 16 whole chicken

Filling:

1 onion, chopped
2 tomatoes, seeds removed and cubed
½ bunch coriander, chopped
3 cloves garlic, crushed
200g plain yoghurt
salt/pepper/ground cumin to taste
1 tablespoon olive oil

For the filling:

■ Mix all the ingredients together in a large bowl and then spoon carefully into cavity of chicken. Use any of the filling left over for the potato recipe which appears below.

For the crust:

■ Mix salt and pepper and egg white to make an easy paste to spread around the chicken. Try and make it as even as possible as it makes a nice golden crust after cooking. Place chicken in baking dish and arrange potatoes around the outside. Cook for 2 hours at 240°C. Set cooked chicken aside for 5 minutes before cracking the crust. Max warns you to be careful of the steam that escapes when you do.

Potatoes:

■ 6 medium potatoes, washed, cut in half and topped with the yoghurt mix. Wrap potatoes in foil and roast with the chicken.

Beef and veal

Mandalay Beef Sibyan (Burmese Beef Curry)

Over twenty years ago, an enterprising young Burmese chef made his way to Australia and set up a restaurant that has introduced Sydney to the chilli-hot tastes of his homeland. Maung-Tauk-Sein, or James Chang as he calls himself, says Burmese people like their food 'very, very hot' but adds with a twinkle, that he has gradually increased many of his regular customers' chilli tolerance over the years. This recipe, which is equally great using chicken or pork, will not burn your mouth, though it can be made hotter with the addition of more chilli powder.

Serves 4

2 tablespoons vegetable oil
1 medium red onion
2 cloves garlic, crushed
2 teaspoons ground ginger
1kg topside beef, cut into 1cm cubes
1 teaspoon fish sauce
1 teaspoon paprika
¼ teaspoon black pepper
½ teaspoon sesame oil
½ teaspoon chilli powder
2 teaspoons curry powder
2 teaspoons tomato paste
2 tablespoons coconut milk
1 teaspoon salt

2 potatoes, peeled and cubed (optional)
1 cup water
Fresh sprigs coriander to garnish

■ Heat vegetable oil in saucepan and saute onion, garlic and ginger for 1 minute. Add meat to saucepan and brown. Add fish sauce, paprika, pepper, sesame oil, chilli and curry powders, tomato paste, coconut milk, salt and potatoes and stir mixture until combined. Add water and cook for 5 minutes or until a thin layer of oil forms on the top. (Cooking time may be less for chicken or pork.) Garnish with coriander and serve with boiled rice.

Plia (Cambodian Beef Salad)

Gently marinated beef served with lots of salad greens and herbs is a very healthy and appealing proposition. Most Thai restaurants serve a similar dish, but with grilled meat and rather different flavours from this Cambodian recipe. It comes from our Khmer friend and colleague Phaline Tuy — who discovered just how appealing this salad can be when she served it at a 'bring a plate' function at SBS Radio where she is a broadcaster. We certainly love it — especially the little touches like fried rice vermicelli and the fact that the meat is cooked only in lemon juice, making it extremely tender.

Serves 4–6

300g lean topside, sliced finely (about 1 finger long, 4cm wide)
lemon juice (enough to cover meat)
salt and sugar to taste
2 pieces galangal — wrapped in foil, grilled for a few minutes and then pounded to a powder

3 pieces coriander root, chopped

2 cloves garlic, finely chopped

packet rice vermicelli

1 head of continental lettuce

2 red or green capsicums (cut in half and sliced)

a stem of tender young lemongrass, sliced very finely

1 small onion, cut in half and sliced

a bunch of mint, curly and/or long (as many types as you can find, usually three, leaves only of course), chopped finely

a handful of roasted peanuts, ground

▉ Place slices of topside in a bowl and squeeze lemon juice over them. Leave to marinate for an hour or so. Squeeze all the juice out of the beef and set the meat aside. Boil the lemon and beef juice mixture, add a pinch of salt, sugar and galangal, the coriander root and garlic. Add more salt and sugar if too sour. Allow to cool.

▉ Deep-fry the rice vermicelli until crispy. Cut the continental lettuce into fine shreds, chop in the capsicum, lemongrass, onions and lots of mint. Add the meat and fried vermicelli, pour the juice mixture over the top and sprinkle with peanuts.

Marita's Sri Lankan Beef Curry

Marita Forbes was the owner/chef of the popular Sri Lankan Cuisine Restaurant in Sydney's Granville for twenty years, a place that lured customers from halfway down the street with the heavenly aromas that wafted from the kitchen. This recipe is one of her favourite dishes, learnt from her mother when she was growing up in Colombo.

Serve with Sri Lankan coconut sambol (see Sauces and Relishes) and spicy Sri Lankan potatoes (see Vegetable chapter).

Marita Forbes

Serves 4–6

1kg stewing beef, diced

1 handful sliced onions

½ teaspoon each of ground ginger and crushed garlic

5cm cinnamon stick

1 sprig of fresh curry leaves

5cm piece of lemongrass

oil or ghee for frying

2 teaspoons chilli powder

4 teaspoons curry powder (dark roast)

salt to taste

¼ cup white vinegar

½ teaspoon ground saffron

½ cup coconut milk

▉ Wash and dry meat, then fry onions, ginger, garlic, cinnamon, curry leaves, lemongrass in a little oil or ghee. When onions are transparent, add the meat, the chilli powder, curry powder, salt, vinegar, saffron and a little water and allow to simmer together with the cup coconut milk.

▉ Let mixture boil until meat is tender. Keep

an eye on the liquid needed and add more water if necessary until beef is soft and sauce is thick.

Moroccan Beef

Michael Guiguis was born in Morocco of Egyptian and Sudanese parents. There were no recipe books in his cooking training — just instinct, familiar flavours and traditions handed down from generation to generation. His first formal training came when he moved to France — to the gastronomic centre that is Lyon, where he worked as an apprentice chef for five years. He then worked his way around Europe, developing a knowledge and love of Mediterreanean flavours in all their guises. He came to Australia in 1979 and still works as a chef.

Serves 4

½ teaspoon rock salt

1 teaspoon cracked pepper

4 x 100g King Island beef fillets

150g unsalted butter

3 cloves garlic, crushed

250g bone marrow (available from butchers or in osso buco cuts)

250g beef stock

1 glass red wine, preferably shiraz

100g caramelised soy sauce (like the Black Elephant brand)

100g sumac (a reddish-brown lemon pepper found in Middle Eastern groceries)

▨ Combine rock salt and cracked pepper in a mixing bowl. Roll beef in the mixture so that it is coated on all sides.

▨ In a cast-iron pan, melt the butter on a high heat, stir in garlic and marrow until caramelised. Seal beef on all sides in the mixture, then brush with soy sauce. Add stock to pan and let it gently simmer and reduce by half, add shiraz and place pan in the oven at 150°C for 20 to 30 minutes.

▨ Place each fillet on a plate and sprinkle liberally with sumac.

Carbonada Criolla (South American Baked Stuffed Pumpkin)

Carbonada Criolla is from Uruguayan chef Diana Pinon who has introduced many to South American fare over the twenty years she's been cooking. This is an example of an unusual and spectacular dish of Chilean and Argentinian origins (hence the corn). South American cuisine is not well-known, but like Mexican cuisine, combines an indigenous element with European influences. You can leave out the meat and substitute mushrooms, the beef stock can be a vegetable one if you like.

Serves 4

1 large pumpkin

soft butter

sugar

olive oil

1kg diced beef

2 onions, chopped

2 red capsicums, chopped

4 cloves garlic, chopped

beef stock

3 tomatoes, chopped

oregano and bay leaf

salt and pepper

500g potatoes, cubed

500g sweet potatoes, cubed
3 ears corn, cut into rounds
4 peaches, cut into halves

■ Wash pumpkin well and cut into the top to create a lid, leaving the stem as a handle. Scrape seeds and fibres from the pumpkin shell and brush the inside with soft butter and sprinkle with sugar. Bake in a preheated oven for 45 minutes. It should be firm enough to hold the filling.

■ Meanwhile, heat the oil in a large heavy-based pan and cook the meat until browned. Remove meat and add onions, garlic, and capsicums to the cooking pan until soft. Pour in the stock and bring to the boil. Add meat and stir in tomatoes, oregano, bay leaf, salt and pepper. Cover the pan and simmer for 15 minutes. Then add the potatoes and sweet potatoes and cook for 10 minutes. Finally, add the corn rounds and peach halves and cook for 5 minutes. Pour the entire contents of the pan into the baked pumpkin, cover with its lid and bake for 15 minutes.

Sabine Gleditch's German Rouladen

Broadcaster Sabine Gleditch grew up eating this delicious dish and was happy to pass on her family recipe along. Buy the best possible beef available and spend time sourcing the right brand of mustard, she advises. The rest is easy.

Serves 6

6 thin (5mm thick) slices of beef fillet — at least 30cm long and 10cm wide
mild but tasty mustard — preferably Thomy, imported from Switzerland and available from delis and some supermarkets
4 medium-sized onions, finely chopped
bacon pieces, finely chopped
salt
white pepper
margarine
sour cream or creme fraiche
wooden toothpicks

■ Spread out slices of beef and coat generously with mustard. Place onions and bacon pieces on top. Add salt and pepper. Roll up the meat carefully, making sure that you don't lose too much of the stuffing in the process and insert toothpicks to hold each roll together.

■ Fry in margarine until golden brown in hot 2-litre casserole dish. Add two tablespoons sour cream or creme fraiche. Lower the temperature slightly to avoid burning but continue frying for another 10 minutes. Add about 600ml boiling water, stir, place lid on top and let simmer for about an hour, occasionally turning and stirring the meat.

■ It's ready to serve after that time, but some people prefer the gravy thickened — which you can do with a small amount of cornflour. Don't forget to pull out the toothpicks before you serve — the meat will keep its rolled-up shape. Serve with peeled boiled potatoes (preferably the Tasmanian bintje variety available from good vegie markets). In Germany rouladen are traditionally served with red cabbage.

Edytta's Israeli Cholent

Translator, interpreter and Jewish humourist Edytta Super is originally from Israel, likes 'real food' — things like cholent in fact, which she

Cholent

Religious Jews are not permitted to cook on the Sabbath, but dishes prepared in advance may be kept hot in a previously lit oven. Enter cholent, a Central European favourite based on beans. Long, slow baking is part of its charm and appeal — enhancing rather than impairing the flavour. Housewives would prepare their cholent on Friday afternoons and take it to the baker's oven where it would cook overnight, and after schul (synagogue) services were over, it would be a fabulous hot dish for the family.

Served either as an accompaniment to roast meats, or as a main course, the baked dish should be quite thick when cooked, not dry but without excess liquid. The addition of meat to these recipes is a modern refinement on a dish once composed exclusively of beans simply because many Jewish families could not afford the meat.

What's interesting is that every family seems to have a different version of this dish, depending on what part of the world they are from. Israeli interpreter Edytta Super makes hers with tomato paste and includes slow-baked eggs in their shells, a decidedly Middle Eastern idea while journalist Peter Ipper, originally from

Hungary, uses a recipe containing ginger and red paprika — very Hungarian touches. It comes from his grandmother's cookbook — like many family heirlooms, a special piece of personal history. Its extra significance comes from the fact that it survived the Holocaust — Auschwitz, in fact, where his grandmother was sent during the war. Miraculously, she returned.

reckons is guaranteed to send the whole family off for a siesta after Saturday lunch. Edytta's version contains eggs baked in their shells — a very special addition.

Serves 6–8

2 large brown onions

oil for frying

6 cloves garlic (fresh please!)

1kg gravy beef, cut into large chunks

4 pieces of beef sparerib

500g borlotti beans, soaked in cold water overnight

8 medium-sized pontiac potatoes, peeled and cut into two or four pieces (not diced)

6 eggs

4 large tablespoons tomato paste

salt and pepper to taste

■ You'll need a fairly large, deep oven dish with a lid, or a big pot which will fit in the oven.

■ Slice the onions and throw into the hot oil, add crushed garlic and toss until golden brown. Add the meat and seal. Place in an oven dish, cover with soaked beans and potato pieces and then arrange the raw, unshelled eggs in between (they will be brown when the dish is ready — beautiful!). Finish off with tomato paste, salt and pepper to taste and water to cover. Put the lid on and place in a preheated oven at about 150°C for about 8 hours. Every 2 or 3 hours, or even after 5 hours, check to see the water is still there and stir once or twice. Reduce heat only if you leave it all night. You may serve it with white boiled rice (although not necessary) and cucumber salad. 'Enjoy! I know you will!' says Edytta.

Peter Ipper's Hungarian Cholent

This recipe comes from a very special memento — the cookbook belonging to journalist Peter Ipper's grandmother. Like its owner, it survived the Second World War. (Peter's grandmother was sent to Auschwitz.) The recipe was sent on to Peter in his new Australian home by his mother, who's holding on to the very precious original.

Serves 8–10

2 cups dried lima beans, soaked overnight and drained

1.5kg brisket

3 onions, diced

¼ cup oil

2 tablespoons salt

¼ teaspoon pepper

¼ teaspoon ground ginger

1 cup pearl barley

2 tablespoons flour

2 teaspoons ground red paprika

■ Use a heavy saucepan or Dutch oven and brown the meat and onions in the oil. Sprinkle with salt, pepper and ginger. Add the beans and barley and sprinkle with the flour and paprika. Add enough boiling water to cover 2–3cm above the mixture. Cover tightly. Cholent may be baked for 24 hours at 120°C or, for quicker cooking, at 180°C for 4–5 hours. Slice the meat and serve with the barley and beans.

Beef Goulash

Polish cooking double act Jerzy and Katrina Karon have been creating authentic dishes at a series of Sydney eateries since they arrived in Australia over a decade ago. This recipe is a favourite for both Jerzy and Katrina not just at home but as part of their professional repertoire.

Serves 4

500g lean beef (without bone)

30g vegetable oil

300g onions

salt and pepper to taste

1 tablespoon sweet paprika powder

1 bay leaf

5 allspice

2 tablespoons tomato paste

a dash of tabasco sauce

2 tablespoons flour

■ Wash meat under cold running water, pat dry and cut into cubes. Heat vegetable oil and fry the meat until browned all over. Peel and slice onion. Add to the meat and cook slowly. Season the meat with pepper, salt, paprika and tabasco. Add 2 cups of water, bay leaf and allspice. Cover saucepan, turn heat down to cook slowly for about an hour. When meat is tender, add tomato paste.

■ Mix flour with cold water (½ cup) add to the meat and cook for 3 minutes.

■ Serve with Irish potato pancake (see Vegetable section). On a serving platter, arrange potato pancake and fill with required amount of goulash. Fold pancake in half. Top with a small amount of goulash, followed by one teaspoon of sour cream and freshly chopped parsley. Serve with a fresh garden salad.

■ Note: Can also be served with latkes (p. 167) or galushka (p. 128).

Polish Marinated Beef

Katrina Karon is an accomplished cook who brought many flavours with her when she arrived from Krakow in 1986. Marinated beef is served throughout Europe but this particular recipe took some hard work and much experimentation on Katrina's part. She'd found her favourite version in a restaurant in her home city and played with ingredients and amounts to reproduce it perfectly.

Note: Leave the meat to marinate for 4 days before cooking.

Serves 6

1kg topside beef

vegetable oil

salt and pepper to taste

¼ cup raisins

100g pumpernickel or rye bread

fresh cream

Marinade:

2 medium onions, peeled and sliced

1 bunch carrots, washed and chopped

1 bunch celery, washed and chopped

5 juniper berries

15 peppercorns

5 allspice

2 bay leaves

250ml red wine vinegar

375ml water

1 glass red wine

■ Place all the marinade ingredients in a saucepan and bring to the boil. Set aside to cool.

■ Wash the beef under cold running water. Pat dry and place in a bowl. Pour cooled marinade mixture over the meat to cover completely. Leave to stand for about 4 days in the fridge, turning the meat occasionally.

- After marinating, lift meat from bowl and dry well.
- Heat vegetable oil in pan and brown the meat on all sides, sprinkling with salt and pepper. Add 375ml of marinade, 1 cup water and raisins.
- Cover saucepan and braise, turning occasionally. Replace the evaporated liquid using marinade and water. After cooking for an hour, add crumbled pumpernickel or rye bread.
- When the meat is cooked, leave it for 10 minutes to rest before carving it, to give the juices time to settle. Carve the meat into slices and serve on a warmed plate. Strain the pan juices through a sieve and make up to 375ml with water. Bring to boil, thicken with fresh cream. Season with 1 tablespoon raisins. Serve with pasta or potatoes and red cabbage.

Veal Medallions Normandy

Apples and apple brandy are native products of France's northern coastal region of Normandy. Appropriately then, this recipe came from a Melbourne restaurant called La Normandie. It was collected by our French colleagues at SBS Radio — who regularly interview chefs for their broadcasts. (Makes great listening!)

Serves 4
2 apples
100g champignon mushrooms
600–800g veal fillet sliced into medallions (slices of around 2cm in thickness)
oil
salt and pepper to taste
50ml calvados
1 glass of cider
80g creme fraiche

- Peel the apples and slice them finely; slice the mushrooms. This is a quick dish, so 8 to 10 minutes before you are ready to eat, sear the meat in a pan with a little oil. Add salt and pepper. Set aside meat.
- Pour off the cooking oil, turn up the heat and flambe with calvados. Deglaze with the cider (which will absorb all the cooking juices). Add the apples, mushrooms and creme fraiche and allow to boil. Simmer for 5 to 6 minutes in order to reduce the sauce.

Serve by first placing the medallions on the plate, then covering with the Normandy sauce. Accompany with potatoes or preserved fruit and a glass of cider or red wine, preferably French.

Chomlek (Simmered Summer Veal)

This dish is from Ohrid, in Western Macedonia — a beautiful lakeside town which is popular for summer holidays. (The lake is said to be the oldest in the world.) Naturally this is chiefly a summer dish and can, in fact, be eaten cold. This recipe is from Violeta Jovanovska, who is a wonderful cook.

Serves 4
500g diced veal or lamb
4–5 onions, cut into eighths
4–5 tomatoes, also in eighths
4–5 capsicums (the long pale green or red ones, roughly chopped)
1 clove garlic
1 teaspoon of red paprika
1 glass white wine

Kefta/Kufta/Koefte/Cevapcici and Keftedes

The Arabic word 'kufta' means 'hand' — hence the name for the kind of hand-rolled minced meat skinless sausages (rissoles or meatballs in more plebeian terms) that can be found all over North Africa and the Mediterranean — wherever the mighty Ottomans once ruled, in fact. The variations come with the types of meat used (although beef and lamb are the prime ingredients) and the herbs, spices and seasonings added to give these delicate little creations their own special taste.

Sudanese restaurateur Tahir Malik suggests using ground beef, ground lamb or both together, flavouring the mixture with coriander, cumin, black pepper and salt, a little fresh mint, some spring onion and binding it all with an egg, a little flour or some wheat germ. The meat is then rolled out into little cigar-shaped *kufta* which are cooked in a stew of onion and vegetables.

Anita Bezjak, of Slovenian origin, takes equal portions of lamb, beef, pork and veal ('make sure the beef is very lean', she says, 'to balance the fattier pork') and simply grates onion into the mix. One onion will do two kilos of meat — so reduce proportions accordingly. She then flavours the *cevapcici* with salt and pepper and a little paprika if feeling so inclined. The finished product is a squat, fat sausage with square edges — like a little lipstick box — shaped in the hands.

The Greeks have made their version of the hand-rolled meatball — *keftetha* — into a higher art form — but as Perth's Kailis family warns us in their family cookbook, 'one simply does not give out information on the *keftetha*'. The book, compiled by four generations of Kailises, goes on to tell us that, 'It's classified. Any written *keftetha* recipe is not the whole story — a comment passed in Greek church between two friends who do not know that you are in earshot reveals "I use mint". So you immediately store that information for your next attempt at the perfect *keftetha* … but do not be fooled into thinking that it comes that easy!' The closest we have come to unearthing the Greek secret is discovering that crumbling stale white bread into the meat mix gives it a particularly smooth texture and that a little parsley (or mint) never goes astray!

■ Cut the onion and tomato into eighths, and the meat, carrots and capsicums into similar sizes. In a heavy-based pot on the stove place a layer of each vegetable, with the meat somewhere in the middle. Drop in a clove of garlic and sprinkle with the paprika and salt as preferred. Pour the white wine over the lot, cover and simmer very, very slowly for a couple of hours.

Lamb and goat

Uncle Tony's Lamb on the Spit

Among the Greek community in Adelaide, Tony Vatsikidis is a legend. For decades now, he has cooked his signature dish — lamb on the spit — for christenings, birthdays, engagement parties, weddings and Greek Easter.

You need to start your preparations the afternoon before your feast and if you are serving this for lunch be up early to prepare the coals.

Serves 30

16–18kg lamb, the freshest and leanest possible
8 cloves garlic
oregano
black pepper to taste
salt to taste
olive oil with lemon juice and oregano

Stuffing:

5 whole onions, peeled
5 lemons, sliced in half
the fat set aside from the lamb
a handful of oregano
6 cloves garlic
black pepper

■ You will need a rotary electric-powered spit and about one-and-a-half bags of wood charcoal. Prepare lamb the night before cooking. Slice off all the fat from the lamb and save. Combine stuffing ingredients.

■ Impale the lamb with the iron spit so it rests under the neck, through the gut and up through the rump. Fill the gut with the stuffing mixture and sew it up with a needle and twine (available from butcher shops). Then secure the front legs together with wire. The sewing is important to stop the lamb from falling apart in the cooking process.

■ Make about eight deep parallel incisions in the side of the lamb and place a garlic clove in each. Dress with a mixture of oregano, black pepper and salt. Cover with a sheet overnight to allow the spices to be absorbed.

■ The next day, start by putting about ¾ of the charcoal on the bottom of the spit tray, light and wait about 30 minutes for the charcoal to get going.

■ If you want to eat at 2pm, light the charcoal really early (around 6am). When ready to barbecue, rearrange the charcoal so that it's concentrated at the sides where the legs will be placed.

■ Put the lamb on the spit at the highest notch and cook for 1 hour in that position. Then place it in the next notch down and baste with a mixture of olive oil and lemon with oregano.

■ Cook for the next 3 hours, moving charcoal around, adding more charcoal and constantly basting with the mixture.

■ The lamb should be ready about 4 hours after you have begun this process. It's ready when a knife slides easily through the meat. When this happens you can slice and serve. Uncle Tony wishes you 'Kali Orexi!' (Good appetite!)

Mrs Vatsikopoulos' Greek Leg of Lamb in the Oven

This recipe is from Adelaide-based Victoria Vatsikopoulos and you'll find it not only smells fabulous as you're cooking it, it's foolproof as well.

Serves 6
1 lean leg of lamb
2 tablespoons oregano
1 teaspoon salt
black pepper to taste
5 cloves garlic
a handful of cloves
1 espresso cup olive oil
juice of 1 lemon

Hassan M'Souli and Omar Majdi

■ Wash leg of lamb, dry and slice off excess fat. Coat the leg with a mixture of oregano, salt and black pepper. Cut about 5 deep incisions in the meat and stuff each slit with a clove of garlic and a clove. Baste with a mixture of olive oil and lemon juice.

■ Place in baking dish and pour half a cup of water in the bottom. Cover with foil and cook in a moderate 180°C oven for 3 hours. In the last 30 minutes remove the foil and allow the leg to brown on both sides.

■ If you like, you can peel some baby potatoes, coat them with a similar mixture of oil and lemon and place them in the dish with the lamb.

Lamb Couscous with Vegetables

Couscous is truly one of the great dishes of the world. It's basically a hard wheat semolina grain which is ground, rolled into pellets and steamed over the spicy stew with which it is served and without which the dish as such does not exist (at least in the minds of North Africans). While 'instant' couscous is available in Australia, it's a poor imitation of how fluffy real couscous can be.

Good couscous takes time. However, if you do want to cut corners, add a step to the recipe on the box by finishing the couscous with steam — placing the grains in either a couscousier or a colander lined with fine muslin. Balance this over the steaming spicy broth for 20 minutes and taste the difference. This recipe is served to great acclaim by Moroccan chef Hassan M'Souli.

Serves 4
1kg lamb shoulder, cut into small chops
2 red onions, diced
1 clove garlic, chopped
1 teaspoon ground ginger
1 tablespoon paprika
1 tablespoon ground cumin
2 bay leaves

1 fresh chilli, chopped

½ tablespoon saffron powder

1 tablespoon fresh coriander, chopped

½ cup olive oil

3 carrots, sliced into quarters

¼ pumpkin, cut into cubes

3 ripe tomatoes

3 parsnips, sliced into quarters

4 zucchini, sliced into quarters

salt and pepper to taste

Couscous:

750g couscous (coarse semolina — not the instant variety)

2 tablespoons olive oil

1 cup cold water

▨ To avoid couscous developing lumps, cover with water and set aside.

▨ Lightly fry lamb, onion, garlic and spices in olive oil and place into the bottom of a couscousier (or a large saucepan), cover with water and gently bring to the boil.

To prepare couscous:

▨ Drain couscous and place evenly on next level of couscousier or use a colander (mentioned above). Once the steam starts to penetrate couscous, allow a good 15 minutes steaming time.

▨ After 15 minutes, remove the couscous from the steamer and place in a large open bowl. Work with your fingers to separate grains. Add 2 tablespoons oil and 1 cup cold water, put back into the steamer and steam for a further 15 minutes.

▨ Add carrots to the meat and cook for 10 minutes, then add pumpkin, tomatoes, parsnip and zucchini and allow to cook evenly.

▨ When couscous and vegies are tender, arrange the grains around the outside of a heated serving platter, placing the lamb pieces in the centre, and the vegetables over the couscous.

▨ Garnish with Moroccan chickpeas (see recipe in Vegetables chapter) and the juices from cooking. If you have a lot of liquid, you can season with further spices or Moroccan harissa (see recipe in Sauces, Relishes and Marinades) for those guests who like a little more spice.

Abbacchio Alla Romana (Roman Spring Lamb)

Italians rarely eat lamb. In fact when they do, it is usually at Easter … and springtime. So mixing up pagan and Christian symbolism, how better to celebrate new life and new beginnings than with a very tender, young spring lamb (abbacchio in Italian)?

This dish was a popular standard when Giuliano Dambelli, co-author Joanna's husband, worked as a cook at the Atlanta restaurant in Sydney's Woolloomooloo. The restaurant has long since closed its doors but the recipe lives on. You can use the sauce ingredients to make a very zingy gravy for lamb roasted separately in whatever way you fancy — or try this casserole version. It would probably work quite nicely with lamb shanks, too.

Serves 6

1 knob of butter

2 tablespoons olive oil

2 cloves garlic, peeled and left whole

1.5kg spring lamb, boned and cubed

a little plain flour, seasoned

1 bay leaf
a few sprigs of rosemary
300ml dry white wine
150ml water
3 anchovy fillets
1 tablespoon wine vinegar
continental parsley to garnish

■ In a baking dish or casserole, melt butter and heat with the olive oil. Add garlic cloves and fry them gently. Dust the cubes of lamb with the seasoned flour and brown them in the butter and oil. Add the bay leaf, rosemary and wine and stir with a wooden spoon until the wine begins to simmer. Add the water and simmer, uncovered, for about 1 hour or until the lamb is tender and the sauce reduced.

■ Remove 3 tablespoons of sauce from the pan and mix it with the anchovy fillets and wine vinegar until you have a smooth paste. Return to the sauce and blend until smooth.

■ Transfer to a warm serving dish and garnish with parsley.

Fasule Me Pasterma (Albanian Lamb and Beans)

This is a recipe from a father and son team, Edi and Elton Kane — first and second generation Albanians. This recipe makes enough for five people — there are five in Edi's family. Allow several hours for preparation!

Serves 5
350–400g dried beans
550g smoked lamb ribs
1 medium onion
5–6 tablespoons olive oil

1 tablespoon paprika
1 tablespoon salt

■ Put beans and lamb together in a casserole and boil with 3 litres of water at medium heat for 2½ hours. Peel the onion, puree in a blender and stir-fry with the oil until the onion takes on a golden colour. As soon as you turn the heat off, stir in the paprika until the mixture is all red. Pour the mixture into the casserole, add salt, put the lid back on and let it simmer for a further 2 hours on a low heat.

■ Serve while still warm with special Albanian bread called kulace.

Fijian Lamb Curry

Formerly of Radio Fiji, where he worked for many years as a journalist, Jai Kumar now manages the radio studios at SBS in Sydney. Like many Fijians, Jai is pretty multicultural in his tastes — enjoying all the Melanesian dishes native to the Fijian islands, but also well-versed in the Indian culinary arts. Jai, who cultivates a dazzling crop of squat, almost triangular Fijian chillies in his garden, says the essential difference between Indo–Fijian and Indian subcontinent food is in the complexity of the spice base. Indo–Fijian is lighter, less dense in spices and more often includes coconut milk (although this 'dry' curry has no coconut in it). For this recipe, we thank Jai's daughters Shalini and Kamini Kumar.

Serves 4–6
1kg lamb chops
2 teaspoons crushed garlic
½ teaspoon crushed ginger

½ teaspoon crushed chilli

2 tablespoons curry powder (masala) as preferred (see Note)

1 medium onion, sliced finely

1 tablespoon oil

salt to taste

2 medium potatoes, quartered

¼ to 1 cup water, optional

chopped fresh coriander

■ Trim fat from chops and cut meat into bite-sized pieces. Mix garlic, ginger, chilli and masala with a little water to form a thick paste. Brown onions in oil in a pan. Add curry paste and fry for about 10 seconds on a medium to high heat, stirring continuously.

■ Add meat and salt, stir well and cover. Lower heat to medium. Allow to cook for about 10 minutes, then add potatoes.

■ Cook until meat is tender, stirring regularly. The meat will cook in the water it 'sweats' in and this water should dry up by the time the meat is tender. If the water from the meat sweating should dry up too quickly add ¼ cup of water and continue cooking.

■ When tender, turn up heat to high and stir continuously to ensure any extra water dries up. Be careful not to allow the meat to stick to the pan.

■ The curry can be served dry or if desired, add ¼ cup of water and cook for a further 3 to 5 minutes on a medium heat for a thick gravy. Up to 1 cup of water can be added depending on the consistency of the gravy required.

■ Serve, garnished with fresh coriander, with either boiled rice, roti or naan or Lebanese bread and fresh or bottled fruit chutney.

■ Note: a simple masala or curry powder usually consists of coriander and turmeric blended with some or any of the following:

peppercorns, fenugreek, mustard seed, cumin or fennel seed. Add cinnamon, ground cloves or ground ginger for extra aroma.

Khoreshe Ghormeh Sabzi (Tangy Persian Lamb)

A fabulous name for an exotic Iranian dish from Teheran, a recipe given to us by broadcaster Asie Kodeiri. What sets this braised meat and vegetable dish apart is the sour flavour of oman or muscat lemon, a kind of musty dried lime, dark in colour with small seeds. They swell with cooking and are then squeezed into the dish to maximise flavour. They also come powdered and are available from any Middle Eastern grocers.

Serves 4

500g diced meat (Asie prefers good lean lamb)

¼ cup chopped onion

100g red beans

3–4 dried oman or muscat lemon, which is also known as black lime (remove the seeds before use), or 1 tablespoon lemon powder

salt to taste

1kg mixed vegetables and greens (suggested are parsley and leeks and, if you were in Iran, fenugreek), chopped

250g margarine

■ Fry the diced meat with the onion. Add the red beans and dried lemons, salt to taste and cover with water. Allow to cook until tender. Meanwhile fry the chopped vegetables in the margarine. Just before the meat is completely cooked, add the vegetables to the main dish and finish cooking together. Serve with rice.

Racks of Lamb in Massaman Curry

When flamboyant Thai chef Prasit Prateeprasen was eight years old and living in the royal city of Aytthaya, he would help his grandmother cook the most fabulous meals. Prasit's family are related to the Thai royal family so they really were preparing and eating food fit for a king — like this fragrant Muslim-style dish. His early training has stood him in good stead — Prasit now owns several restaurants in Sydney.

Serves 4

4 racks of lamb (6 cutlets each)
2 x 250ml cans coconut milk

Sauce:

12 cardamom pods
12 cloves
6 star anise
4 tablespoons cumin seed
¼ cup coriander seed
dried chilli to taste
2 tablespoons red curry paste (see recipe in Sauces, Relishes and Marinades under Three Thai Curry Pastes)
2 tablespoons tamarind puree or to taste
3 cans coconut milk

To make the sauce:

Roast cardamom, cloves, star anise, cumin, coriander and dried chilli then pound to a powder — a coffee grinder is very useful if you have one. Mix the spices, 3 cans of coconut milk, curry paste and tamarind puree together and bring to boil until thickened.

To prepare the lamb:

Trim as much of the fat as possible then place in large pan with 2 cans of coconut milk and boil until tender. When it's cooked, add the

Rita and Bill Fenelon

curry sauce and boil for 3 minutes. Serve with steamed rice and fried whole peanuts.

Rita Fenelon's Irish Stew

Rita Fenelon is the warm face behind the counter at Emerald Meats, helping husband Bill in the shop. This is her own recipe for Irish stew which she cooks on the stove top if she's home. When she's working, she leaves the casserole in the oven, sets the timer and comes home to the glorious aromas of this Irish national dish.

Serves 4

1.5kg of lamb forequarter chops (or chump chops with the fat trimmed)
1kg potatoes
2 large onions
2 cups (approx) chicken stock or water with 2 chicken stock cubes dissolved
1 tablespoon chopped parsley and thyme (mixed)
salt and pepper to taste

■ Peel and slice potatoes and onions. Place a layer of potatoes in saucepan or casserole dish then a layer of meat and finally the onion. Season each layer and repeat once more, finishing with a layer of potato. Pour liquid over — enough to come halfway up the casserole dish.

■ Simmer on top of stove (very gently) for about 2 hours or cook in a moderate 180°C oven for 2 hours or until meat is tender. Check halfway through to see if a little more liquid is needed.

Khasi ko Tarkari (Nepalese Goat Curry)

Growing up on a blend of Nepalese, Bhutanese, Muslim, Chinese and Tibetan cuisines has had a lasting effect on effervescent chef Mary Dorjee. She was born in Kalimpong, a hill station in the district of Darjeeling and has a mission, she says, to 'recreate and capture the magic flavours and textures' of her youth. She's in the right field, running a successful catering business with her sister Pauline Yip.

'Mealtimes at home were always an adventure. We looked wide-eyed as steaming momos (steamed dumplings) or dhal-puris (lentil-stuffed bread) were accompanied by succulent meat dishes and mouth-watering homemade vegetarian achaars (pickles),' she says. This is a favourite recipe.

Serves 4

⅔ cup vegetable oil
1 whole head garlic, peeled
2.5cm fresh ginger, peeled and chopped
1 large onion, finely chopped
1 teaspoon fenugreek seeds
1 cinnamon stick, 5cm long
1 teaspoon black mustard seeds
2 bay leaves
6 cardamom pods, bruised
½ teaspoon ground turmeric
1 tablespoon ground coriander
2 tablespoons ground cumin
2 teaspoons salt
1 teaspoon sugar
2 tablespoons tomato paste
4 fresh red chillies, chopped
4 tablespoons white vinegar
1kg goat meat, diced
250ml water
4 tablespoons fresh coriander, chopped

■ Grind the garlic and ginger with a little water to make a paste. Set aside.

■ Heat the oil in a deep heavy-based pan over a medium/high heat and fry the onion until golden brown. Remove onion with a slotted spoon.

■ In the same oil, fry the fenugreek seeds for a few seconds. Then add the mustard seeds, bay leaves, cinnamon stick and cardamom pods. Fry for a few more seconds. Do the same with the ginger and garlic paste, then add the fried onions and stir. Add the dry spices — turmeric, ground coriander and cumin — add salt, sugar and tomato paste and stir until the spice mix separates from the oil. Finally add the fresh chillies and the vinegar, add the goat meat completely coating the meat in the spices. Stir-fry for about 5 minutes. Pour in the water and bring to the boil. Cover and let the curry simmer for about 45 minutes, stirring a few times. Before serving hot with boiled rice garnish with fresh coriander.

Pork

Tony Marino's Porchetta (Spit Roasted Pork)

Tony Marino loves to eat. A self-taught butcher who grew up in the Abruzzi region of Italy, he says food is his life, with nothing more pleasant than gathering his extended family around him for a big feast. Tony came to Australia in 1960, following the beautiful Elisabetta who later became his wife. The couple settled on the outskirts of Adelaide and started a butchery and later a smallgoods business that has now grown into an empire. Tony started curing his own prosciutto using methods he had picked up in Italy. At one stage the whole family would gather around in the evenings to help the prosciutto cure perfectly by massaging the salt gently into the flesh for an even flavour and tender texture. Now Tony has machines to do this work and a factory filled with well over a thousand prosciutti at any one time. As well, he's famous for zampone or stuffed pig's trotter and this delicious pork cooked on the spit.

With competition being what it is, Tony was reluctant to give us exact amounts for his seasoning, but experienced cooks will be able to use this as a guide.

You'll need to buy or hire a spit roaster

Serves 20, depending on the size of the pig

1 whole pig (deboned — get your butcher to do this! Remove

Tony Marino with grandson Riccardo

the trotters and carefully slice around the backbone so that the entire length of bone is removed. You should be left with the head and entirely deboned trunk.)
20 cloves garlic, peeled and chopped finely
dried rosemary
bay leaves
ground nutmeg
fennel seeds
salt and pepper to taste
sugar
strong twine
a large upholstery needle

■ Sprinkle garlic generously around entire insides of pig. Mix together the other spices, Spreading open the inside cavity, fill it with the mixture. Roll the meat back to its original shape and with strong twine and a large curved upholstery needle, sew pig back up the middle, looping it around the entire pig every handspan or so. Roast on spit for up to 4 hours. Rest the meat for 10 to 15 minutes before carving in rounds.

The Alice Springs Filipino community

Lechon (Filipino Suckling Pig)

Around Australia, no Filipino get-together is complete without a roasted pig on the spit. And there is a certain pecking order to determine who does which job. In the Alice Springs Filipino community, Philips Tucio is seen as the master of the lechon (and has been for most of the twenty years he has been in Australia).

Serves up to 20, depending on the size of the pig
1 whole pig, intestines and trotters removed
20 stalks lemongrass (pound the white fleshy ends with a hammer before using)
a handful of bay leaves
3 peeled onions, cut into quarters
2 handfuls of garlic cloves
salt and pepper to taste
1 cup of Filipino soy sauce (sweeter and stickier than the Chinese variety)
extra soy sauce and vegetable oil for basting

■ Stuff the pig with the lemongrass, bay leaves, onions, garlic and soy sauce mixture. The pig is basted every 20 to 30 minutes with a mixture of soy sauce and vegetable oil. Depending on the size of the pig, it will usually take 2 to 4 hours to cook.

Philips says no party is complete without lechon and usually no-one goes home empty-handed. The leftovers are divided between the party-goers and eaten later cold or woven into a number of Filipino dishes such as humba (see below).

Annabelle's Humba (Sweet and Sour Pork)

Annabelle and her nine brothers and sisters all grew up eating humba on Negros Island, Visayas, in the Philippines. Without refrigeration, this was the perfect way of preserving leftover pork from lechon or roast pig on the spit. 'We usually had plenty of lechon left over after a fiesta celebration (a patron saint's day celebration) or after attending parties, as hosts usually give leftovers to the guests to take home,' she explains. 'The vinegar preserves the meat even without refrigeration.' Even now, across the seas in the warm desert location of Alice Springs, Annabelle still loves humba as the perfect meal for a busy person.

Serves 2–4
500g roast or fresh pork, chopped into bite-sized pieces, fat on
2 teaspoons minced garlic
3 bay leaves
1 cup vinegar
2 teaspoons salt
pinch sugar
1 cup Filipino soy sauce (Silverswan brand)

■ Combine all ingredients in a saucepan. Bring to boil, then simmer until pork is tender. Serve with steamed rice. Leftover roast pork from pig on the spit (lechon) may be used instead of fresh pork meat.

Annabelle Johnson

Pork Adobo
(Filipino Sweet–Savoury Pork)

A simply made recipe, the sweet-savoury adobo is one of the Philippines' national dishes. This recipe is from Andy Cabrera, who picked it up from his cousin, who is a chef.

Serves 4

1kg pork belly, cut into serving pieces
8 cloves garlic, diced
1 cup white vinegar
1 cup sweet Filipino soy sauce
oil for frying
pepper

■ Wash the pork belly pieces. Place in a pot and add garlic, vinegar and soy sauce to cover. Allow to boil without stirring. Simmer until the sauce has thickened and reduced. At this point, remove the meat and fry it in a little oil. Return it to the sauce and bring back to serving temperature. Add pepper to taste.

Pork Porkolt (Paprika Stew)

Setting the record straight on one popular Hungarian dish has become the mission of translator Kate Johnson (who has been closely associated with the Hungarian community since coming to live in Sydney over twenty years ago). What we think of as 'goulash', the popular paprika-fragrant Hungarian stew, is actually called 'porkolt' in Hungary while what the Hungarians call 'gulyas' is in fact a 'lot wetter' — it's a hearty meat soup. Like a true Hungarian housewife, Kate grows her own cherry paprika and then hangs them in bunches in the kitchen to dry until she's ready to use them for porkolt.

This recipe was taught to her by her dear friend Zoli.

Serves 4

1 large onion
oil (although traditionally people used to use lard)
1 generous tablespoon of good-quality paprika
1 kg lean, diced pork
salt to taste
2 cloves garlic
1 teaspoon caraway seeds
2 tomatoes
1 green capsicum
1 cherry paprika (or substitute dried chilli)

■ Chop onion into small pieces and sauté in the oil. Don't get the pan too hot or you'll burn the paprika, which goes in when the onion has softened. As soon as you've stirred in the paprika, add the meat, diced small, and stir around to coat it with the paprika-onion mixture. Add the salt, crushed garlic, caraway and a splash of water. Cover and let simmer while you cut up the tomatoes and green capsicum, then add them, along with the cherry paprika or chilli. Stir, cover and continue to cook gently, adding a little water when needed. It should be tender and ready to serve in about 50 minutes.

■ Serve with rice, mashed potato, buttered noodles, crusty bread or homemade nokedli pasta or galushka (dumplings made of flour and eggs dropped into boiling water to cook — see Gabriel Carr's recipe, p. 128).

■ Note: This dish mustn't have a lot of liquid at any stage, Kate warns, and like a risotto, needs to have an eye kept on it. You can't put it on and go shopping! It can also be made with other meats, including game. Some of the cooking water can advantageously be replaced with white wine. And if you reduce the garlic and paprika and finish the sauce with stabilised sour cream, you have a pork paprikas.

Bigos (Polish Pork and Sauerkraut)

Bigos is pretty close to being Poland's national dish. The mixture of pork, sausage and sauerkraut is eaten throughout Poland but differs depending on which region you're from — the area around the Baltic being quite different from the mountains and that being quite different from the cities. This recipe is from Krakow, from Sydney chef Katrina Karon.

Serves 4

5 dried mushrooms

1.5kg sauerkraut (the best, says Katrina is either Polish or German from a good delicatessen)

5 allspice

2 bay leaves

1 teaspoon cumin seeds

300g Polish salami or kransky sausage

2 tablespoons butter

500g roast pork

2 onions

2 tablespoons tomato paste

freshly ground black pepper to taste

■ Wash the dried mushrooms and leave in a bowl covered with cold water for 1 hour. Wash the sauerkraut in a colander under running water and drain. Put 3 cups of water in saucepan, add sauerkraut, allspice, bay leaf, cumin seeds and mushrooms and cook slowly for about 30 minutes.

■ Chop the Polish salami into bite-sized pieces and fry in butter until brown. Set aside. Chop the pork into bite-sized pieces and fry, making sure you save the juice.

■ Peel and chop the onion and fry it in the juice from the pork. Add the pork and onion to the sauerkraut and cook slowly.

■ When sauerkraut and meat are cooked, add the salami. Add the tomato paste and freshly ground black pepper to your taste. There should be very little sauce. Serve hot with fresh bread or potatoes.

Pork Malabar

'It's a bit like an Indonesian rendang only with stronger flavours,' says Indo–Fijian chef Barbara Brewer. Her father was from Kerala, near India's legendary Malabar Coast, and his use of spices still influences Barbara's cooking today. 'In fact, he taught me to cook,' says Barbara. Nowadays when she prepares a family get-together she has daughter Anne and three daughters–in–law to help her in the kitchen.

Serves 4

½ cup vegetable oil

2 medium onions, sliced

4 cloves garlic crushed, or 1½ teaspoons paste

2.5cm piece fresh ginger or 1½ teaspoons paste

a few curry leaves

1 tablespoon ground coriander

1 tablespoon garam masala

½ tablespoon ground cumin

1 teaspoon ground turmeric

1 teaspoon hot chilli powder or to taste

1½ cups water

500g diced pork

1 tablespoon brown vinegar

1 teaspoon brown sugar

1 cup coconut milk

½ cup dessicated coconut

■ Heat oil in a heavy-based frying pan. Add the onions and when they start to brown, add the garlic, ginger, curry leaves and stir over a gentle heat. Add all the powdered spices and ½ cup of water. When the oil floats to the top (about 10 minutes), add meat and salt. Stir to mix and coat all the pieces of meat. Add the rest of the water.
■ When all the liquid has evaporated, add vinegar and sugar. When meat is tender pour in coconut milk.
■ In a separate frying pan, roast coconut. It will take about 30 to 40 seconds. Add to the curry. Stir and take off heat.

Gordana's Sarma (Serbian Sour Cabbage and Smoked Meats)

Sarma is the Serbian national dish — combining sauerkraut–like cabbage with a selection of smoked meats and rice. It's filling and very Middle European — great for a really hearty winter meal and a perfect excuse to visit a 'continental' butcher and try out some of their terrific smoked meats.
This recipe comes from Gordana Gamboz, a Serbian broadcaster in Melbourne.

Serves 6

3 small cups of rice

1 onion

500g minced meat (Gordana uses half beef and half pork)

1 tablespoon hot red paprika (Hungarian)

1 sour cabbage head (from Serbian butcher or even a supermarket)

selection of smoked meats such as bacon, rebra (ribs) or smoked hock (susena kolenica)

1 tablespoon white flour

oil for frying

salt and pepper to taste

■ Boil water for rice. Cook it until still well underdone. Chop and fry onion in a separate pan, and when soft add mince. Mix in paprika. Mix with the rice to make the filling. Roll 1 tablespoon of rice and mince mixture into each cabbage leaf and close. Place a layer of these in a large pot (4–5 litres), then a layer of bacon and a couple of smoked ribs or hock. Continue until pan is full. Put in water to cover and cook very slowly for 2½ to 3 hours. When it's ready, fry flour in oil, cover with water and simmer a little. Pour over the finished dish. Season.

An Australian St Patrick's Day

There's a small street in the Sydney beachside suburb of Harbord that comes alive each St Patrick's Day (17 March) with displays of Irish dancing, interesting renditions of old chestnuts like 'Danny Boy', and that magic black brew, Guinness, on tap. In fact, the butcher shop in Lawrence Street is a drawcard for many Irish expatriates in Sydney and beyond.

While some Irish pubs in Australia colour their beer green (much to the horror of the Irish back home), the proprietors of Emerald Meats colour their hair green and serve up treats that would mist the eyes of any homesick Irishman.

Dublin-born Bill and Rita Fenelon have made a point of offering a home away from home for the past twenty years. Crubeens, tender boiled ham hocks, are perfect with a creamy-topped glass of Guinness from one of the kegs brought in especially for St Pat's Day. Then there's iron-rich black pudding which is an essential part of an Irish breakfast, along with sausages, bacon, eggs and lashings of tea and toast.

Intriguingly, Bill has come across some new flavours in Australia that have enhanced the recipes handed down to him from his family. For instance, ham and bacon is smoked back home using juniper branches. In Australia, Bill was at a loss to find the fragrant wood so he made his own mixture of sawdust and juniper berries and reckons his hams taste even better here!

As the Irish say: 'Slainte go foil.' (To your good health!)

Dany Chouet's Cleopatra Cassoulet

Cassoulet is a French winter classic … but the French have many versions of this more than hearty dish. This one is 'authentique' thanks to Danny Chouet of the exquisite Cleopatra restaurant in the Blue Mountains, NSW.

Meats:
1 small neck of pork (scotch fillet)

1kg lean pork belly

800g pork skin without fat

6 thick pork sausages or chipolatas

12 confit duck legs (start three days beforehand, see p. 86)

Marinade:
half a head garlic, finley chopped

1 bunch flat leaf parsley, finely chopped

salt and pepper to taste

1.5l dry white wine

1 tablespoon whole black peppercorns

1 large bouquet garni (fresh thyme, parsley stalks and bay leaf)

Vegetables:
1kg white Great Northern Beans or cannelini beans

1 bay leaf

1 whole brown onion, studded with cloves

Cooking liquid:
60g duck fat

250g smoked pork speck, diced

3 to 4 onions diced small

3 medium carrots diced (1cm cubes)

4 large very ripe tomatoes, peeled, deseeded and chopped (or one 800g tinned Italian peeled tomatoes)

pepper

1.5l chicken or pork or duck stock

1½ heads garlic, peeled

Topping:
breadcrumbs

1 clove garlic

1 bunch flat parsley

The day before serving:

▪ Mix together the garlic and parsley from the marinade ingredients.

▪ Remove excess fat from the neck and tidy the meat. Pierce holes along the meat and insert salt, pepper and the garlic and parsley mixture deeply. Tie up with string like a roast.

▪ Leave the skin on the pork belly, but remove the bones and keep aside.

▪ Arrange the pork skin flat on a board, season normally with salt and fresh ground pepper, then spread thickly with the garlic and parsley mixture. Roll like a thick sausage and tie with string at 1.5cm intervals.

▪ Place the three cuts of meat in a large container. Cover with 1.5l of white wine, sprinkle over one tablespoon of whole black peppercorns and immerse the bouquet garni. Cover and place in the fridge. Before going to bed at night, turn the meats in the marinade.

On the day of serving:

▪ Place the beans in a large pot, cover generously with cold water, add the studded onion and the bay leaf. Bring to the boil and cook for about 30 minutes.

▪ Strain the beans in a colander and refresh. Discard the onion and bay leaf. Leave the beans to drain. Take the meat from the marinade and strain, reserving the marinade.

▪ Heat the oven to 200°C and roast the neck only, basting often with a little marinade. Cook for about 1¼ hours and then set aside.

▪ At the same time, in a large thick-based pot, fry the smoked speck with the duck fat, then add the diced carrots and diced onions.

Saute gently for about 15 minutes avoiding browning. Add the tomato flesh, and reduce to a nice thick consistency. Season with freshly ground pepper only. Add the drained beans, mix together with the sauce, pour in the remaining strained marinade and bring gently to the boil. Bury the pork belly, skin roll, and bouquet garni in the beans. Chop the rest of the garlic and add to the beans and bring up the level of liquid with the chicken stock (you should have about 2cm of liquid above the beans). Do not stir the mixture. Let it simmer, covered, for at least 1½ hours, maybe more, checking the meats with a skewer to see if they are done. Remove the meats as soon as they are cooked. Set aside with roast pork and let cool down. Pour beans out of the pot into a bowl and stir to equalise the flavours. Discard the bouquet garni.

To serve:
Preheat oven to 200°C.

Half fill a large earthenware gratin dish with beans. Thickly slice the roast pork and the pork belly, slice the skin thinly, grill the pork sausages on one side only, remove the confit duck leg from the fat. Arrange, in alternating slices embedded into the beans, the duck legs, pork neck slices, belly slices; skin slices and sausages. Bury all the meats halfway into the beans and pour the roast pork jus all over.

Mix together the breadcrumbs, one large crushed clove of garlic and the chopped Italian parsley and sprinkle generously all over the top. Drizzle a little liquid duck fat on top of the breadcrumbs to crisp them. Bake in the oven for 30 to 40 minutes until golden brown on top, very hot and sizzling around the edges. This can be reheated the next day.

Cassoulet Confit Duck Legs

If these confit duck legs are to be used for the cassoulet, they must be started at least three days beforehand. Confit duck legs may be preserved in the refrigerator for up to two months, as long as they are completely covered with duck fat, and no air bubbles remain.

Makes 12 legs
12 duck legs (whole Maryland)
1 bunch fresh thyme, plucked
1 branch fresh rosemary, plucked
1 bay leaf, crushed
2 garlic cloves, crushed
salt and pepper
nutmeg
2kg rendered duck fat or goose fat

Clean the duck legs but leave all fat on them. Combine the thyme, rosemary, garlic, bay leaf. Place the duck legs in a large mixing bowl or plastic container, rub them on both sides with the herb mixture, season normally with salt and equal amounts of freshly ground pepper and nutmeg. Cover tightly and leave in the refrigerator overnight — preferably for 24 hours.

The next day, melt the duck fat in a large saucepan or casserole dish over a very low heat. Meanwhile, remove the legs one by one and thoroughly wipe dry with kitchen paper. When the fat is warm, but not bubbling, plunge the legs carefully into the pot. Cook very slowly, barely simmering, for 2 to 3 hours. The confit is cooked when easily pierced by a wooden skewer. Remove the duck legs from the pot and set aside in a ceramic or strong plastic dish. When the fat is lukewarm, pour it through a fine sieve over the meat. When it has thoroughly cooled, cover and place in the fridge.

Barbecues

The idea of grilling meats (and to some extent vegetables) over hot coals in the open air may go back to the days when humans first discovered fire and what it could do to a bit of raw flesh, but many millenia later the concept still exercises a powerful attraction. So much so, in fact, that the modern descendant of our ancestors' campfires — the barbecue — is as contemporary as it is universal. From the Balkans to the Philippines no festive occasion would be without a whole lamb or suckling pig on the spit. At the churrasco or parillada of Brazil and South America, every edible part of the cow gets a roasting (including the large and small intestine, delicious we're told). The Koreans have so refined the idea that their 'charcoal barbecue' restaurants feature tiny gas grillers on every table so that diners can sizzle strips of tender marinated beef (bulgogi) to be dunked in sesame dipping sauces, or succulent beef ribs (kalbi) where the meat is tastiest around the bone. At the other end of the scale the Aussies have perfected the fine art of the sausage sizzle, white bread and tomato sauce included.

But visit any Australian public park with barbecue facilities on a sunny Sunday and you will be amazed at the variations on the basic barbie theme: everything from marinated Chinese chicken wings to spicy Spanish sausages, grilled Lebanese kebabs, whole Vietnamese fish with lemongrass and ginger and Italian char-grilled vegetables richly doused with olive oil. For charcoal heaven, don't forget a good marinade, an interesting salad and of course, a selection of sauces — all guaranteed to make your grill-feast into a multicultural extravaganza.

Bush meats and game

Kangaroo à la Ghan with a Bush Tomato Barquette and Kumara wedges

Colin Edwards is a 'coordinating chef' with Qantas Catering, a huge operation providing meals not only for air passengers on thousands of flights out of Australia, but also for train

Colin Edwards

travellers on such magical journeys across the Australian desert as the famed 'Ghan' route from Adelaide to Alice Springs, and the Indian Pacific across the Nullabor Plain from Sydney to Perth.

Working on the Ghan, Colin became inspired by the spectacular, uniquely Australian countryside he was passing through and decided that uniquely Australian ingredients — both plants and meats — could be incorporated into the menus offered in the train's dining cars. He began working with the strong indigenous flavours of desert raisins (also known as bush tomatoes or akadjura), native pepperleaf, bunya nuts, lemon aspen, kakadu plums and lemon myrtle. Not only do diners love them, but Colin himself has developed an 'immense passion for these unique products', becoming 'almost obsessive' in his quest to discover their potential.

Serves 8
8 200g kangaroo fillets
100ml macadamia oil
1g ground native pepperleaf

Glaze:
½ cup veal or brown stock
8 whole native pepperleaves, ground

■ Trim the kangaroo of connecting tissue and silver skin. Marinate in macadamia oil and ground pepperleaf. Cover and chill for 3 hours.

To prepare the glaze:
■ Reduce the stock to a syrupy consistency. Remove from heat and season with pepperleaf.
■ Heat a flat grill plate until very hot. Seal kangaroo well until browned. Continue

cooking until medium rare. Remove from plate and rest in a warm oven for 10 minutes to finish the cooking process. This will relax the meat fibres for tenderness.

■ Arrange plate with two tablespoonsful of glaze. Slice kangaroo fillet across the grain and lengthways, or on an angle working along the fillet. Serve with kumara wedges, bush tomato barquette and steamed bok choy and garnish with fresh sage leaf.

Bush Tomato Barquette

100g plain flour, sifted
50g butter
pinch of salt
25ml water
bush tomato chutney — either commercial brand or add 1 part ground bush tomatoes (akadjira or desert raisins) to 10 parts tomato chutney

■ Sift flour, rub in butter well until the mixture resembles breadcrumbs. Dissolve salt in water and mix into the flour and butter mix. Do not overwork. Mould into a ball, cover and refrigerate for 30 minutes. Roll out thinly and line barquette or small tartlet moulds. If using a round mould, 4cm is ideal. Bake blind and cool. Fill with bush tomato chutney.

Kumara Wedges

1kg sweet potato (preferably the orange, kumara variety)
vegetable or olive oil

■ Peel potato and cut into 6cm lengths. Store them in cold water until ready for use. Drain well and pat dry with absorbent cloth. Mix lightly with oil and season. Spread them evenly onto a baking tray and roast in a hot 220°C oven for approximately 30 to 40 minutes.

Kangaroo Fillets with Beetroot Puree

When we were first given this recipe (some years ago now!), kangaroo meat was not yet legal for human consumption in several Australian states. Since then it has become a common sight on restaurant menus — although still rarely served in private homes. Its gradual appearance in supermarkets should change all that. South Australians, however, have been enjoying this lean, tender meat for many years — no wonder then that it was a South Australian who gave us the recipe. Aboriginal journalist Charlton Buzzacott grew up in the tiny town of Quorn in the rugged Flinders Ranges in South Australia and got this recipe from a restaurateur friend.

Serves 6

6 kangaroo rump fillets (1 per person)
black pepper, freshly ground
4–5 tablespoons butter
2–3 tablespoons virgin olive oil
5 medium-sized beetroot
200ml beef stock (preferably homemade but Campbell's beef consomme will do)
salt to taste

■ Roll the fillets in freshly ground pepper. (If you like, sprinkle also with half a teaspoon fresh thyme.) Melt butter and oil in heavy-based frying pan. Add fillets and seal quickly on both sides in the hot pan. Lower heat to medium and cook for 2 to 3 minutes (fillets should be pink inside).

■ Boil beetroot until soft, then puree. Add beef stock for a 50–50 mix of beetroot and stock. Add salt and pepper and reduce gently to sauce consistency. Pour onto plate and arrange kangaroo fillet on top. Sprinkle with freshly chopped parsley.

Variations:

■ Try coriander in the beetroot mix — add towards the end of the cooking.

■ Serve with couscous and squash and perhaps a potato.

Rack of Crocodile with Lemon Aspen Salsa

More tourists than locals are tasting crocodile, one of the 'new' Australian meats which, we've discovered, is very easy to cook. One of a handful of Aboriginal chefs in Australia, Danni Murray was born in Quilpie, Queensland and raised in Quorn in the Flinders Ranges. As a child she used to collect and cook bush peaches or quandongs. Now, however, she's covering the range of bush flavourings, developing their strong sharp tastes for use in everything from sauces and salsas to main courses and desserts. Her recipe calls for crocodile but any firm-fleshed white fish steak or cutlet may be substituted.

Serves 4

1 quantity lemon aspen salsa (see pp. 176–7 in Sauces, Relishes and Marinades)
1 rack of crocodile ribs which can be divided into 4 cutlets 1.5cm thick (cut along the rib line to divide into cutlets or use 1kg crocodile fillets)
salt and pepper to taste
2 tablespoons vegetable oil

■ Season cutlets with salt and pepper and drizzle with vegetable oil. Place crocodile cutlets on a char-grill or barbecue and cook until done to taste. Danni advises that crocodile needs to be thoroughly cooked but not overdone as it can become leathery.

Arrange salsa on a large plate, add crocodile cutlets and decorate with sprigs of coriander.
■ Serve with salad vegies and crusty damper.

Emu Fillet with Yoghurt

In the dusty plains north of Perth, two German expatriates run a thriving business raising emus. Both Karsten and Gerlind Bobardt just love their work, and have developed a range of recipes based on emu. This recipe calls for what are known as 'inside' fillets, one of the best cuts from the large bird.

Serves 2

4 slices emu inside fillet
salt and pepper to taste
butter
¼ cup white wine
2 tablespoons natural yoghurt

■ Season the meat with salt and pepper. Sauté the meat quickly in the butter. Drain off butter and add wine and reduce. Add yoghurt and cook for 2 minutes. Serve.

Emu Rump with Avocado and Mustard Cream

Gerlind Bobardt's German heritage shows through with this recipe for emu, featuring a heavy cream sauce.

Serves 2

English mustard
2 tablespoons sour cream
3 thin slices of emu rump, flattened
salt and freshly ground pepper

butter
½ avocado, sliced thinly

■ Mix English mustard with sour cream. Season the meat and cook in butter for 1 minute each side. Remove and place on plate. Arrange avocado on top of meat then spoon cream mixture over the top.

Stuffat Tal-Fenek (Maltese Rabbit Stew)

Rabbit is the national dish of Malta, made into stews or pies. Broadcaster Vivienne Kost often makes stuffat tal-fenek and like many Maltese in Australia, says she usually buys her rabbits privately to be sure of freshness.

Serves 4
1 rabbit, jointed
seasoned flour
2 onions, sliced
oil for frying
4 cloves garlic
2 carrots, chopped
2 tablespoons tomato paste
1 cup red wine
1 250ml can peeled tomatoes
1 cup boiled peas

■ Roll rabbit pieces in seasoned flour. Fry onions in oil until golden. Add garlic and chopped carrots. Add rabbit pieces and fry until golden brown. Add tomato paste, wine and tomatoes and bring to boil. Add some water if necessary.
■ Place contents in casserole dish and bake for 1½ hours at 150°C.
■ The Maltese way of eating rabbit is to serve the sauce with spaghetti as a first course and the rabbit pieces as a second course.

Baked Rabbit with Pork and Fennel Stuffing

When David White was growing up in the 1950s, he hated his mother's rabbit casserole. It wasn't until many years later that he discovered how marvellous rabbit could be when he sampled the peasant-style Tuscan variety. This recipe is easy once you've found a source for good-quality rabbit. As for the stuffing, David says you can use ready-made Italian pork and fennel sausages if you can find them. And a tip on the rabbit: you know you have a good one if there's a layer of fat under the backbone when you look inside the cavity.

Serves 2
2 pork and fennel sausages or 200g minced pork, a little extra garlic and 1 teaspoon fennel seeds
1 clove garlic, chopped
1 medium-sized rabbit
1 cup olive oil
1 cup white wine
kitchen string

■ Take the skin off the sausages and mix crushed garlic through the pork and fennel. Stuff the rabbit and sew up well with kitchen string.
■ Place in a baking dish and add olive oil, rubbing well over the skin. Cook at 190°C for 15 minutes. Pour wine over the rabbit and return to oven, basting every 10 minutes. Top up wine if necessary. Test using a skewer. Serve with borlotti or cannelini beans.

Mix and Match

Some of the recipes in the Sauces, Relishes and
Marinades chapter go wonderfully with plain
grilled meats. Try the tomato Chermoula sauce
with whole or filleted fish, Moroccan harissa
with sausages or chicken and the Portuguese
piri piri is a natural (and traditional)
accompaniment to charcoal chicken.

Korean dipping sauces are great with thin slices
of grilled meat — and of course Korean
kimchi (from the Sauces, Relishes and
Marinades chapter) is the ideal side dish.
Vietnamese pickled vegetables (in Sauces,
Relishes and Marinades chapter) go beautifully
with any barbecued chicken or fish as does
Spanish escalivada or Moroccan chickpeas (in
the Vegetable chapter).

For a good salad selection, see the Salad section
for potato, couscous, and avocado salad or
tabouli.

Cretan Stifado (Hare Stew)

Cretan Chrysoula Georgilaki speaks evocatively of the customs and countryside of home, of the wild hare caught on the mountain side, its meat strongly perfumed with the thyme that grows naturally all over the hills. Truly Cretan Stifado requires hare, but at a pinch, Chrysoula says, rabbit or even veal can substitute. This recipe is from her grandmother.

Serves 4

2kg tiny onions (available from Greek grocers)
1 cup olive oil (Cretan is best)
1 hare, cut into pieces — around 1–1.5kg (or rabbit or veal)
1kg tomatoes, peeled and crushed
1 teaspoon tomato paste
5 bay leaves
pepper to taste
salt to taste
2 teaspoons ground cumin
2 cups boiling water

■ Chop a couple of the onions and saute them in a little of the olive oil. Add hare, cut into pieces, and let it brown. Add the whole peeled onions, tomatoes, remaining oil, tomato paste, bay leaves, pepper, salt, cumin and two cups of hot water. Cover tightly and leave on a low heat to simmer for 1½ hours. Do not open — that's Chrysoula's grandmother's secret. That way none of the juices disappear.

Christian's Australian Venison with a Swede and Sweet Potato Puree Served on a Red Currant Jus

Christian Heidenreich is a classically trained Austrian chef who came to Australia via Asia to explore new food frontiers. Food in Europe is standing still, he believes, whereas here we are still developing a cuisine that combines the best of Mediterranean and Asian cooking styles. He's got one of the best environments in Australia to practise his art — Christian is executive chef at the Sheraton Mirage Resort in Port Douglas. This dish combines a little bit of what he calls his 'wiener schnitzel, sacher torte, schmaltz heritage' — the venison and red currant sauce, and some of what he's learnt along the way — the still crisp, wok-fried vegies.

Serves 2

Red currant sauce:

100g red currants (frozen)
50g red currant jelly
100ml port
100ml red wine
300ml game stock (your own is best but prepackaged game or beef stocks are also suitable)
Chopped onion, garlic, celery, leek and carrots (equal quantities)
20g sugar
vegetable oil
salt and pepper to taste

Sweet potato and swede puree:

150g each sweet potato and swede (peeled and chopped into mid-size pieces)
30ml each milk and cream
pinch of cumin
salt and pepper to taste

Stir-fried Asian vegetables:

60g mixed Asian vegetables (pak choy, bok choy, choi sum, kay lan, snow peas)

sesame oil

one birdseye chilli (chopped finely)

ginger

garlic

soy sauce

Venison:

400g trimmed Australian venison loin

salt and pepper to taste

vegetable oil

parsley

To prepare sauce:

■ Heat a small amount of oil in a heavy-based saucepan and sauté vegetables until nicely coloured. Add sugar, red currants and red currant jelly and stir well. Add alcohol and reduce by half then add stock and reduce to a thick sauce consistency. Strain through a fine strainer and season with salt and pepper.

To prepare puree:

■ Boil vegetables till soft, drain and mash as finely as possible. In a small saucepan, bring milk and cream to boil then add cumin, salt and pepper. Add to vegetable mash.

To prepare vegetables:

■ Chop into large chunks — for example cut the bok choy in half. Stir-fry in sesame oil with chilli, ginger, garlic and a little soy sauce.

To prepare venison:

■ Season the venison with salt and pepper and pan-fry in a little oil until medium rare. (This gives the best flavour and nutritional value). Allow to rest for 3 to 4 minutes then slice into medallions, arrange neatly on a plate, add vegetables, puree and sauce and garnish with parsley.

Seafood

Kokoda (Marinated Fish)

A favourite around the Pacific, kokoda (pronounced kokonda) is actually a raw marinated fish dish, served chilled or at room temperature and prepared a day in advance. No-one would ever know it hadn't actually been cooked and it's a guaranteed success. The recipe comes courtesy of former colleague David Gardiner, a broadcaster in his native Fiji who has also worked as a chef. In his many years with SBS Radio and TV he was considered quite an authority by his Fijian colleagues and was always ready to talk food!

Serves 4–6

4–6 filleted Spanish mackerel, cubed (you can use any firm, white-fleshed fish)

10–12 lemons

1 large tomato, diced

1 can coconut cream (preferably Samoan-made)

1 medium onion, diced

2–3 chillies, diced

½ green capsicum, diced

salt and black pepper to taste

½ teaspoon hot paprika

2 spring onions, diced

■ Place the cubed fish into a stainless steel or glass bowl and pour the juice of 5 or 6 lemons (depending on size) over it. Marinate in refrigerator, covered, for at least 8 hours (12 is better). Drain in colander then add juice from remaining lemons, coconut cream, tomato, onion, chillies and capsicum. Add salt and black pepper to taste and garnish with paprika and spring onions.

■ Hint: Don't chill the finished dish to extreme temperatures as the coconut milk can become a little chalky.

■ Traditional accompaniments are boiled and mashed sweet potato (kumara) or cooked green bananas (plantains). The bananas are boiled in water until soft (test them with a skewer), then peeled and mashed. Alternatively, they can be boiled without their skins in a pot of coconut cream with a little salt. The Tongans serve kokoda on a bed of diced iceberg lettuce.

Pearl Meat Kilaw

Pearl meat is the flesh from the giant pinctada maxima, the pearl-bearing oyster found particularly off the north-western coast of Australia in the Kimberley Region. Our Malaysian-Chinese chef friend Tony Tan was delighted to have had the opportunity to invent a recipe especially for this very precious form of seafood, a rare delicacy indeed. He does stress that you could use the marinade with any firm, white-fleshed fish, just in case your budget (or local seafood outlet) doesn't run to pinctada maxima.

Serves 2

250g pearl meat substitute, sliced or shaved horizontally

2 tablespoons ginger juice, or to taste

2 tablespoons lime juice

zest of 2 limes

1 red chilli, seeded and minced (not a birdseye)

1 stalk lemongrass, tender part only, minced finely

1 tablespoon coriander stems, minced finely

salt and freshly milled black pepper to taste

2 tablespoons fresh coriander leaves

2–3 tablespoons julienne of spring onions, soaked in iced water

■ Place pearl meat in a bowl and toss in the rest of the ingredients except for the coriander leaves and spring onions. Cover and refrigerate for 45 minutes to 1 hour. Add coriander leaves, toss and divide over four plates. Serve garnished with spring onions on top.

Geoff's Oysters with Tangy Barbecue Sauce

Geoff Pickard and Andrea Coles farm oysters in one of the most beautiful spots in Australia — Great Oyster Bay on Tasmania's Freycinet Peninsula. Surrounded by bird life and the quiet of nature, the two go about their days tending their oysters in the intertidal river and at the deep-sea leases that are looked over by spectacular mountains rising straight from the sea. They often eat oysters straight from the shell, but nothing is better, says Andrea, than oysters on the barbecue with a dollop of Geoff's sauce.

Serves 4
24 oysters on the half shell

Sauce:
250ml (1 cup) tomato sauce
6 tablespoons fresh lemon juice
3 tablespoons vegetable oil
1 large tablespoon brown sugar
2 tablespoons Worcestershire sauce
8 drops tabasco
150ml water
½ teaspoon dry mustard
1 teaspoon garlic salt
1 large onion, finely chopped

Place sauce ingredients in a saucepan and simmer for 8 minutes over a low heat, stirring regularly. (Sauce can be prepared and kept in the fridge for several weeks).

Spoon sauce over oysters and place on rack over hot barbecue coals until sauce just starts to bubble. Then eat and enjoy!

Andrea Coles

Skewered Oysters

While Andrea Coles swears her Pacific and Angazi oysters are best straight from the sea, over the years she and partner Geoff Pickard have developed recipes for cooked oysters too.

Makes 8 sticks
2 tablespoons butter
1 clove garlic
40 button mushrooms, washed
salt and finely ground black pepper to taste
1 teaspoon finely chopped parsley
48 fresh oysters
8 satay sticks (pre-soaked in water)

Melt the butter in a large frying pan and saute crushed garlic for 1 minute. Add mushrooms and seasoning and cook a further 1 to 2 minutes. Toss in parsley and cook a further 30 seconds. Thread satay sticks with oysters, alternating with mushrooms (6 oysters, 5 mushrooms per stick).

■ Cook on grill over low heat for 1 to 2 minutes, turning often.

Barramundi in Paperbark with Wattleseed Cheese Sauce

Raymond Kersch was one of the first Australian chefs to concentrate an entire menu on bush food. Many have followed his lead in using the sharp fresh flavours of the Australian bush. Ray grew up in inner Sydney and really discovered bush flavours through visiting his brother who works with Aboriginal people in the Kimberley in Western Australia. While the paperbark gives a slightly smoky flavour, Ray says it also slows down the cooking time, allowing the fish to cook more gently and thoroughly.

Serves 4
Cheese sauce:
200g Taleggio cheese or cheddar, grated
1½ cups cream
¼ cup white wine
1 teaspoon finely cracked black peppercorns
2 teaspoons wattleseed

Barramundi:
1kg barramundi fillets, divided into 4 portions
dried bush tomato powder
dried lemon myrtle powder
roll of paperbark (can be bought from gourmet food shops)

To prepare cheese sauce:
■ Combine all ingredients in a pot. Bring to boil, thicken with cornflour or arrowroot until sauce has a paste texture for spreading on top of barramundi. Allow to cook before using.

To prepare barramundi:
■ Coat top of barramundi with wattleseed cheese sauce. Sprinkle half of fillet with dried bush tomato and the other half with dried lemon myrtle.

■ For 4 separate parcels, place each portion on a large piece of paperbark and wrap around sides of fillet. Bake in a moderate 180°C oven for 12 to 15 minutes.

Amok (Cambodian Fish in Banana Leaves)

Kim Ley Chau has had a number of trips back to Cambodia since he left sixteen years ago, always to visit family. Along the way, he collects new recipes for his restaurant on Sydney's Oxford Street.

Spend a bit of time getting the wrapping of the parcels right and you'll be rewarded with a clever way of serving beautiful steamed fish. You can use your own washed banana leaves cut into lengths or buy them at many Asian grocery stores. If you just can't find them or don't have the time, the recipe will work without them. Kim says at home he would use a fish similar to a large catfish for amok but says in Australia, the fish of the tropical north — barramundi — is just perfect.

Serves 4
1 stalk lemongrass
1 small knob galangal
1 small knob fresh turmeric (or ½ teaspoon ground turmeric)
700g skinned fish fillets, barramundi for choice, cut into 1–2cm pieces
400ml coconut cream (Mae Ploy brand the best)
1½ tablespoons good red curry paste, (try Maesri brand or

see Sauces, Relishes and Marinades chapter)

8 fresh kaffir lime leaves, sliced finely

2 tablespoons fish sauce

1 tablespoon sugar

1 tablespoon finely chopped fresh coriander

1 teaspoon chilli powder

4 banana leaves (optional)

100g Chinese broccoli leaves

■ In a blender, process the lower fleshy part of lemongrass stalk with peeled galangal and turmeric. In a large bowl combine fish, coconut cream, curry paste, kaffir lime leaves, fish sauce, sugar, coriander and chilli powder. Adjust fish sauce or sugar if necessary — the taste should be sweet and spicy with a hint of salt.

■ If you're using banana leaves, soften by warming them in the sun or quickly placing them over a low heat, one at a time. Cut into 30cm lengths. Put one leaf on top of the other, with the lines of the leaves running at right angles to each other. Use scissors to trim the edges neatly. To fashion a square container, fold up the four sides and secure using a toothpick.

■ The banana leaf bowls can be substituted by four bowls of 500ml capacity. In either case, line each bowl with the broccoli leaves then spoon ¼ of the fish mixture into each.

■ Place in a steamer over a wok of simmering water and steam for 20 minutes or until cooked. Serve hot with jasmine rice.

Kailis Fillets in Herb and Vinegar Sauce

Three generations of the Perth-based Kailis family published a commemorative cookbook when Uncle Peter Kailis turned 70. Everyone in the family contributed recipes: the six children (including Uncle Peter) of George Palass. Kailis and his wife Evangelia, the first Kailis to settle in Australia, and the many offspring of those six children, now all adults themselves! As the family is in the seafood business, naturally the fish chapter is rich in great suggestions. This recipe is from Uncle Theo George Kailis (Peter's brother).

Serves 8

8 fish fillets (150g each 15-20mm thick) or 8 whole herring

3 cloves garlic, cut into slivers

plain flour (optional)

4 tablespoons olive oil

½ cup mixed herbs

1 cup malt vinegar

salt and pepper to taste

■ Insert slivers of garlic into fish. Dredge in flour (optional).

■ Heat oil until smoking. Fry fish for 3 minutes on each side for fillets or 2 minutes each side for herring. Remove from pan and sprinkle with half mixed herbs.

For the sauce:

■ Heat oil until smoking. Add vinegar, salt and pepper and remaining mixed herbs. Cook for 2 minutes, stirring. Pour sauce over fish and serve with a side salad.

■ Note: Where it says mixed herbs use dried or fresh thyme, oregano and parsley. Be careful when pouring vinegar into hot oil as it may ignite. Remove pan from stove before adding vinegar.

A Fishy Tale

The Mendolia name in Western Australia is synonymous with sardines and anchovies — the result of a long hard slog by two generations of the family. When Sicilian fisherman Francolino Mendolia arrived in Perth in the early 1950s and started working on lobster boats, he was struck not by the lobsters but the first-class sardines and anchovies that the Aussie fishermen regarded merely as bait.

What he noticed was that the quality of the fish from the clear cold waters off Western Australia, was far above anything he had ever seen in the Mediterranean. An enterprising young man, he imported Sicilian fishing nets and, working up to 18 and 20 hours a day, gradually saved enough for his own boat.

Eventually his sons joined the business and Francolino wanted to push further — this time starting a factory that would process the brimming loads of fish the family caught.

It took many years, but eventually Francolino's son Jim realised his father's dream, with help from the rest of the family. In 1988 he established the Bella del Tindari and Auschovy (anchovy fillets) brands. Early on, the whole family used to help with the filleting of fish, but mechanisation has meant an expansion into new products such as crumbed sardines.

'Years ago, Australians were used to white tasteless fish,' says Jim. 'But we've helped to change that — besides being high in Omega 3, sardines and anchovies are very tasty fish — they've got a lot of oomph.'

Jim says his proudest day was the first Fremantle Sardine Festival which he'd organised and which has now become a huge annual event in January, attracting thousands to a big cookout in a large park on the water's edge. His father by then was wheelchair-bound after a stroke but, says Jim, 'He was so proud of that festival — it was more than he'd ever dreamt of'.

See recipes for barbecue sardines and sardine ripiene (Rosa's stuffed sardines).

The Mendolia family with Maeve O'Meara

Sofia and Svein Oddsson

Sofia's Salmon in Champagne Sauce

Sofia Oddsson and her husband Svein are salmon experts from Iceland, who came to Australia when Svein was offered a job in Tasmania with an aquaculture company. They then branched out to start their own little smokehouse, Southern Delights, curing and marinating salmon in the traditional Icelandic way as well as making a range of sauces. Sofia's blue eyes sparkle as she recounts tales of how her ancestors would bury whole salmon wrapped in wild herbs in the frozen ground as a means of preserving the beautiful rose-coloured fish — the early means of making gravlax (literally 'grave salmon').

Serves 6
12 servings of gravlax (from delis, fishmongers or fish markets)
12–24 blanched asparagus spears
12 slices swiss cheese

Champagne sauce:
1 generous cup creme fraiche or sour cream
3 fish stock cubes, crumbled into a little water
½–¾ teaspoon cayenne pepper
1–2 tablespoons butter
1 cup champagne

■ Arrange the gravlax salmon on an oven-proof dish with asparagus on top. Place a slice of the cheese on each asparagus. Place in a hot oven for 5–8 minutes until the cheese bubbles and turns golden.

To prepare the champagne sauce:
■ Heat up creme fraiche and fish stock over a low heat until warm. Add cayenne pepper to taste, then the butter and champagne. Remove the salmon from oven, place on serving plate. Drizzle sauce over the top and serve with crusty bread or garlic bread.

Barbecue Sardines

This recipe is from Sicilian cook 'Mama' Rosa Mendolia, the 'Queen of Sardines' in Fremantle. She migrated four decades ago with her late husband Francolino, a fisherman also from Sicily. Through sheer hard work, he bought a couple of fishing boats of his own and with son Jim, established a canning factory. The family can also boast starting a hugely popular sardine festival in summer, to which thousands flock to eat the delicious freshly caught sardines. This recipe is an old family favourite.

Serves 6
24 fresh sardines
salt

Rosa Mendolia

the heat of the plate or grill. Generally the fish is cooked when it comes away easily from backbone. Keep a regular check while basting with dressing. Any remaining dressing may be used as a dip for the additional taste.

Sardine Ripiene (Rosa's Stuffed Sardines)

Rosa Mendolia's stuffed sardines are delicious, easy to make and great for family dinners. She has been making this recipe for her large family for over forty years and finds it takes no time at all, especially as she has her own bottled Italian tomato sauce ready to use. In fact, her cooking is so good that every day her grown-up sons come home for lunch with their mum. 'If we haven't turned up by a certain time, Mum will track us down!' laughs son Jim.

Dressing:

1 cup olive oil

¼ cup water

2 cloves garlic

salt and pepper to taste

1 tablespoon dried oregano leaves

2 tablespoons chopped fresh parsley

■ Remove heads and gut from sardines and wash clean. Sardines can be prepared several hours ahead and stored in refrigerator.

To prepare the dressing:

■ Combine all ingredients and place in a shallow dish.

■ Place sardines on an oiled hotplate or grill, lightly sprinkle fish with salt and brush well with dressing. Turn occasionally, however, after sardines have been turned the first time, sprinkle with salt and dressing on the underside.

■ The cooking time will vary according to

Serves 10 to 12

2 eggs

salt and pepper to taste

a dash of milk

3 handfuls breadcrumbs

1 handful fresh finely grated parmesan cheese

Italian flat-leaf parsley, finely chopped

24 whole sardines or 48 fillets

light olive oil for frying

1 bottle good Italian tomato sauce (or make your own — you'll need 1 litre)

■ Butterfly the sardines into fillets and remove spine. This is easy to do yourself, just run your finger along the backbone from top to bottom.

■ Beat the eggs together with salt and pepper, milk, breadcrumbs, parmesan cheese and parsley — this should have a fairly thick consistency. Spoon between sardine fillets to make fat little sandwiches.

█ Fry the parcel in light olive oil, turning fish halfway. Be careful not to move the fish too much. Add tomato sauce, turn down heat to low and cook gently for 30 minutes.

█ Serve with a large bowl of green salad with a good garlicky dressing and a loaf of crusty Italian bread for mopping up the delicious tomato sauce.

Gefilte Fish

The Schenker family, have long enjoyed this recipe which was passed onto them from grandmother Mitzi and grandfather Otto. Nothing could be more typical of Jewish cuisine than these minced fish balls, but the interesting thing is that the recipe varies considerably from country to country. Some people like it very sweet, others abhor the idea of sugar. This version comes somewhere in between.

Makes about 20 balls

Fish:
1kg minced mixed fish
1 large onion, grated
1 large carrot, grated
2 eggs
1 cup water
2 teaspoons sugar
1 teaspoon salt
1 teaspoon ground ginger
¾ cup coarse matzo meal

Simmering liquid:
2 litres water
2 onions, roughly chopped
2 carrots, sliced
salt to taste
a little sugar

█ Mix all ingredients for fish together and let stand for 30 minutes. Form into balls (golf-ball sized) and lower gently into a large pot full of the combined simmering liquid ingredients. Simmer gently.

█ Try and keep the balls to 1 layer if possible. Let simmer with lid on for at least 1½ hours. (Longer does not spoil the fish.)

█ Take out balls one at a time with slotted spoon, and arrange in dish with sliced carrots to decorate.

█ To the remaining stock, add powdered gelatine (check proportions on the packet but roughly 1½ tablespoons) and stir until well dissolved. Strain over fish balls in dish and refrigerate until set. Serve with horseradish or beetroot/horseradish mix. (See Ukrainian beetroot relish in the Sauces, Relishes and Marinades chapter.)

Gumbo (Alabama Seafood Stew)

This recipe from chef Forrest Moebes is a rich dark spicy dish full of plump prawns, oysters and yabbies. The yabbies are optional, depending on your budget. Crabmeat is a great addition if you really want to show off. You can make the base days in advance and simply reheat and add seafood.

Serves 4

1kg medium prawns with head and tails

5 cups basic seafood stock

¾ cup butter

2 cups onion, chopped

2 cups celery, chopped

2 cups red and green capsicum, chopped

3 tablespoons gumbo file powder (see note)

1¼ cups homemade tomato sauce (made from chopped onions, seeded chopped tomatoes and a dash of white wine)

12 shucked oysters

1/2 kilo yabbies

Seasoning mix:

1 teaspoon cayenne pepper

1½ teaspoons sweet paprika

1 teaspoon salt

1 teaspoon black pepper

1 teaspoon fresh thyme, chopped (dried as substitute)

1 teaspoon fresh oregano, chopped (dried as substitute)

Note: gumbo file is ground okra, available at Middle Eastern delis.

▨ Peel prawns and use heads and tails to make seafood stock.

▨ In a large heavy soup pot, melt butter over medium heat.

▨ Add onion, celery and capsicum. Increase heat to high and add gumbo file and seasoning mix. Cook for 5 minutes, stirring constantly.

▨ Reduce heat to medium, stir in tomato sauce and cook for an additional 5 minutes. Add seafood stock, bring to the boil then lower heat and simmer 45 minutes.

▨ To serve, bring gumbo to the boil, add the whole yabbies and a minute or two later, the peeled prawns. Cover with lid and cook for a further minute until seafood is cooked. Serve with rice.

Seb's Mar I Muntanya (Catalan Seafood and Chicken in Chocolate and Nut Sauce)

Seb Bosch is a young Hobart restaurateur who's following in the footsteps of his mother Pilar and father Francisco, both born in Catalonia, Spain. When they emigrated to Tasmania with Pilar's sister Ramona and set up a restaurant, they changed the way many Tasmanians thought about food. 'When we came,' says Pilar, 'People didn't go out to dinner often, olive oil was still sold in pharmacies and when we were collecting mussels at the beach, people came up to us and asked us why we were collecting bait!' Seb chose this wonderfully flavoured dish as it's typical of Catalan cuisine and also because all of its ingredients show something of a history of Spain — the cocoa came from the New World; the cinnamon from the new spice routes through the Indies; the pinenuts a Moorish influence — more recently, the Moreton Bay bugs and prawns, an Australian influence. Grab a

Pilar and Seb Bosch

mortar and pestle and daydream as you're pounding. The name of this wonderfully fragrant dish translates as 'sea and mountains'.

Serves 4

½ cup olive oil

4 large chicken drumsticks, seasoned

8 medium-sized Moreton Bay bugs, cut in half along spine

8 green king prawns

1 cup finely sliced leek

2 tablespoons parsley, chopped

2 cups fish stock

salt and pepper to taste

1 cup pureed canned or vine-ripened tomatoes

Picada:

1 tablespoon hazelnuts

1 tablespoon pinenuts

1 tablespoon roasted almonds

1 tablespoon chopped parsley

½ teaspoon dried thyme

1 teaspoon cocoa powder

½ teaspoon cinnamon

2 bay leaves, crushed

2 cloves garlic

A good splash of Chinchon (Spanish aniseed liqueur)

■ Place all the picada ingredients in a pestle and pound until it makes a smooth, glossy paste.

■ In a 30cm-wide terracotta pan (or heavy-based frying pan), add the olive oil and heat. Fry drumsticks until cooked thoroughly.

■ Add all the seafood to the pan, sprinkle leek and parsley over and season with salt and pepper. Cover and cook for 5 minutes.

■ Add the picada, pureed tomatoes and fish stock. Cover and cook for a further 10 to 15 minutes. If the cooking liquid has thickened too much, add more fish stock to achieve what Seb calls 'spoon-coating consistency'.

Serve immediately. The whole pan can be brought to the table. Bon profit!

Alvin's Malaysian Fish Curry

This recipe from Malaysian chef Alvin Tan is definitely Malaysian in flavour — that wonderful blend of ethnic Malay, Chinese and even Indian influences.

Serves 4

1½ cups water

½ tablespoon tamarind pulp (mix with ¼ cup water or use 2 dried tamarind slices)

400g blue-eye cod, jewfish or snapper cutlet

6 okra

½ tomato, quartered

1 baby eggplant, cut into wedges

1 red chilli, slit halfway lengthwise

1 green chilli, slit halfway lengthwise

150ml canned coconut milk

Ingredients (A):

5 tablespoons oil

1 small onion, thinly sliced

3 cloves garlic, thinly sliced

½ thumb-size piece ginger, thinly shredded

1 sprig fresh curry leaves

1 star anise

2cm cinnamon stick

3 cloves

1 teaspoon black mustard seeds

½ teaspoon fenugreek seeds

Ingredients (B):

½ onion, pounded fine

2 tablespoons fish curry powder (mixed into a paste with some water)

½ tablespoon chilli powder

■ Heat oil in wok and fry ingredients (A) until onion is soft and transparent. Add ingredients (B) and continue to fry until fragrant or oil seeps through.

■ Add coconut milk, water and tamarind juice. Bring to the boil, add the fish cutlet, okra, tomato and eggplant and simmer until cooked. Add the sliced chillies. Transfer to a soup plate. Garnish with fried shallots, chopped coriander and sliced chillies.

Manikakis Ockie

Greek-born George Manikakis caught his first octopus when he was five years old — a few decades later it is still his favourite seafood. When he migrated to Australia 30 years ago, he managed to find a coastal spot that has ensured him a steady supply all these years. He still goes 'ockie' hunting several times a year — venturing out at low tide with a long-handled hook (for dragging them out of their holes — always marked by a ring of shells from discarded shellfish) and a bucket of oil and sand. The oil and sand mixture is thrown on the ripples to cut glare and flatten the surface, making it easier to see the bottom and those telltale piles of empty shells. Each creature is beaten 40 times on the rocks, to break the muscle fibre, then the tentacles are brushed up and down over a rocky surface to release a sticky white foam. 'Then the flesh tears just like paper,' says George. It certainly makes for the tenderest ockie you'll ever taste, especially when cooked in its own juices in the traditional Greek way by George's wife Helen.

Helen Manikakis

Serves 4–6

1 large octopus (around 1kg, washed and cleaned but still whole)

1 cup red wine vinegar

1 cup olive oil

2 onions, cut in quarters

3 bay leaves

■ Place the octopus snugly in a deep saucepan. Cover and simmer for about 20 minutes, allowing it to release its own juices. Simmer uncovered for another 10 minutes so that the juices reduce, then add the vinegar, olive oil, onions and bay leaves. You will not need salt. Cover and cook for another 20–30 minutes, until the tentacles seem tender and the sauce thick.

■ Remove the octopus, then cut into large pieces — tentacle by tentacle and dividing up the head. Pour over the sauce and garnish with the cooked onions. 'Too good,' says George.

Prawns Buzzara

'The Italians copied this dish from us,' says Dennis Valcich defiantly. A proud Croatian from the beautiful Dalmatian coast, Dennis has worked as a chef and restaurant manager for many years and recently produced an English-language Croatian cookbook featuring many of the regional specialties of his homeland. His particular part of Croatia is famous for seafood (and yes, Dubrovnik was part of the Venetian empire, so there is a connection). Be careful, though, if you listen to Dennis for too long he'll have you believing his claim that Marco Polo was Croatian. One thing's for sure, the cross-fertilisation across the Adriatic between Italy and Croatia has certainly not harmed either cuisine!

Serves 4
1kg medium to large green prawns
olive oil
4 cloves garlic, finely chopped
1 teaspoon finely chopped continental parsley
pepper, salt or Vegeta vegetable salt (optional)
1 glass dry white wine
4 peeled tomatoes, finely chopped
1 tablespoon breadcrumbs (optional)

■ Remove prawn whiskers, rinse and drain. Heat oil in a large, deep frypan and add garlic, fry for a few seconds, then add prawns. Toss them in pan for a few minutes. Add seasonings (parsley, pepper and salt/Vegeta). Cover and simmer briefly, occasionally tossing pan.
■ Add wine, stir and cover. Cook for a further few minutes, then add tomatoes and sprinkle with breadcrumbs (if used). Toss and cook for a further 3 to 4 minutes.
■ Serve on a large platter with lots of crusty bread, bibs and finger bowls. The dish may also be made with mussels or scampi.

Stuffed Calamari

Another brilliantly easy recipe from Dennis Valcich, a seafood master in his own right.

fresh calamari tubes (4 or 5 to a kilo)
olive oil
pepper and salt to taste

Stuffing:
1 tablespoon finely chopped garlic
1 cup fresh breadcrumbs
½ teaspoon Vegeta vegetable salt (optional)
pepper and salt to taste

■ Carefully remove head from the calamari tube by inserting two fingers and pulling slowly. Remove the backbone, make a small cut at the tip of the tube, rinse and drain.
■ Mix ingredients for stuffing, place a small amount of mixture in each tube, reattach the heads. Cover the base of the baking dish with olive oil and heat it in a preheated moderate oven for 3 to 4 minutes. Roll calamari in the hot oil, season and lay them in the dish. Sprinkle with the rest of the seasoning and place in oven to bake for approximately 40 minutes, turning calamari once while cooking. Remove from tray and slice into rings. They can be served with a little oil drizzled on top, chips, salad and baby spinach.

Muqueca de Camarao (Bahia Prawns)

Bahia is the most 'African' region in Brazil — due to the fact that it was where the European colonists brought the first cargoes of African slaves. (Brazil's first capital, the city of Salvador, was in the Bahia region). To this day Bahia has retained its African heritage and its culinary influences, including the use of palm oil which is used in this and many other recipes. A heavy, dark orange oil that can be found in paste or liquid form, it's strong in flavour and gives a unique taste to any dish. You can find it in specialty grocery stores — Portuguese, South American or Spanish. This recipe comes from Paulo Weinberger, who was born not in Bahia but in Brazil's modern-day centre, Sao Paulo.

Serves 4

4 tablespoons safflower or peanut oil

2 large onions, sliced thinly

1kg cooked king prawns, cleaned and peeled

1 tablespoon crushed garlic

3–4 tablespoons palm oil (do not overdo, it is strong)

1 can coconut milk

½ tablespoon salt

black pepper to taste

■ Fry onions in safflower oil until golden brown. Add prawns and continue frying for a few minutes, stirring well. Add garlic. When garlic has browned, add palm oil, mix well, pour in coconut milk and season.
■ Cook over a medium heat until it boils, then simmer for about 20 minutes, checking regularly.

Alain's Garlic Prawns

Alain Fabregues is a French chef who settled in Western Australia and built himself a restaurant in the hills behind Perth around ten years ago. He'd already collected accolades for his work back home — with the equivalent of a knighthood from the French government for his services to the food industry. At The Loose Box in Mundaring, Alain whips up delicacies like these prawns which he suggests be drizzled with a good local olive oil. The one made by the monks at New Norcia, south of Perth, is what he recommends. Each step takes a short time but you'll need to work quickly to make sure the final dish is hot and appetising.

Serves 1

4 tiger prawn tails

3 teaspoons pureed garlic, thyme, parsley, salt and pepper

1 large zucchini

¼ cup reduced fish stock

¼ cup cream

100g unsalted butter

1 tomato, diced

1 teaspoon good-quality olive oil

chopped chives, finely chopped

■ Clean tiger prawn tails and brush with 1 teaspoon of the garlic puree mixture. Wrap in cling wrap and steam for a few minutes. Set aside and just before presenting, cut prawns in half lengthways.
■ With a fine mandolin, make some 'spaghetti' from the zucchini, toss quickly in a pan with some butter and a pinch of salt for just a minute — make sure the zucchini stays al dente.
■ For the sauce, infuse fish stock with cream and add 2 teaspoons garlic puree mixture. Be careful not to boil the sauce.

Alain Fabregues

Serves 4 as an entree

4 x 250g marron

salt and pepper

1 lemon

1 bunch chives

100ml virgin olive oil

3 cloves garlic

1 soup spoon of tomato paste

3 tomatoes

juice 3 oranges

3 whole oranges

150ml fish stock

a dash of tabasco

sugar

a little cornflour

Each individual serving is set out on the plate inside a steel ring. On the bottom, arrange the zucchini spaghetti, then the prawns in an overlapping flower shape.

Pour some of the sauce over the prawns and the rest around them, then remove the ring. To garnish, spoon over some warmed diced tomato which has been mixed with olive oil, salt, pepper and chives.

Marron Maltaise

'What luck we have in Western Australia to have this marvellous crustacean — the marron,' says French master chef Alain Fabregues, who delights in the freshness and quality of the produce of his adopted country. 'I've tried many recipes [for marron] but this one is by far the best — it's original, it's colourful, it's light and it enhances the sweet flavour and texture of the marron.'

Immerse the marron in boiling water for 2 minutes, then refresh in cold water. Split each marron in two, clean it, crack the claws open and put on a tray, facing upwards.

Season with salt and pepper, a few tears from a lemon, a good pinch of thinly sliced chives and a few drops of virgin olive oil. Allow to marinate for 30 minutes.

Peel the garlic cloves and slice them thinly so they look like sliced almonds. Blanch, peel and dice the tomatoes. Segment the oranges, making sure no seeds or skins are left.

Heat a saucepan, add a little of the olive oil and let it heat up. Add the sliced garlic, stirring with a wooden spatula until it's transparent. Add the tomato paste and let it cook to the point where it's just about to burn at the bottom of the pan. Add the orange juice and fish stock. Keep on stirring and cook for 5 minutes.

Check the seasoning and add pepper, salt, tabasco and sugar as desired.

Remove from heat and let the temperature go down at least 15°C before adding a bit of

Take One Fish

An easy and impressive dinner party meal? A whole fish (especially if you have someone on hand who can neatly serve it for you without including too many bones!)

We include suggestions ranging from an Italian baked fish to a ginger and lemongrass Timorese recipe. Try Kylie Kwong's classic Chinese, Filipino sweet and sour, Nonya barramundi and Lebanese samke harra. It's worth checking the Sauces, Relishes and Marinades chapter for interesting flavours to add to whole fish, or indeed fillets. Try serving the finished grilled fish with something spicy, tangy or creamy from the same chapter. Preserved lemons, for a start!

Some of the dips in the Mezze/antipasti chapter — like tzadziki or roasted garlic and black bean dip (especially with fish steaks like tuna) — make good sauces to put on the side as do muhammara and zhug from our Sauces, Relishes and Marinades chapter. And some of our vegetable dishes are just meant to accompany fish, like Vietnamese pickled vegetables, escalivada or Pacific-style baked taro leaves with coconut milk.

cornflour mixed with water. Bring back to the boil and repeat the process until, says Alain, 'the liaison is at its peak' — in other words, you have a smooth flavoursome sauce without lumps.

To cook the marron:

■ You will have to do this twice, maybe three times because they will not fit in one pan. In a large skillet, add some olive oil and heat until it smokes. Place the marron in the skillet, flesh facing down. Cook and give them a nice golden colour before turning them over onto the other side to finish cooking.

■ Place the marron on four heated plates, crossing the claws over the head to steady them on the plate.

To finish the sauce:

■ Bring the sauce to the boil again, add the orange segments and diced tomato and pour over the marron. Sprinkle with finely sliced chives and serve.

Singapore Chilli Crab

Singapore chilli crab is reason alone for a quick trip to Singapore and yet is so easy to make at home. This recipe is from Alvin Tan at the Seri Nonya Restaurant, Sydney. It can also be made with mud crab. Don't be put off by the tomato sauce in the recipe — it's used throughout Singapore and adds to its distinctive taste.

Serves 4

3 tablespoons fresh garlic
2 tablespoons fresh ginger
1 teaspoon fresh lemongrass
½ medium onion

8 tablespoons oil
2 fresh red chillies
¾ cup tomato sauce — Maggi, Ayam or Heinz brands
¼ cup sweet chilli sauce — Ayam brand for preference
1½ teaspoons salt
1½ tablespoons sugar
2¼ cups water
4 fresh blue swimmer crab, cleaned and halved or 2 x 800g mud crab, quartered and claws lightly smashed
1 egg, beaten
4 slices white bread, toasted

■ Blend the garlic, ginger, lemongrass, onion and chillies to a fine paste, using ½ cup of water to moisten the mix. Heat oil in large wok or pot. Add the blended ingredients and fry until fragrant. Add the tomato sauce, chilli sauce, salt, sugar and water. Stir, and when it comes to the boil, add the crab. Allow to simmer, cover and stir occasionally for approximately 10 to 15 minutes. (Mud crab will take an extra 5 minutes). Turn off the heat, add the beaten egg to sauce and mix well. Serve with triangles of toast to mop up the sauce.

David White's Seafood Salad

When SBS's Head of Production David White was the executive producer of the current affairs program *Dateline*, reporters returning from overseas assignments would be debriefed as much about their culinary adventures as their journalistic endeavours! David's own culinary explorations have taken him around the world and even seen him spending his whole Christmas holiday in Lyon, one of the gastronomic capitals of France. When it comes to cooking, David's motto is: 'The simpler the better using the best and freshest produce'.

Serves 2
1 live green crab
mixed salad leaves
walnut oil
Maggie Beer's verjus

■ Boil the crab until cooked. Cool and take the flesh out. Mix dressing using a little more oil than verjus and toss the lot together in a large bowl.

■ David likes to use prepared Chinese barbecued squid. You can see the plump yellow squid in the windows of Chinese barbecue shops. Use the soy mixture it is served with as the basis of your salad dressing, chop the squid into fine rounds and serve tossed with mixed salad leaves.

Kim Yang

Kim's Baby Barramundi and Nonya-style Sauce

Softly-spoken chef Kim Yang grew up in East Timor eating Portuguese-style food, a culinary legacy of colonisation. Kim worked around Australia as a chef before deciding to settle in the tropical splendour of Darwin, a city he loves for the variety of Asian vegetables to be found. 'There are three types of basil easily available, and everything is so fresh,' he says. These days Kim's skill is exercised specialising in Thai and Nonya-style (a blend of Malay and Chinese) food.

This is a real show-off dish as the butterflied fish looks beautiful and with its fragrant sauce, tastes marvellous too. Kitchen scissors are a real help in butterflying the fish. Set aside 45 minutes preparation time.

Serves 2
4 cloves garlic
1 teaspoon ground red chilli
½ teaspoon belachan (dried shrimp paste)
3 pieces lemongrass, thinly sliced then minced
1 thumb-sized fresh turmeric
1 cup oil
½ cup minced onion
2 tablespoons maltose
1 tablespoon chilli paste in soya oil
½ tablespoon sugar
1 teaspoon salt
1 tablespoon tamarind
2 baby barramundi, 450–500g
Note: Ingredients such as belachan and maltrose are available in most Asian food stores.

■ Blend garlic, chilli, belachan, lemongrass and turmeric together. Heat oil in a saucepan until it begins to smoke, then add the minced onions. Saute for about 3 minutes, then add the blended ingredients. Reduce heat and cook for a further 10 minutes. Add the remaining ingredients, except barramundi and saute for another 5 minutes and taste.

▪ Scale the barramundi and cut open lengthwise — butterfly cut.

Heat a cast-iron hot plate smeared with a little oil and place fish with its skin-side down to seal flesh. Continue for about 3 minutes, then apply the nonya paste on the top of the fish. Place under a grill for approximately 6 minutes without turning until the fish is firm when touched. Garnish with julienned red capsicum and fresh mint leaves.

▪ This dish goes well with water spinach with sambal (in the Vegetables chapter) and steamed rice.

Kailis Whole Fish

The Kailis family is quite a gang. It all began way back in 1914 when grandfather George came to Australia from the Greek island of Castellorizo and opened a fish shop in Perth. Some eight decades later, his four grandsons run a business that operates across Australia and even exports to Asia. And they certainly know their seafood. It's great to watch Theo Kailis baking a large snapper with his mother Sophie's tangy tomato salsa. A very easy meal — and the finished dish is perfect with some steamed rice, lemon wedges and a Greek salad. Theo's tip: Always score the fish through to the bone to help it cook. And undercook rather than overcook as the fish will keep on baking in the pan once you take it out of the oven. Allow about 30 to 40 minutes for this (depending on the size of the fish). A small snapper would be done in just 20 minutes,

while a 2kg monster would take a good 35 to 40 minutes.

Serves 6
1 whole fish, approx 1kg

Sophie's Tomato Salsa:
4 medium-sized carrots
3 sticks celery
2 red capsicums
2 green capsicums
6 tomatoes, peeled
2 brown onions, diced
4 cloves garlic
1 red chilli
1 green chilli
oregano
basil
2 teaspoons tabasco
olive oil
4 x 425g cans tomato soup or 1.5 litre Italian-style tomato cooking sauce

▪ Coarsely chop all fresh vegetables, except brown onions. Place vegetables, herbs and tabasco together in a blender and blend until finely chopped.

▪ In a large saucepan sauté onions in olive oil until transparent. Add blended vegetables and tomato sauce to saucepan and allow to simmer for 30 to 45 minutes.

▪ Spread the salsa generously over a whole, cleaned fish. Bake in a moderate 180°C oven for around 30 to 40 minutes, less for a small fish.

Kylie Kwong's Steamed Whole Fish with Ginger and Shallots

Kylie Kwong grew up in Sydney — in what she describes as a typical Asian extended family. Her family's presence in Australia dates back to the gold rush and her prosperous ancestor Kwong Sue Duk from Guangdong Province who first came to Australia in the early 1800s. (He eventually founded a world-wide dynasty of Kwongs — across South-East Asia, America and Australia.)

Her mother and grandparents were renowned for their cooking, and as head chef at Sydney's Wockpool Restaurant, Kylie is definitely continuing the family tradition of great food. Her steamed fish with ginger and shallots is a classic — combining the yin and yang of Chinese philosophy, with an appreciation of life's dualities and the faith that harmony arises from the proper blending of opposites.

'I find my passion for food and cooking stems mostly from my childhood memories,' Kylie says. 'That excitement I felt every afternoon about the evening's meal, smells of ginger and soy sauce chicken, steamed egg with Chinese mushrooms, the sounds of the sizzling wok or the loud thud thud of my mother's Chinese cleaver chopping up roast duck, going to the fish shop with Mum to choose the best whole Murray perch!'

Choose your best whole Murray perch, a superb coral trout or a super-fresh snapper and try this out.

You will need a wok and a Chinese steamer basket big enough to hold the fish. Make sure the basket lid fits properly!

Serves 4

one whole fish, one with sweet, light flesh
½ cup fresh, very young ginger (pinkish on the outside and very crisp)
⅓ cup chicken stock
splash yellow bean soy sauce
2 whole Chinese cabbage leaves, blanched
½ tablespoon castor sugar
½ cup yellow bean soy
1 cup shallot stems, julienned in 4cm lengths
1 teaspoon sesame oil
½ cup peanut oil

■ Score whole fish several times, place on white Chinese cabbage leaf on a plate and place in steamer basket. Splash with yellow bean soy, cover with half the julienned ginger and pour over the chicken stock. Cover. Steaming takes about 10 minutes depending on size of fish — check that flesh is firm through to bone before removing.

■ When fish is ready, place peanut oil on stove and heat to smoking point. It will start to make a pinging sound as fine bubbles are released. Garnish cooked fish with castor sugar, the rest of the ginger, yellow bean soy, half the coriander and half the shallots. Next comes a splash of sesame oil and a little of the stock it cooked in. When oil is smoking, pour very quickly over fish. It will sear and seal the ginger and shallots and bring out all their aroma. Quite a party trick!

■ Garnish with the rest of the shallots and coriander and serve immediately.

Note: Kylie's chicken stock is made in the classic Chinese way, with shallot stems, ginger and a Spanish onion. See our Soup chapter for details.

Ikan Furak (East Timorese Fish with Ginger and Garlic)

Coconut oil is an important part of this Timorese dish. It is a heavy oil, full of saturated fats, but just this once! It does give a special flavour to the fish and reflects the importance of coconuts in the Timorese diet. We got the recipe from Melburnian Maria Gabriela Carrascalao, originally from East Timor, who tells us coconut oil can be bought in most Asian grocery stores.

Serves 4
2 tablespoons coconut oil
1 whole or filleted fish (1kg)
juice of 2 lemons
1 knob fresh ginger, grated
1 clove garlic, chopped finely
pinch of saffron
hot chilli to taste

■ Grease large flat pan with small amount coconut oil, add fish and cover with lemon juice, ginger, garlic, saffron and hot chilli. Cook uncovered on low heat for 30 minutes and serve with vegetables — perhaps chopped green pawpaw fried in coconut oil and a small amount of garlic, and rice.

Filipino Sweet and Sour Fish

Rhonda Cabaron moved a long way from her home in the Philippines to Alice Springs but all her favourite recipes came with her, including this one which she learnt while a student in Cebu City. With fresh fish flown south from Darwin, this is an easy dish to prepare for the regular get-togethers held by Alice Springs's small but close-knit Filipino community.

Rhonda Cabaron

Serves 6
3 large red snapper (weight that adds up to 1kg)
salt to taste
vegetable oil
1 onion, sliced
4 cloves garlic, crushed
1 green capsicum, julienned
1 red capsicum, julienned
1 large golf-ball sized knob ginger, sliced into thin strips
2 carrots, julienned
1 tablespoon sugar
2 tablespoons vinegar
1 tablespoon thick soy sauce, preferably Filipino brand
4 tablespoons sweet chilli sauce, preferably Thai brand
1 chicken stock cube
½ cup water
vegetable oil

■ Rub the skin of fish with salt, then with a sharp knife cut 3 slits into each side of the fish. Fry in a small amount of vegetable oil until cooked and crisp on the outside.

■ In a large saucepan or wok, stir-fry the onion and garlic for a couple of minutes, then add capsicum, ginger and carrot. Stir well and add sugar, vinegar, soy sauce, chilli sauce and chicken stock cube crumbled into water.

■ Cook until vegetables are almost at the al dente stage, lower heat and add whole fish — gently heat through and serve with steamed rice.

Samke Harra
(Middle Eastern Chilli Fish)

The centrepiece of a luscious Lebanese meal (after enjoying a tableful of mezze) is often a whole poached fish served with a spicy, sauce. This particularly scrumptious version of a traditional recipe comes from the combined creativity of former chef George Haddad and his former assistant, Katherine Witbreuk, these days a chef in her own right. George too has gone on to bigger things. But there are many in Hobart still mourning the days when George, his wife Anne and Katherine fed the Tasmanian capital out of the once legendary Ali Akbar restaurant.

Serves 4–6
one whole fish, of the light, sweet, white variety
½ cup diced celery
½ onion, diced
¼ leek, finely sliced
white peppercorns
a bunch of parsley stalks
2 bay leaves
a sprig of fresh thyme
2 teaspoons fennel seeds
1 coriander root

The Haddad family

Sauce:
1 cup walnuts, finely chopped
1 bunch coriander, finely chopped
1 bunch parsley, finely chopped
2 chillies, finely chopped
500ml fish stock
500ml white wine
pomegranate pips and coriander leaves for garnish

■ Place fish in a roasting pan with the celery, onion, leek and herbs. Cover with foil and place in a 190°C oven. Cook for 20 to 40 minutes, depending on the size of the fish.

■ Meanwhile, prepare the sauce by reducing the wine and fish stock until only one cup of liquid remains. Add walnuts and stir until well mixed. It should have the consistency of a light paste.

■ When the fish is ready add the other ingredients to the sauce and season. Add strained fish juices from pan. Place fish on serving plate and spoon over the sauce. Garnish with pomegranate pips and coriander leaves.

Bacalhau Com Queijo (Portuguese Salt Cod with Cheese)

'You can't talk about Portuguese cuisine without bacalhau,' exclaims caterer and enthusiastic foodie Fatima Barroso who, under the banner of 'Exclusive Cuisine', feeds many luminaries around Sydney. Dried cod fish is in fact quite delicious — well-rinsed of its salty preservative it cooks up to a sweet, tender and quite rich texture. The ultimate comfort food, really, especially when teamed with fried potatoes and grated cheese!

Serves 6
350g salt-dried cod (bacalhau in Portuguese shops, baccala in Italian delis)
650g potatoes, peeled
3 tablespoons flour
4 tablespoons water
3 eggs, separated
salt and pepper
300ml tomato sauce (made by reducing tinned tomatoes with garlic and/or onion)
110g grated cheese
oil for frying

■ Soak the cod for 24 hours in cold water, changing it occasionally. Boil it with the potatoes until the potatoes are tender. Remove from heat and drain. Slice the potatoes and break the fish into smallish pieces, discarding skin and bones.

■ Make a batter with the flour, a little salt, water and the egg yolks. Beat well. In a separate bowl beat the eggwhites and fold into the batter.

■ Divide batter into two portions. In one mix the sliced potatoes and in the other the pieces of cod. Fry spoonfuls of each mixture (separately) until golden. Assemble layers of both fried cakes in a fireproof dish and cover with tomato sauce. Sprinkle with grated cheese.

■ Bake for 15 minutes at 200°C on the top shelf, to melt the cheese. Alternatively, place under the grill.

Fatima Barroso

Noodles, pasta, dumplings and rice

Iranian Rice

Jimmy Ghafari swears this is the best rice recipe in the world. It involves a fair bit of work, demanding lots of rinsing and draining. The boiled rice is finished off in the oven. 'Iranians love big plump grains of rice, especially to go with Persian curries,' says Jimmy. 'And rice is the basis of all our meals, so cooking it properly is very important.'

Serves 10–12

6 cups Basmati rice
½ cup of vegetable oil mixed into 1 cup of hot water

■ Wash rice 6–7 times, to rinse out the starch. The water should be nearly clear by the time you've finished — and do it gently so as not to break the grains. Put rice in a large container, cover with cold water and add 2 large handfuls of salt. Mix through and leave rice for 8 to 10 hours. Strain the rice but don't wash it.
■ Put 2 litres of water to boil in a large pan on the stove. When boiling, add the rice and cook until it reaches an al dente stage. Strain and rinse with cold water.
■ Place in a small baking tray and add hot water and vegetable oil mix. Cover with aluminium foil and cook in a 250°C oven for 25 to 30 minutes. Serve immediately.

Israeli Festive Rice

Festive rice can be eaten on its own as a main dish, or with meat, or with vegetables. 'It's all optional,' says Edytta Super who gave us this Israeli recipe, 'but you must enjoy it'.

Serves 6–8

1kg packet of rice
250g slivered almonds
olive oil
½ packet of black currants

■ Cook rice as preferred. Toss slivered almonds in a dash of olive oil, taking care they don't burn, as they cook really fast. When they're ready, remove from the pan and fry the black currants. They will also need only about a minute or two. Then add to the rice, mix well and bake in a moderate 180°C oven for about 20 minutes.

Tamarind Rice

'This is poor man's food,' says Indo-Fijian caterer, Barbara Brewer. 'Tamarind is a good preservative so this rice could last people for days. Women would wrap it in a ball and carry

Barbara Brewer

it in their saris when they were working or walking the roads.' Poor man's food or not, it became so popular when Barbara ran a small takeaway restaurant that she was selling frozen packs of it for her customers' TV dinners.

Serves 2

2 tablespoons vegetable oil

½ teaspoon each of mustard, fenugreek and cumin seeds

1 small onion, finely sliced

a few curry leaves

2–3 dried red chillies, broken in halves

½ cup tamarind juice (made with walnut-sized piece of tamarind soaked in water)

2 cups cold rice (leftover is excellent)

salt to taste

■ Heat oil in wok. When hot, put in seeds but be careful not to put your face too close as they sputter in oil. Add onion and when it starts to brown, add curry leaves and chillies. Stir and add tamarind juice. When it starts to bubble, add rice (without lumps) and salt. Stir to coat rice. Turn heat low until all the liquid has been absorbed and rice is hot and fluffy.

Nasi Empit (Malaysian Compressed Rice)

A recipe from Malaysian chef Alvin Tan, this compressed rice dish is designed to accompany satays. (See the recipes for satay marinades on pp. 188–9.)

Serves 4 as an accompaniment

2 cups rice

2½ cups water

½ teaspoon salt

■ Wash and drain rice. Place rice, water and salt in rice cooker (or saucepan). Mix to dissolve salt. When rice is cooked, mash a little with a potato masher to break up the grains. Transfer rice to a tray lined with cling wrap. Place another tray on this and put a heavy object on top to compress the rice for 3 to 4 hours. Cut into 2cm cubes. This can also be frozen for later use.

Barley and Rice Pilaf

Vegetables and spiced rice, laced with the strong flavour of a good olive oil. The use of pulses and grains, wild greens, oil with lemon or vinegar is typically Greek and a wonderful way to eat. This salad can be made with plain long grain rice, or for something different, wild rice — just to add an extra contrast to the sweet smoothness of barley.

Serves 4

3 large leeks, sliced into thick rounds

¼ cup olive oil

1 cup rice (wild rice, brown rice or plain white long grain), rinsed

1 cup barley

½ cup olive oil

⅔ cup raisins

1 cup chopped walnuts

salt and pepper to taste

2–3 tablespoons of balsamic vinegar or lemon juice if preferred

■ Toss the leeks in ¼ cup of olive oil then place in a baking pan and roast in a preheated 200°C oven until dark and caramelised (about 30 minutes). In the meantime, boil the rice until just tender and drain well. The barley must also be cooked — for about 10 minutes in salted water. Rinse with cold water and drain.

■ Place the barley in serving bowl and toss in around ½ cup of oil, adding the rice, leeks, raisins, walnuts, salt, pepper and vinegar. Serve warm or at room temperature.

Arroz A Brasiliera (Brazilian Rice)

This flavoursome way of preparing steamed rice with a little oil and garlic makes a great accompaniment to any number of dishes — not least, of course, to Brazilian beans (see p. 158). Combine the two and you have one of Brazil's national dishes. After sixteen years in Australia, Paulo Weinberger still cooks in a 'mainly Brazilian style' which includes regular serves of rice and beans! 'Of course, unless you have nothing else, you eat it with meat, salad, a fried egg — as an accompaniment, in other words,' he stresses.

Serves 4
2 tablespoons oil (Paulo prefers olive oil)
1 tablespoon crushed garlic
2 cups of white (or brown) rice
4 cups of water
1 tablespoon salt

■ Heat oil in saucepan over moderately low heat for 1 minute, add crushed garlic and wait until it turns a golden colour. Add rice, mix well with wooden spoon and leave it frying for about 6 minutes, stirring every couple of minutes. Add water and salt and stir. Cover and increase heat until water boils. Reduce to simmer and cook for 15 to 20 minutes (longer for brown rice), until dry and cooked. If dry

and not cooked enough, add a little boiling water, cover and check again in another 5 minutes.

Abla's Chicken Rice

Abla Amad was born in Lebanon. She always loved cooking and her home in Melbourne was always full of people. Her secret dream was to open a little restaurant where she could serve home-style food on a wider scale. Almost twenty years ago now, her dream came true and Abla's was born. Since then she has been feeding half of Melbourne on her fresher-than-fresh tabouli, crisp kibbeh, piquant eggplant dip and other traditional treats.

This is a lesser-known dish — sweet with allspice and cinnamon and crunchy with pinenuts and almonds. It is not difficult to prepare and quite a sight to behold as you take away the ring tin it is moulded in to display an appetising mound of chicken, rice and Middle Eastern spices.

Serves 6–8
1 large boiling chicken
2 cups slivered almonds
1 cup pinenuts
500g lean lamb mince
2 cups of water
2 cups long grain rice, washed
salt and pepper to taste
allspice, cinnamon

■ Place chicken in stockpot, cover with cold water, bring to boil and simmer until cooked (about 1½ hours). Reserve 2 cups of stock. Brown the almonds and pinenuts in oil and set aside.

In a deep saucepan brown the mince in a little oil and add half the pinenuts. Add 2 cups of stock and 2 cups of water to mince, then the rice. Season with a little salt and pepper. Cover and cook on low heat until all liquid is absorbed (about 20 minutes). You can stir it occasionally.

Meanwhile, bone the chicken and slice meat finely (removing skin).

Mix the toasted almonds and remaining pinenuts with allspice and cinnamon, then press the mixture into the bottom of a ring mould cake tin (the kind used for kugelhopf). Line the tin with slices of chicken, then fill middle with rice and mince mixture. Press in firmly. Place face down over serving platter and leave until serving. Lift off the mould and you should have a decorative ring of rice with a delicious, fragrant topping.

Zap Gum Lo Mai Fan (Bea's Savoury Sticky Rice)

Before she moved to Australia, Bea Hutcheon was one of Hong Kong's unsung foodies, acting as translator for Mrs Lisa Fong, one of the former colony's most famous chefs. In Australia, she has carried on the tastes of home. This simple recipe is made for busy chefs — just remember to leave time to soak the glutinous rice and mushrooms. This recipe is for microwave ovens.

Serves 2
3/4 cup glutinous rice
2 tablespoons small dried shrimps
2 black dried mushrooms, stems discarded
1¼ cups water mixed with white wine
¼ cup long grain rice
2 Chinese sausages (lap cheung — use lighter coloured ones)
1 tablespoon minced fresh coriander

Sauce:
2 teaspoons light soy sauce
2 teaspoons dark soy sauce
½ teaspoon sugar
2 teaspoons oil
black pepper to taste

Wash glutinous rice and soak in cold water to cover for at least 3 hours or overnight. Wash shrimps and mushrooms and soak in the water and white wine for same period.

Later or next day: drain glutinous rice and discard water. Drain shrimps and mushrooms and save liquid in measuring glass. Dice mushrooms and shrimps if too large. Wash long grain rice, drain and mix with glutinous rice, diced mushrooms and shrimps.

Place in Pyrex casserole (only half full). Lay washed sausages on top. Pour over the reserved liquid plus enough cold water to make 1¼ cups. Cover casserole, leaving a small opening. Place on top of a small towel (to catch drips) on the turntable. Microwave on high (100% power) for 15 minutes, stirring twice.

Meanwhile, mix together sauce ingredients. Remove sausages and dice but leave rest in microwave oven to stand 5 minutes.

Stir coriander into rice with sausages and seasoning sauce. Cover and microwave for another 3 minutes on high. Let stand for 5 minutes before serving.

Rice is Nice

As most of us know by now, it takes more than one kind of rice to make a pilaf — or rather, the best rice for that classic Persian dish of fluffy, buttery grains would have to be basmati yet you'd never use anything less than plump arborio grains for a really authentic risotto. Asian cuisine delights in perfumed jasmine rice, shiny glutinous or sticky rice for desserts and cakes and the highly refined japonica strain for sushi and other Japanese specialties.

Long and short grain black rice is popular in Thailand and Indonesia and makes truly spectacular desserts while the lesser known red rice (enjoyed in Sri Lanka, for example) has the nutty flavour of its brown cousin but requires several hours soaking before cooking. Spain has its Calasparra — the ultimate paella rice — while the Lombardy region of Italy is famous for a whole range of superb risotto rices like arborio, carnaroli and vialone nano. You can smell the perfume of the paddy fields around the city of Kut in southern Iraq, where chicken biryani is almost a national dish (highly fragrant rice cooked in chicken stock, and tossed with shredded chicken, spices, onion and strands of egg vermicelli).

Rice can be steamed and fried, compressed into squares or rolled into deep-fried balls. It can be a salad, a sweet, a sushi roll or 'savoury' with mince meat and tomato. The Vietnamese love to re-fry their rice with tomato and oil to make 'com tam' or broken rice, usually served with a crumbed pork chop and maybe a fried egg. And what could be more sensual than a bowl of freshly made rice flour noodles sliding around in a full-bodied beef or chicken stock?

Paella

'Valencia', with its traditional restaurants found along the promenade in the old city, 'is said to be the birthplace of paella,' Spanish language broadcaster Nati Sangiau says. After two hundred years under the Moors, 'the way it is served gives away its origins. You will eat it in the Arab fashion. The paellera (literally the place where the paella is made) is set down in the centre of the diners and each person is given a wooden spoon to pick out what he or she wants, the same way North Africans eat their couscous.'

Paella can be made with various ingredients but the most authentic, the Valenciana version, is always with seafood, chicken and diced pork. Nati stresses that this is an expensive dish, not one to be concocted with leftovers, but with a preferred combination of the best and freshest ingredients, whatever you choose. For cooking it, a wide round dish with sides high enough to allow the rice to double in size can be placed on a stove or, better still, the barbecue. Create a base of saffron-flavoured rice plus as many ingredients as you like — quantities depend on you.

Serves 6
400g chicken pieces

seafood — mussels in shell (a couple per person, black ones are best), green prawns (a couple per head), clams, yabbies, crab claws, calamari rings, fish fillets cut in thirds

200g pork, diced

olive oil for frying

1 onion

1 capsicum

2 fresh tomatoes or 4 canned

salt to taste

2 cups short grain rice

4 cups water (including water containing saffron)

4 strands saffron (see note)

brown paper for covering dish when cooked

■ Fry chicken and pork in olive oil. Set aside once cooked, then fry onion in chunks, capsicum in strips, tomatoes in slices. Arrange ingredients in paella dish and salt to taste. Warm them then add the rice (Nati suggests 2 cups for a normal-sized dish but says as long as the water used is double the amount of rice you can't go wrong. Remember too that it will swell in size). Cook the rice for a moment, mixed in well with the other ingredients, then pour water and saffron over.

■ At this point, add the seafood, as it doesn't need long to cook. Stir a touch and then don't stir again until the dish is cooked (about 20 minutes). Shake the dish gently and move it around over the flame to ensure even heat (that's why a barbecue is best for this dish) but resist the temptation to stir. When it is still al dente, turn off heat and cover with brown paper. Allow it to complete 'cooking' for another 5 minutes with heat extinguished.

■ Serve — with wooden spoons, if you like!

Note: Safffron strands should be mashed with a mortar and pestle and left in hot water a while to release their colour. Alternatively, a hint from Casa Iberica, one of Melbourne's favourite sources of fresh, good-quality saffron: dry toast the strands for a few minutes in a heavy-based pan, then simply add to the water to be poured onto the paella ingredients. Don't be fooled into using artificial colouring — usually turmeric — instead.

Nao Fukushima's Sushi

Nao Fukushima left his home in the northern island of Hokkaido many years ago and has spent much of his time in Australia teaching Japanese to businesspeople, housewives, students and those simply interested in things Japanese. Part of his course involves talking and learning about food and he occasionally has his classes at home and demonstrates his rather free-form cooking. (Nao likes nothing better than to head off into the bush or to the ocean with a fishing rod, a sharp knife, some wasabi paste — the green horseradish paste that's delicious with sushi and sashimi — a bottle of soy sauce and fisherman's luck.)

Serves 4 as an entree

2½ cups short grain rice (Australian rice is very good)
vinegar dressing (mix 4 tablespoons vinegar with ¼ cup sugar, 2 teaspoons salt and 2 tablespoons mirin or dry sherry)
nori (green sea vegetable paper)
1 fillet very fresh ocean trout, slice across the grain into thin slivers
spring onion, cut into strips
Lebanese cucumber, cut into thin slivers
wasabi paste (can be bought as powder and mixed) or in tubes
soy sauce

▢ Put rice in colander and wash under running water, rubbing the rice by hand until water runs clear. Put into saucepan and cover with cold water to 1cm above the level of the rice. Turn on the heat and allow the rice to reach the boil. When it's boiling, turn down to a simmer and cook covered for 15 minutes without lifting the lid.

▢ Turn off the heat and leave for 15 minutes, still with the lid on, so the flavour settles. Take off the lid and mix the rice with a bamboo or wooden spoon. The fresh oxygen, says Nao, mingles with the grains for a great taste. While rice is still hot, mix with the vinegar mixture and toss vigorously so every grain is coated.

▢ Cut the nori paper into rectangles a bit smaller than your hand. Put a thin layer of sushi rice on the paper, add a sliver of ocean trout, spring onion, cucumber and small amount of wasabi paste and roll into a cigarette shape.

▢ Serve with a small bowl of soy sauce and 'just touch the sushi to the soy sauce and eat it,' says Nao.

Risotto alla Milanese — alla Riccardo Schirru

Risotto, risotto, risotto … Purists say you will never find a good one in a restaurant. Certainly if you consider that a real risotto is simmered slowly with the gradual addition of a fragrant broth, gently bathing the swelling rice grains, then it's hard to imagine how you could even expect a restaurant kitchen to attempt to cook it to order. A former colleague of ours, journalist and broadcaster Riccardo Schirru, will go down in our memory as a *buongustaio* as only Italy can make one — a lover of fine food and wine who can talk gastronomy for hours at a time, and always has some new discovery when it comes to eating out or shopping to cook at home. His recipe for a Milanese risotto is a classic rendition of a classic dish, with the delicacy of saffron and the richness of a little bone marrow in the stock.

Serves 4 as an entree
25g butter
1 small onion
350g rice (Italian arborio rice — Calrose is a poor substitute)
a good dash of dry white wine
1 litre good chicken stock (simmering on stove)
3–4 saffron strands (pounded to a powder and left to soak in a little hot water or broth)
25g bone marrow (from osso buco meat)
a little more butter
parmesan cheese, freshly grated

▉ Melt butter and fry onion until soft. Add rice and allow to cook a little without changing colour. Throw in a dash of white wine and let bubble away until just a little is left. In the meantime, have chicken stock simmering in a saucepan on the stove and saffron already pounded to a powder and diluted in hot water or a little of the broth. Add the bone marrow and the stock a cupful at a time, only adding as rice absorbs it. Pour in the saffron as rice becomes tender. It should take about 20–25 minutes for the rice to be creamy, not dry. Let it stand for a few minutes after mixing in a little more butter and parmesan cheese, then serve.

Risotto Della Nonna

'This is a dish my grandmother used to make,' says Italian TV executive Claudio Paroli, a keen cook from the northern Italian region of Lombardy — home of rice not pasta, butter not oil and lots of parmesan cheese.

Serves 2
65g butter
1 onion

1 cup arborio rice
3 or 4 Roma tomatoes, peeled
1 litre chicken stock
pinch of salt
tiny pinch of sugar
1 teaspoon cinnamon
handful of grated parmesan cheese
1 egg
black pepper to taste

▉ Melt the butter and sauté the onion until translucent. Add the arborio rice, stir it over low heat until opaque white ('no burn marks on the rice, please', says Claudio), then add tomatoes and slowly, by the ladleful, some of the homemade stock. Add more stock only when the rice has absorbed the previous ladleful. Add a pinch of salt and a touch of sugar. Keep stirring. Midway through the cooking process (the rice takes about 20 minutes to cook) add half the ground cinnamon. About 10 minutes later add the rest. Away from the heat add parmesan and an egg, stirring quickly. Grind in black pepper to taste. Done.

Riso Alla Siciliana

John Portelli and his wife Rosemary di Santo-Portelli run the Enoteca Sileno in Melbourne's North Carlton — a treasure-trove of exquisite produce and fine Italian wines. John is the ultimate food enthusiast. He can tell you all about pasta-producing techniques, discuss the qualities of Sicilian sea salt, wax lyrical about tiny olives or pungent dried porcini mushrooms. So what do John and Rosemary eat at home? In summer, Rosemary tells us, they love this dish from John's family region, the island of Lipari in the Eolian group off Sicily.

Serves 4

300g carnaroli rice (see note)
a couple of anchovies (If salted, rinse off the salt and remove the bones. If in oil, drain them.)
1 onion, chopped finely
extra virgin olive oil
balsamic vinegar
half a glass of dry white wine
juice of 3 medium-sized lemons
salt and pepper to taste
3 ripe tomatoes, washed, halved, centre removed and diced
marjoram
50g pitted tiny black olives

■ Fill a saucepan with plenty of salted water and bring it to the boil. Before adding the rice to it to cook, put the anchovies on a dish and place it over the boiling water. Mash the anchovies with a fork and allow to melt down a little. This will only take 2 minutes. Remove the dish with the anchovies and add the rice to the boiling water. Turn down the heat and allow the rice to cook.

■ In the meantime, sauté the onion in the olive oil. Spray with the balsamic vinegar and allow to evaporate. Add the white wine, lemon juice and mashed anchovies. Mix all the ingredients well and then pass through the food processor for a short minute (or you can press them in the mortar).

■ When the rice has cooked, drain it and place it in the serving dish. Pour the 'salsina' (sauce) of anchovy, white wine and lemon juice over the rice, adding a little salt and pepper if needed.

■ Just before serving add the diced tomatoes, heated through in a little hot olive oil. Sprinkle

with marjoram and olives. Serve hot.

Note: Carnaroli is a fine variety of short grain rice, perfect for this sort of dish, a substitute could be arborio (risotto rice) or at a pinch, Calrose.

Galushka (Hungarian Spaetzli)

This recipe for galushka (not to be confused with goulash or gulyas) comes to us courtesy of culinary charmer Gabriel Carr. With his silky voice and European good looks, Gabriel once hosted his own TV show, worked for many years for SBS TV as a subtitler and voice-over artist, and can often be spotted playing a 'continental gentleman' in TV ads. Cooking is among his many talents. His published collection of lady-killing food sensations, entitled *Seducer in the Kitchen*, features this under the heading 'Recipes for a Hungarian rhapsody' and is, naturally, for two people. Naturally too, it is to be served with a sauced dish, like porkolt (see pp. 81–2) or veal paprika.

Serves 2

1 cupful of flour
1 egg, beaten
½ teaspoon of salt

■ Combine ingredients with just enough water to make the mixture the consistency of ice-cream about to melt. Let stand for about an hour. Pour onto a floured board. Boil salted water in a saucepan and, with a knife, flick 1cm square bits of the dough into the water. When all the pieces have come to the surface, strain and serve.

Zganci (Slovenian Buckwheat)

Barbara Zagar, who gave us this recipe, says zganci is one of Slovenia's great undiscovered dishes. Don't be put off by the name or the idea that this may be complicated to make, says Barbara, once you master it you won't be able to stop showing off your newly acquired skills! The texture is a little like rice when it's fluffed up with a fork. The taste is fairly bland, she says, but that makes it the best choice to serve with stronger dishes such as meats, sauerkraut, pork crackling, bacon and even with milk or sour milk as a breakfast dish.

Serves 4

1kg buckwheat flour
3 litres water
salt to taste
150g oil or lard or butter

▦ In a large saucepan, put the water on to boil. Add salt.
▦ Sift the flour then add to the boiling water. Cover and boil slowly for 10 minutes without stirring. Remove from heat and make a long thin hole in the middle with the end of a wooden spoon. Cook slowly for 30 minutes.
▦ Remove from the heat and decant half of the cooking water and put aside. Add some of the oil or butter to the mixture and mix well with a fork. (The best sort is the fork used to carve meat.) The idea is to make it crumbly, to give it the consistency of rice. If it's too dry, add some of the water you've put aside.
▦ Transfer into a serving dish and top with the rest of the oil or butter or lard.

The Marino family

Marino Family's Polenta

This recipe is from the Abruzzi region of Italy, which Adelaide butcher Tony Marino left almost four decades ago. You need a large table to enjoy polenta in the authentic Abruzzese way. It's great fun and an arresting way of serving food — each family member is armed with a spoon and eats their way into the middle of the table. The Marino family have guessing competitions about the shape that is left once everyone has eaten. (Note: They have never once eaten the table clean!)

Serves 20
Sauce:
1 large onion, chopped
4 cloves garlic, crushed
1 stick celery, chopped
1 dozen quail, seasoned with salt and pepper, legs tied with string
1.5kg pork and veal mince
3 thick fresh Italian sausages
4 chicken wings
1kg stewing veal
1 tin sliced mushrooms

20g dried Italian porcini mushrooms covered with water and soaked for 20 minutes (reserve liquid)

3 litres homemade tomato sauce (or 8 cans peeled tomatoes, finely chopped)

1 cup white wine (the Marinos use riesling)

Polenta:
1kg polenta

3 litres water

good pinch of salt

To prepare sauce:
■ In a large saucepan, heat olive oil over high heat and add onions and garlic, stir quickly and add celery. Add quail, pork and veal mince, sausages, chicken wings, and stewing veal and cook for about 20 minutes until the meat turns golden brown. Stir occasionally. Remove sausage, quail and chicken wings and set aside.

■ Add the mushrooms, tomato sauce and wine. Pass mushroom liquid through a cloth serviette and add to sauce. Cook for 1½ hours over slow heat to bring out full flavour. Just before serving, add sausage, quail and chicken to the sauce.

To prepare polenta:
■ Boil water and add polenta gradually and stir continuously for 20 minutes with large wooden spoon. (You have to have a few muscles to keep this up!)

To serve:
■ Bring pot of polenta to table — wooden or laminex — and spread mixture evenly over surface to height of 1.5cm. Spread sauce evenly over polenta, carefully placing sausages in the middle of the table and dotting quail and wings at regular intervals.

■ Grab a group of hungry family and friends, arm them with spoons and ask them to eat their way into the centre. Children have a great time guessing what shapes are made as the polenta disappears.

Franca Manfredi's Gnocchi

Franca Manfredi was born in Gottolengo, near Brescia in Northern Italy. Cooking was always in the family — her mother ran a boarding house and was a wonderful cook. It's a talent Franca has inherited and passed on to her son Stefano (Steve). When they migrated to Australia in the 1960s, however, they had no thought of ever opening a restaurant — let alone creating one of Sydney's finest and most upmarket establishments (Restaurant Manfredi and now, belmondo)! Overseeing the kitchen is Franca's job. Ever the perfectionist, she still handmakes the pasta (the finest in Australia) and her glorious gnocchi. You certainly need a light hand for this dish and speed is important, Franca thinks, for rolling the little dumplings off a fork as fast as you can. 'She's been clocked in at 200 gnocchi a minute,' adds Steve. He marvels at the aerodynamic quality of these luscious morsels. The marks left by your fork are perfect for concealing a little well of sauce and the gentle indentation made by the thumb as they are pushed across the fork prongs helps them bob up more quickly to the top of a boiling pot, perfectly cooked and never soggy.

Serves 6
1.5kg of boiled desiree potatoes (boil them with their skins on)

a handful of good parmesan cheese

a good sprinkling of salt and likewise of nutmeg

a scant 200g of plain flour
3–4 egg yolks

■ Peel the potatoes while still warm and mash with a potato ricer or mouli. Form them into a flat-topped heap in front of you, sprinkle over parmesan cheese, salt and nutmeg. Make a small well in the centre and fill with about half the flour. Pour the egg yolks on top of the flour and mix them in with the flour first, then mix the lot — with your hands of course, as if kneading bread. The mixture should be soft and potatoey, not too sticky. Use flour on your hands and the rolling surface.

■ Sprinkling more flour on the rolling surface, divide the mixture into several snakes of dough, about the diameter of the hole formed between your thumb and forefinger. Cut the snakes into 3mm lengths.

■ Sprinkling more flour, take a fork and hold it upwards in front of you with the prongs facing down and away from you. Put each gnocco (singular of gnocchi) on the bowl of the fork and gently push it down across the prongs. This will leave a small thumb indentation in one end and a set of grooves on the bottom edge of the dumpling. Don't press hard, you are almost flipping them!

■ Have ready a pot of boiling salted water. Throw in about 20 of the gnocchi and wait until they bob up to the surface. That means they are cooked. Drain them and serve with a tomato sauce or burned butter and parmesan.

Burned butter

■ Burned butter is simple to make once you get the hang of it. Melt about 15g of butter per serve in a small saucepan. Once it has melted, give it an occasional stir. When you see it start to froth, stir again. The minute you see it starting to brown, turn off the heat. The heat in the saucepan should continue to cook it. Pour over the gnocchi dressed with a little parmesan. The hot butter will melt the cheese and make a lovely sauce for the gnocchi.

Pierogi (Polish Ravioli)

The Polish version of the Russian pirozhki (which usually come large and fried) is a little more like ravioli, only with a hearty cheese and potato filling. You can serve a few with a winter stew or as an entree, like pasta. The recipe comes from Polish journalist Isabel Sendlak.

Serves 4–6
1kg mashed white Polish cheese
500g mashed boiled potatoes
salt and pepper
500g flour
water
butter
sour cream

■ Mix cheese and potatoes, and add salt and pepper to taste. Make a pastry dough of flour and water (no eggs), and roll out to around a 3mm thickness. Cut into small rounds, using a cup. Fold in half over a spoonful of cheese and potato mixture, pinch the edges and form the crescent-shaped pierogi.

■ Boil water in a large saucepan. Drop pierogi into the boiling water and cook for about 5 minutes. Remove, place in a bowl and add a spoonful of butter. Shake around to melt butter and prevent sticking. Serve hot with butter and sour cream.

Varenyky (Ukrainian Dumplings)

For Ukrainians, there's nothing that conjures up home quite as much as well-filled plump varenyky (crescent-shaped dumplings served with onions which have been fried in butter or sour cream). Ukrainian broadcaster Liana Soipetsky, who has given us the following recipe, points out that you can make these with a savoury or a sweet filling and says either version is very easy to make.

Every cook has a different way of preparing the dough — good versions should be tender and that depends on the amount of water you use. Try cool water for a softer dough that prevents quick drying.

Makes about 48

1½ cups water

¼ cup cooking oil

1 egg

4½ cups flour

1 teaspoon salt

Mushroom filling:

1 small onion, chopped finely

3 tablespoons butter

2 cups cooked mushrooms

salt and pepper to taste

2 egg yolks

To prepare dumplings:

■ Combine water, cooking oil and egg and blend well. Add flour and salt. Knead the dough until smooth and soft. Put in a lightly oiled bowl and cover. Let the dough rest for about 20 minutes. Roll out on a floured board, thinner than for pie crust, and cut out with a round biscuit cutter or into 5–6cm squares. Put about a teaspoon of the filling on each piece. Fold over forming a half circle and pinch the edges together with your fingers to seal in the filling.

To prepare the filling:

■ Cook the onion in butter until tender. Add the mushrooms and cook together for about 10 minutes. Season with salt and pepper. Remove the mixture from the heat and beat in the egg yolks. Chopped dill may be added for flavour. Cook the mixture well.

■ Place each finished varenyky on a clean tea towel. When you have used all the dough, cook them by dropping a few at a time into a pot of boiling water. Stir with a wooden spoon a few times to prevent sticking to the bottom. When cooked they will float to the top (about 10 minutes). Remove them with a slotted spoon to a colander and drain thoroughly. Place in a deep dish, coating them generously with melted butter. Toss very gently to coat them evenly and prevent them from sticking. Serve with sour cream or fried chopped onions sauteed in butter until golden.

■ Varenyky may be made in a large quantity, refrigerated and reheated without any loss of quality. Place cooked varenyky on a biscuit sheet and freeze individually. Next day, put them in plastic bags and keep in freezer. To reheat, pan-fry in butter until golden in colour, turn and fry other side.

Char Kway Teow (Malaysian Fried Flat Rice Noodles)

In Malaysia, every town has its own char kway teow man, who has a mobile cooking service — basically a wok and dishes of fresh ingredients

Alvin Tan

which are flung together on the spot for this marvellous stir-fried noodle dish. Malaysian friends remember listening for the char kway teow man's bell, their mouth watering at the sound of it. Like the mobile service, Malaysian-born chef Alvin Tan cooks this delicious dish many times every day in his restaurant.

You can adjust the amount of chilli according to your heat tolerance. Add more soy sauce if you prefer it sweeter.

Serves 4 for entree or 2 for main course (this is the ideal amount to make in a wok)

1 tablespoon vegetable oil

1 teaspoon fresh garlic, roughly chopped

6 large prawns, peeled and deveined

300g fresh flat rice noodles (available from most Asian grocers)

½ Chinese sausage, sliced thinly

thick dark soy sauce to taste

1 teaspoon light soy sauce

1 tablespoon fish sauce

1 tablespoon water

½ tablespoon fresh red chilli, pounded

pinch pepper

1 egg

100g fresh pippies, clams or vongole (optional)

30g garlic chives — washed and cut into 5cm lengths

100g bean sprouts

■ Heat wok until hot. Add oil and fry the garlic until light brown. Add the prawns, toss quickly and put in the noodles and the sausage. Add the dark soy sauce, light soy sauce, fish sauce, water, chilli and pepper. Stir-fry over high heat for about 1 to 2 minutes.

■ Push noodles to one side of wok. Add some oil and break in the egg. Cover the egg with noodles and allow to cook. Stir and mix well. Add pippies, clams or vongole, chives and bean sprouts. Stir-fry until the beansprouts are just cooked and remain crunchy. Transfer to a plate and serve with additional pepper and light soy sauce.

Prasit's Pad Thai

Prasit Prateeprasen sells hundreds of serves of pad thai every week through his Sydney takeaway outlet. And it's no wonder as pad thai is one of the great dishes of the world. A Thai variation on the Chinese concept of stir-fried noodles, it's easy to make, full of flavour and combines the textures of rice noodles, fresh sprouts and chives, prawns and meat.

Serves 4

250g rice noodles (the thin flat kind)

¼ cup oil

3 cloves garlic, minced

4 tablespoons dried shrimp

Noodles

Turn down a concrete driveway on Canterbury Road in Sydney's inner-western suburbs and you'll find a small scrubbed factory that greets you with the faintest hint of egg aroma. Inside the radio is playing popular Chinese songs and a large stainless steel machine is gently folding a continuous sheet of satiny wonton skins back and forth. This is Jang's Noodle Manufacturers, a business started in 1964 by Kam Hoon Jang, an enterprising Cantonese migrant who was one of the first to make noodles for the local Chinese community.

David Ap and James Jang

Son James Jang, with his mobile phone permanently welded to his belt, has carried on the business since his father's death and continues the push for higher quality. He has found that the best ingredient is frozen eggs. 'They're absolutely fresh and we use a lot of them — they give better elasticity and help bind the noodle.' He has thoroughly researched the best sorts of flour too — with just the right amount of moisture and water absorption.

Down the road, James' cousin David also runs a noodle business started by his father, Dick, around the same time as Kam Hoon rolled out his first egg noodle. Dick Ap Pty Ltd also boasts a lot of stainless steel but the scent here is of rice noodle being gently steamed. This is where some of the country's best rice noodles — in sheets, in flat ribbons or fine strands — and wheat noodles, the yellow-coloured

Hokkien noodles, are manufactured.

Of course, these are just a few varieties amongst the endless types of fabulous, comforting noodles made around the country. As well as egg and rice and wheat noodles, there are bean thread noodles, buckwheat noodles and potato noodles which are heavy and chewy and very popular in Korea.

A good noodle should have a chewiness and texture and not be overcooked. When you're buying fresh noodles in the supermarket they should always be soft and should not form a hard sticky block in the packet, nor should they be too yellow (if they are, we're told, they're full of food colouring!). Check use-by dates and use within a couple of days of buying.

Prasit Prateeprasen

½ cup fish sauce

60g sugar or palm sugar

2 tablespoons tamarind puree or vinegar

1 egg, beaten

1 tablespoon roast chilli, crushed

2 slices tofu, diced and fried

¼ cup chopped garlic chives (2.5cm long)

¼ cup roasted peanuts, crushed

1 cup or more fresh mung bean shoots

8 large fresh green prawn cutlets, stir-fried until cooked

50g lean pork or chicken, thinly sliced and deep-fried or wok stir-fried

coriander sprigs

chopped shallots

lime wedges

■ Soak the noodles in cold water for 30 minutes or until soft, drain and set aside.

■ Heat a large wok until hot, add oil and garlic and dried shrimp, stir-fry until golden brown.

■ Add noodles and stir-fry until translucent. Reduce heat if mixture is cooking too quickly. Add fish sauce, palm sugar and tamarind juice or vinegar. Keep stirring until ingredients are well mixed. Make a space in the middle of the wok and stir in the beaten egg. When it's half-cooked, stir in the roast chilli, tofu, chives, peanuts, mung bean shoots, prawn cutlets and pork or chicken.

■ Place on a large dish and garnish with coriander, shallots, more bean shoots (if desired) and lime wedges which you squeeze over the noodles just before eating.

Mines Frites (Egg Noodles, Mauritian-style with a Fresh Garlic Sauce)

Like char kway teow and pad thai, one of the most popular dishes on the tropical isle of Mauritius is Chinese in origin. In fact, Chinese migrants make up a considerable percentage of the population — and the locals have embraced Chinese cuisine as their own (as they have Indian and French styles, ingredients and techniques). Quite a culinary paradise! As it is quite hard to find this dish in Australia (given the absence of Mauritian restaurants), we were thrilled to learn the secret of mines frites — thanks to one of our few Mauritian restaurateurs, Alain Albert. His little 'cafe creole' with the charming name of 'Katkoko' is tucked away in Sydney's Newtown. 'Katkoko' is creole for 'quatre cocos' — literally 'four coconuts' but referring to somewhere that's 'back of beyond', somewhere so remote there's only a few stray coconuts and that's it!

Serves 4

4 portions of Chinese dried egg noodles

1 cup vegetable oil

2 chicken breasts, cut into small pieces

8 dried Chinese sausages, sliced diagonally

250g of small green prawns, shelled and deveined

1 medium-sized onion, diced

2 cloves garlic, crushed

¼ teaspoon fresh ginger, crushed

¼ cup salt-reduced soy sauce

1 cup fresh coriander, finely chopped

1 cup spring onions, finely chopped

Garlic sauce:

3 cloves garlic, crushed, with a pinch of salt

¼ cup white wine vinegar

¾ cup cold boiled water

¼ teaspoon raw sugar

½ bunch garlic chives, finely chopped

1 teaspoon white rum

1 small green chilli (optional)

▦ Cook egg noodles quickly in a pan of boiling water for approximately 2 minutes. Drain, sprinkle oil over them and set aside.
▦ Heat 2 tablespoons of oil in a wok and cook the sliced chicken breast until golden. Remove from the wok and set aside.
▦ Repeat the process with the sausages and the prawns, adding more oil to the wok if required. When cooking the prawns, make sure that they are not overcooked. It is best to remove them from the oil when the edges start to curl up and the flesh is slightly opaque.
▦ Put the remaining oil in the wok and bring the heat right up. Add the onions and quickly cook until soft but not brown. Add the garlic, ginger and return the chicken, sausages and

prawns to the wok. Combine well. Add the soy sauce and the noodles and stir-fry until the noodles are hot and well coated. Finally, add the fresh coriander and the spring onions, toss well and serve accompanied by the garlic sauce.

For the sauce:

▦ Combine all ingredients in a bowl. If a hot sauce is required, the chopped up green chilli may be added. Spoon a little over the noodles. The sauce keeps well in the fridge for days.

Kylie's Hot and Sour Szechuan Noodles

There's nothing retiring about Szechuan cooking. It's full of robust flavours or, as creative Chinese-Australian cook Kylie Kwong puts it, 'a balance of salty, sweet, vinegary (sour) and hot, with the numbing effect created by Szechuan pepper'. Inspired by classic Szechuan hot and sour dishes, Kylie put together this clever blend of tastes to make the kind of noodle salad that goes with almost anything — from a lightly steamed fish to some plain barbecue soya chicken, even an omelette. It's a great recipe from a very special chef. Kylie is one of the few bright young cooks around who really knows about Chinese food culture — she grew up with it. Make sure you have fresh noodles and take care in selecting your sauces. There are dozens of different kinds of soy, for example. This recipe calls for the sticky sweet Indonesian variety known as kecap manis, and the light, really refined Japanese salt soy. Chinese black vinegar is pretty powerful, as is Chinese chilli oil — so go easy at first.

Serves 2 – 4

500g fresh shanghai or hokkien noodles
1 Lebanese cucumber, finely sliced on a diagonal
3 Chinese white cabbage leaves
½ cup shallots (julienned)
½ cup Chinese pickled mustard greens, julienned
½ cup Chinese pickled leeks, finely sliced
½ large red fresh chilli, finely sliced

Sauce:

½ cup sweet soy sauce (Indonesian kecap manis)
¼ cup Chinese black vinegar (Chiang Kiang brand)
¼ cup Japanese soy sauce
2 tablespoons Chinese chilli oil
2 teaspoons Szechuan pepper, dry roasted and ground
2 tablespoons shallots, finely sliced in rounds
extra Szechuan pepper as required

■ Bring a pot of water to the boil and cook fresh noodles for a few minutes until they are soft but still hold some bite. Mix the sauce ingredients in a salad bowl and stir vigorously. You can adjust the flavours to suit your tastes, remembering that each sauce has its own strong, unique kick.

■ Add the cucumber, white cabbage, shallots, pickles and chilli to the sauce followed by the cooked noodles (which you have rinsed after cooking in very hot water to remove excess starch). Add a generous pinch of additional Szechuan pepper to finish.

Squid Ink Linguine with Mixed Seafood

Melbourne–based restaurateur and pasta master Bill Marchetti has his own brand of fabulous noodles — which includes the colourful Studio Marchetti black linguine, flavoured

Bill Marchetti

with nero di seppia (squid ink). The contrast with this luscious white seafood sauce looks quite amazing on the plate and tastes pretty wonderful too.

Serves 4

75ml virgin olive oil
2 cloves garlic, finely sliced
400g mixed seafood, cleaned and sliced
salt and freshly ground black pepper to taste
100ml dry white wine
100ml fish stock (see Soups chapter)
300g squid ink linguine
2 tablespoons chopped continental parsley

■ Heat the oil in a frypan and saute the garlic to a light colour. Add the seafood, season and

Perfect Fresh Noodles

Here are some tips on cooking perfect fresh noodles:

- Make sure you use a large enough pot. James Jang says the noodles need to be able to move as they are being cooked.
- Add a good pinch of salt to the water.
- Have the water on a rolling boil before you add the noodles and make sure you add them all at once. Gently loosen any noodles that have stuck together.
- Test by removing one strand and eating it.
- Do not overcook. James says fine egg noodles need just a few seconds; Hokkien and Shanghai noodles around 5 minutes.
- Rinse quickly in hot water and serve at once or add to soup or a stir-fry.

For a fresh noodle recipe, try one from James Jang's niece's — the talented Kylie Kwong's hot and sour Szechuan noodles pp. 136–7.

saute until it begins to colour. Add the white wine, then when the seafood is nearly cooked, add the hot fish stock. Toss the seafood with the cooked pasta and parsley.

Tomato and Basil Sauce (for Egg Fettuccine)

Restaurateur Bill Marchetti loves his pasta. 'A plate of spaghetti with some good oil and parmesan cheese…nothing better,' he sighs, although his other favourite is simple 'aglio, olio e peperoncino' — garlic, oil and chilli. Simple noodles and a simple sauce are definitely the way to go when you're hungry and short on time. Here's his quick tomato and basil sauce, which goes perfectly with egg fettuccine or tagliatelle — or even simple spaghetti.

Serves 4

2 cloves garlic
½ cup virgin olive oil
600g peeled, seeded, diced Roma tomatoes
½ cup pureed canned tomatoes
salt and freshly ground black pepper to taste
¼ cup shredded fresh basil
300g egg fettuccine

■ Fry the garlic cloves in the oil until they begin to colour slightly. Add Roma and canned tomatoes. Season. Reduce over a high heat for 4 to 5 minutes. Add basil. Remove garlic cloves and toss the rest with cooked pasta.

■ Remember pasta should be cooked with plenty of freshly boiling water and lots of salt. Don't ever let it get mushy, make sure it has a good bite to it.

Gino Di Santo's Orecchiette Con Broccoli (Orecchiette with Broccoli)

Orecchiette are handmade pasta shells typical of the Puglia region in south-west Italy (the heel of the boot). The name orecchiette means 'little ears' — which is a close approximation of their shape. They are actually formed with the imprint of a thumb pushing into the pasta dough. The little indentation is perfect for a solid, chunky sauce like this broccoli mash. This is a favourite dish of Luigi (Gino) di Santo, founder of Melbourne's famed Enoteca Sileno — a small deep cellar of a shop full of marvellous wines imported from every region of Italy. (The name Enoteca means 'wine merchant's'.) Enoteca Sileno also sells some of the finest, and purest gourmet Italian products you could find — fine preserves and oils, olive pastes, sun-dried tomatoes, perfect tiny salt-preserved capers and lots and lots of 'craftsman's' pasta — non-industrial pasta from all over Italy. The perfect place to buy your orecchiette, in fact, although you can find 'little ears' in any good Italian grocery store.

Serves 6

two heads of broccoli
2–3 cloves garlic
extra virgin olive oil
½ teaspoon chilli paste, or fresh chilli to taste
500g orecchiette pasta
salt and pepper to taste
parmigiano reggiano cheese (good-quality eating parmesan)

■ Cut, peel and trim the broccoli heads removing the outer skin of the stalks. Cut the heads into smaller pieces, put into at least a 6-litre pot of water. Salt if required.

■ Boil for about 8 minutes until broccoli is tender, then lift the cooked pieces out of the water with a slotted spoon and place in a large frypan in which you have sautéed the garlic lightly with extra virgin oil. Add about 3 ladlefuls of the broccoli water and the chilli paste, cover and simmer very gently.

■ Toss the orecchiette into the simmering water in which the broccoli was cooked, then bring them up to the boil. Check cooking time according to brand, but the real, handmade ones will take about 20 minutes to cook. Break down the broccoli in the water and chilli mixture into a broccoli mash. Season to taste.

■ When the pasta is cooked, drain well and combine with the broccoli. Toss in the pan for a few minutes, then serve, sprinkling each portion with parmigiano reggiano and a drizzle of raw extra virgin olive oil.

Salads and dressings

Mountain Dressing

This dressing gives a nice tang to fried foods (chips, falafel, meatballs or fritters) or even a mixed leaf salad with croutons. Turkish-inspired and recreated by Joanna.

Makes ½ cup
good splash olive oil
1 teaspoon white wine vinegar
1 tablespoon Bulgarian-style yoghurt
freshly chopped dill
salt and pepper to taste

■ Combine olive oil and vinegar, then blend in yoghurt in a food processor or beating vigorously by hand. The mixture should end up quite liquid. Season to taste with dill, salt and pepper.

Dieter Winter

Pumpkin Seed Oil Dressing

Austrian-born Dieter Winter is the perfect person to ask about salad dressings. A former chef, he now grows a variety of herbs and lettuces in the middle of the Australian desert. In the late 1980s he bought a two-hectare block just outside Alice Springs and started a small market garden. Through trial and error he built up the business and now supplies most of northern Australia!
To make this salad dressing, you need pumpkin seed oil, very popular with Central Europeans. You can find this strongly flavoured oil in 'continental' delicatessens, especially those that specialise in products from former Yugoslavia and some of the larger gourmet-oriented supermarkets like Woolworths. Look for a bottle with pictures of pumpkins on the front (in Croatian, for example, it's called 'Bucino ulje').

Makes ½ cup
pumpkin seed oil
olive oil
1 clove garlic, crushed
white wine vinegar
English mustard
1 egg yolk
salt and pepper to taste

■ Crush a clove of garlic in a bowl. Mix in a splash of pumpkin seed and olive oils in equal proportions. Add white wine vinegar and English mustard to taste. Season. Just before using, drop in an egg yolk and beat into mixture.
■ This dressing goes wonderfully with mixed lettuce, finely chopped cabbage with a sprinkle of caraway seed, or still-warm boiled potatoes with some wafer-thin slivers of onion.

Classic Vinaigrette

This dressing goes beautifully with avocado, tomatoes, mixed leaves, even mixed with mayonnaise over potatoes — it's Joanna's standard when all else fails!

Makes ½ cup

1 clove garlic
1 teaspoon Dijon mustard
good splash olive oil
2 teaspoons red wine vinegar
salt and pepper to taste

■ Rub the inside of a bowl with crushed garlic clove. Splash in the olive oil, red wine vinegar and mix. Finish with the Dijon mustard and salt and pepper to taste.

David and Rosie's Eggier Than Egg Mayonnaise

Rosie Penman is a wonderful cook and caterer who ran demonstrations for years at David Jones in Sydney. It was there that she befriended David Mar, a foodie from way back. Ever since he saw Rosie do this with mayonnaise, he's used her recipe for cos lettuce salads — 'or other fairly robust greens,' he says, 'given that it is soooo cholesterol-y!' Nice with potato salad too.

Makes 1 cup

1 egg yolk
oil (your choice)
mustard
tarragon vinegar
2 grated hard-boiled eggs
salt and pepper to taste

■ Put egg yolk in a mixing bowl and beating slowly, add your choice of oil to make up a mayonnaise. Flavour with mustard and vinegar. Add the grated eggs and process further if you want a creamy dressing. Finish with salt and pepper.

Susie Wallace

Susie's Raspberry Vinaigrette

This is one of the prettiest salad dressings you could ever hope to find and, according to our source, playwright and videotape editor Susie Wallace, it goes beautifully with any green salad or simply with sliced fresh avocado and crusty bread. 'Do nothing to compromise its wonderful rich redness,' she advises. It was passed to her from a Hobart flatmate, Robert Jarman, who makes the recipe without balsamic vinegar — Susie added it for extra tang.

Makes 1 cup

¼ cup homemade raspberry jam
¼ cup olive oil (Susie has also made it with canola)

¼ cup red wine vinegar

¼ cup balsamic vinegar (optional)

fresh raspberries (optional but worth it if you can get them)

■ Mix raspberry jam and oil together thoroughly. Add vinegar/s slowly and to taste. Stir in the fresh raspberries trying to avoid crushing them.

Banana Flower Salad

This is one of Thai legend Prasit Prateeprasen's signature dishes, one he says would never have caught on when he came to Australia almost twenty years ago and discovered that lemongrass, sweet basil and galangal were almost impossible to find. This is now one of his most popular creations, a great accompaniment to Thai curries and steamed rice.

Serves 4

300g fresh banana flowers (approx 1 flower) available from Thai or Vietnamese grocery stores

lemon wedges

1 stalk lemongrass

4 Kaffir lime leaves (fresh, not dried)

200g green prawns or chicken breast fillets

2 large red chillies/banana chillies

½ 400ml can coconut milk

2 tablespoons palm sugar or white sugar

1 teaspoon chilli powder or flakes or to taste

2 sprigs fresh mint leaves (use leaves only)

¼ cup tamarind puree, more if desired

2 tablespoons chilli paste in oil

4 tablespoons coarsely ground roast or fried peanuts

2 tablespoons fried crispy onion or shallots

2 tablespoons Thai fish sauce or to taste

2 sprigs coriander leaves

■ Slice banana flower thinly (cross-section) and soak in water with a few lemon wedges for approximately 30 minutes.

■ Slice lemongrass very thinly, using the thickest part of the stem only. Slice kaffir lime leaves very thinly, taking out middle rib. Slit and devein prawns, slice chicken fillet very thinly as for stir-frying. Slice chilli thinly to use as a garnish.

■ Boil coconut milk, put in the prawn or chicken pieces and cook until tender. If prawns are used, be careful not to overcook them. When cooked, drain the chicken or prawns and set aside.

■ Drain the sliced banana flower and put it and all other ingredients except sliced chilli and coriander in a large mixing bowl. Stir well with spatula or fingers until well blended.

To serve:

■ Place the mixed salad on a platter with outer petals as decoration, then scatter cooked chicken pieces or prawn around the salad. Garnish with coriander leaves and sliced chilli. Finally, sprinkle a few drops of coconut milk over the top of the salad.

Moroccan Carrot Salad

Many years ago, co-author Maeve tasted the most heavenly and refreshing salad in the little village of Imlil in Morocco. It goes beautifully with grilled meats or is great on its own as a palate-cleanser. This recipe is from Sydney restaurateur Hugh Foster.

Serves 4

500g sweet young carrot, grated

2 juicy navel oranges, peeled, cut into small segments with

pith removed (reserve the juice)

orange juice (from cut oranges)

juice 1 lemon (roughly equal to amount of orange juice)

pinch of salt

1 teaspoon sugar (or more to taste)

cinnamon or ground cassia

■ In a large bowl combine carrot, orange, orange and lemon juice. Add salt and sugar and adjust to taste. Dust with cinnamon or ground cassia.

Variations:

■ Try adding grated red radishes, chopped parsley or coriander.

Couscous Salad

Couscous is one of the most delicious grains in the world and has been eaten throughout North Africa for centuries. Made of hard wheat semolina, it requires a lot of work — grinding, rolling into pellets and steaming. We've developed a lifelong passion for couscous: Joanna from North African food in France, Maeve from travelling in Tunisia and Morocco, where she enjoyed it the traditional way with spicy stew and as the basis for this salad. It's even better if you use non-instant couscous but the fast variety is vastly improved by steaming over chicken stock for 20 minutes.

Serves 6–8

375g packet instant couscous

good chicken stock

generous pinch saffron strands

good splash olive oil

1 red onion, finely chopped

2 cloves garlic, finely chopped

1 birdseye chilli, finely chopped

large handful pistachio nuts

handful currants

zest 1 lemon

zest 1 orange

generous knob of butter

mint leaves

coriander leaves

■ Prepare the couscous by pouring into bowl, add boiling water according to instructions. Turn out into a large square piece of muslin add saffron strands, wrap and place into colander. Steam over chicken stock for 20 minutes. Set aside.

■ Heat olive oil in large pan over medium heat and add onion, garlic and chilli and cook until onion is transparent. Add pistachio nuts, currants, lemon and orange zest and cook a further minute. Fluff up couscous with a fork, adding a good knob of butter, then add the cooked mixture. Garnish with mint and coriander leaves and serve.

Fattoush
(Lebanese Summer Vegetable Salad)

This refreshing, traditional Middle Eastern salad features the nice crunch of fried Lebanese bread. From father-and-son chef team Fouad and Ali Sayed

Serves 4

1 round of Lebanese bread, either white or wholemeal

vegetable oil for deep-frying

2 Lebanese cucumbers, finely diced (if very fresh there's no need to peel)

2 tomatoes, finely diced

Fouad and Ali Sayed

Fouad and Ali Sayed are a remarkable father-and-son chef team who prepare some of the best traditional Lebanese food in town. They also share an unusual skill, learnt by Fouad in Lebanon when he started in the restaurant industry at the age of sixteen. He has the ability to remember what each customer likes and what they ordered on their last visit to the restaurant. He has never written down his customer's preferences — they are all simply remembered.

Son Ali has been learning the same skill and says the appreciation that rewards his ability to remember makes it all much easier. 'I have such respect for Dad and for his love of food which he has passed to me as well,' says Ali, 'He is my inspiration'.

Indeed, Fouad seems to have an instinctive relationship with food — it is a genuine love affair and his customers benefit with a huge range of mezze — fresh salads, dips and little snacks, then main courses of whole baked fish, grilled chicken with a pure garlic sauce and endless meat dishes.

On working with his son, Fouad says it is the great joy of his life. 'It makes me very happy to be giving everything I've got to my son and do you know — I think he'll be better than me,' he says proudly. Fouad made sure that Ali completed catering college as well as getting a degree in hospitality management. 'He has had more advantages and more training and he started even younger than me so I'm sure he'll do well,' says Fouad. 'It's a hard job but we love it.'

Fouad and Ali Sayed

½ cup radish, finely diced
½ red capsicum, finely diced
½ green capsicum, finely diced
4 spring onions, finely diced
2 tablespoons mint, finely chopped
½ cup parsley, finely chopped

Dressing:
juice 1 lemon
¼ cup extra virgin olive oil
salt and freshly ground pepper to taste

■ Deep-fry the Lebanese bread. Drain on absorbent paper and when cool, crumple in your hands until it breaks into fine pieces.
■ Combine the rest of the ingredients with the bread and toss with the dressing. Serve.

To prepare dressing:
■ Combine in a screw-top jar by shaking hard.

Israeli Avocado Salad

Israel is the home of avocados. So who better than Israeli expat, Robert Lebovits to give us a way of using them in a salad. Incidentally, Robert has done very well out of dips and salads in his adopted land — with his Savion range. (Any member of Sydney's Jewish community will tell you about Savion, Robert's kosher restaurant in the beachside suburb of Bondi.)

Serves 6
juice 3 lemons
3–4 ripe avocados, diced
1 bunch shallots, stems only, chopped
½ punnet cherry tomatoes
3–4 pickled cucumbers, diced
100g black olives, pitted

■ Add lemon juice to diced avocado. Then add other ingredients and gently mix into a delicious flavoursome summer salad.

Japanese Wakame Salad

Mitsuo Nakanishi runs a classically designed Japanese restaurant on the east coast of Tasmania — called Kabuki by the Sea. He loves to use local ingredients, like the iodine-rich wakame seaweed harvested along the Tasmanian shores.

Serves 2
50g dried wakame
180g cucumber (preferably Lebanese or telegraph variety)

1 cup rice wine vinegar
⅓ cup white sugar
1 teaspoon toasted white sesame seeds

■ Soak wakame in cold water for 15 to 20 minutes. Drain and cut into 2cm slices. Slice cucumber thinly, quartering it lengthways first. Gently boil the vinegar and sugar together until syrupy and reduced by half — this takes 10 to 12 minutes. Allow syrup to cool then fold in wakame and cucumber. Serve chilled and garnish with sesame seeds.

Max's Salad Nicoise

From Cannes to Cairns…Chef Max Pantacchini was born in Cannes and spent his early years working in some of Europe's major hotels before being transferred to Australia with the Hilton chain. After some years as executive chef, Max and wife Francoise set up their own fish-smoking business on the outskirts of Cairns where they specialise in Tasmanian salmon and ocean trout and local fish such as barramundi and Murray wrasse. Not surprisingly, his recipe centres on smoked fish! And incidentally, salad nicoise is from Max's birthplace in the south of France. Hot-smoked tuna is a style of smoking — it has nothing to do with spices.

Serves 4
500g hot-smoked fillet of tuna (from good fishmonger, smokehouse or fish market, or use cooked fresh tuna or a can of top-quality tuna)
½ cup olive oil
sprig of rosemary
sprig fresh thyme
8 roasted garlic cloves, mashed

8 Roma tomatoes, cut into 6 wedges
1 bunch spring onions, chopped finely
½ bunch fresh coriander, chopped finely
small handful black olives of your choice
4 potatoes, boiled with skin on, cooled and cut into large slices
mixed salad leaves to serve

Dressing:
oil from the tuna marinade
red wine vinegar
grated cooked egg yolk
salt and pepper to taste

■ Slice the whole fillet into large slices and marinate in olive oil, rosemary, thyme and roasted garlic cloves for 2 to 3 hours or preferably overnight.
■ Remove tuna from marinade, reserving it for the dressing. Add the sliced Roma tomatoes, chopped spring onions and coriander, whole black olives and sliced potatoes. Drizzle oil of tuna marinade that you've skimmed from the top, and red vinegar over the salad, then the egg yolk and add salt and pepper to taste.

Kolyva (Greek Whole Wheat Salad)

Kolyva is a memorial dish — taken to church to commemorate the passing of a loved one. After the service it is distributed in small white paper bags to members of the congregation. James and Evelyn Konstantinidis, on the other hand, serve it to diners at their Sydney restaurant. It's a far cry from the days of James's youth in New Zealand, where he learned about cooking standing on an upturned apple box helping his

James Konstantinidis

Cook the wheat in a large saucepan of salted water for approximately 1½ hours or until wheat splits. Remove and drain. Towel dry to absorb excess moisture. In a large bowl mix all ingredients together with the wheat. Mound kolyva on a platter. Garnish with fresh basil and almonds.

Serve as a side dish with the main course or on its own.

Tabouli (Burghul and Parsley Salad)

The national dish of Syria and Lebanon, tabouli is at its best in summer when the tomatoes are sweet and ripe and the mint, parsley and spring onion are at their absolute best. Remember to leave time for soaking the burghul (cracked wheat, which is sold in two ways — coarse and fine). This recipe goes back generations in broadcaster and teacher Hussam Cheebo's family. Serve at room temperature to get the best from the mix of ingredients.

father fry fish and chips for the family 'chipper'. 'We would then drive to the local pubs and sell packets of fish and chips to the ravenous patrons (6 o'clock closing), not catered for in those days by the pub bistros which flourish today.' His career led him to the Greek island of Milos where the family owned a cafe and eventually to Australia where James likes to feel he is part of a renaissance — the re-emerging of quality Greek food.

Serves 4

2 cups whole wheat, soaked overnight

½ cup sesame seeds, toasted in 140°C oven for 10 minutes

½ cup chopped walnuts

½ cup sultanas

½ cup mixed basil and parsley, chopped

½ cup pomegranate seeds

4 teaspoons sugar

1 teaspoon quality ground cinnamon

pinch salt

fresh basil

blanched almonds for garnish

Serves 4

¼ cup fine burghul

2 cups chopped parsley

½ cup finely chopped spring onion

¼ cup finely chopped mint

¼ cup olive oil (try to get Lebanese — if not, Hussam says Spanish oil is good, particularly Carbonel brand)

2 tablespoons fresh lemon juice

1½ tablespoons salt

½ teaspoon freshly ground pepper

2 firm ripe tomatoes

crisp lettuce leaves (Lebanese lettuce for preference — it's long and thin and looks like cos lettuce. Hussam says it's available from Asian food shops and large fruit and vegetable markets)

¼ cup lemon juice mixed with ½ teaspoon salt

Place burghul in bowl and cover with 2 cups of cold water. Soak for 30 minutes and then drain though a fine sieve, pressing with the back of a spoon to extract liquid. Spread on a cloth and leave to dry.

Wash parsley well, shake off excess water and remove thick stalks. Wrap in a tea towel in the refrigerator until crisp and dry. Put burghul into mixing bowl and add spring onions. Mix by hand, squeezing as you go so the burghul can absorb the onion flavour. Chop parsley fairly coarsely, measure the required amount and add to burghul with mint.

Beat olive oil with lemon juice and stir in salt and pepper. Toss well. Slice tomatoes, discard seeds and gently stir into salad. Arrange lettuce in salad bowl and place burghul salad on top. Serve with a jug of the lemon juice and salt mixture on the side.

Vivien's Potato Salad

Journalist Vivien Altman has learnt much from her mother about cooking. 'She's of Russian/Polish/Jewish background and spent a good part of her childhood in Berlin,' Vivien explains. 'This recipe has been handed down from her but its origins are unclear. It's been a family favourite and tastes even better,' says Vivien, 'after being in the fridge overnight.'

Serves 4
500g potatoes, peeled
½ small onion, grated
1 egg yolk
1 teaspoon each of salt, dried mustard, sugar
4 tablespoons white vinegar
6–7 tablespoons cold pressed olive oil

2–3 tablespoons cream
Dill or parsley to finish, very finely chopped

Boil potatoes and leave them to cool. Place in a bowl and mix grated onion through the potatoes.

Place the egg yolk in a separate bowl and add the salt, mustard and sugar. Add the vinegar and mix in slowly, add the oil and then the cream — it should be a thick creamy consistency.

Pour the dressing over the potatoes and add a generous amount of dill or parsley. Place in the fridge for a couple of hours before serving.

Gabrielle Kervella's Favourite Goat's Cheese Salad

Gabrielle Kervella has been widely acclaimed for her superb fresh and matured goat's cheeses, produced by a modest flock in the paddocks of Gidgegannup in Western Australia. The cheese-making methods and techniques she once learned in France have all had to be re-learned or adapted to the harsh Australian conditions and educating the average consumer here has not always been easy. 'People would even hold their noses when they heard I was selling goat's cheese,' she remembers. The road to her present success has been a steep and rocky one but it certainly hasn't diluted her enthusiasm and dedication. Nor has she tired of the cheese itself. This is a favourite recipe of hers, adapted from the famed American publication, the *Chez Panisse Cookbook*.

Serves 6

12cm rounds of fresh goat's cheese

¼ cup virgin olive oil

3–4 sprigs of fresh thyme

1 cup fine breadcrumbs

1 teaspoon dried thyme

4 handfuls of mesclun lettuce (rocket, lambs lettuce, small oak leaf and red leaf lettuce or chervil)

1 day-old baguette (French stick), sliced into about 24 rounds

½ cup butter

2-3 cloves of garlic

Vinaigrette:

½ cup olive oil

2–3 teaspoons of red wine vinegar

salt and pepper to taste

■ Marinate goat's cheese rounds in olive oil and fresh thyme. Leave for 24 hours.

■ Mix together breadcrumbs, dried thyme and prepare vinaigrette by whisking together olive oil, vinegar and seasoning.

■ Melt the butter and brush each bread slice with it. Bake the buttered rounds in a moderate 180°C oven for about 5 to 7 minutes, until the croutons are a light, golden brown. While still warm, rub them with crushed, whole garlic cloves. Dip marinated cheese slices in the breadcrumbs, and place on a lightly oiled baking dish. Bake in a preheated 200°C oven for about 6 minutes until cheese is lightly bubbling and a golden brown. Toss the lettuces with enough vinaigrette to lightly coat and arrange leaves on round salad plates. Place a round of cheese in the centre of each plate, browned side up, and arrange the croutons around the cheese.

Vegetables

Escalivada
(Catalan Char-grilled Vegetables)

Sounding more like a passionate Spanish dance, escalivada is a lovely fresh mixture of char-grilled vegies, simply drizzled with olive oil and sprinkled with freshly cracked pepper. 'Escalivar' is the Catalan word for cooking over hot embers — char-grilling is a perfect way to prepare this simple dish with its smoky flavour. A great dish for summer. This is a recipe passed through the generations of a Hobart-based Spanish family — the Boschs.

Serves 4
2 red capsicums
2 green capsicums
2 scallions
1 eggplant
olive oil
salt to taste
cracked pepper to taste

■ Rub the outside of all the vegetables with liberal amounts of olive oil. Place them on a rack over hot coals or on a char-griller. Let the skin of the vegetables toast and roast until it starts to crack and peel off. It's all right if the skin turns black but care must be taken not to burn the vegetable beyond the skin. Rotate frequently, making sure the heat penetrates the vegetables — especially the eggplant.
■ Peel the eggplant and capsicum. With your fingers, tear them into thin strips. Arrange on a platter and season with salt and freshly cracked pepper and drizzle with more oil. Serve at room temperature.

Wok-Fried Four Seasons Beans

We loved this dish so much when we visited Singapore for the food festival held each July that we pleaded with its originator, chef Sam Leong at the Four Seasons Hotel to demonstrate it for us. The secret, we learnt, is to have all your ingredients ready, sliced and close to hand so your cooking is fast and seamless. This can easily be made a vegetarian dish by removing the pork and substituting mushrooms or firm tofu.

Serves 4
500g French beans, topped and tailed and sliced in half
80g minced pork
corn oil for frying
small piece pork fat, cubed (optional, available most butchers)
2 cloves garlic, crushed
1 tablespoon hot bean paste (available from Asian grocery stores)
2 tablespoons Chinese wine
1 tablespoon oyster sauce
1 dessertspoon soy sauce
1 dessertspoon cornflour mixed in a little water

■ Over a medium hot wok, deep-fry the beans for 1 minute, stirring gently. Drain beans and remove most of the oil from the wok to leave just a light coating of oil. Stir-fry the pork for just under 1 minute and then set aside. Add the pork fat to the wok and fry for about a minute, then add the garlic and bean paste. Stir-fry for 10 seconds then add the bean and pork.
■ Add Chinese wine, oyster and soy sauces and stir through (tossing the wok is great if you have confidence and a firm wrist). Add a little water to moisten if necessary. Finally, add the cornflour mixture, stir through well and serve immediately.

Misayko Tarkari
(Himalayan Mixed Vegetable)

This recipe is from chef and caterer Mary Dorjee who grew up eating dishes such as this in the hill station of Kalimpong in the Darjeeling district of India. While she misses the marvellous tea and the mind-boggling views of the Himalayas, she has brought the cuisine she grew up on to Australia. Mary's mother experimented with blends of Nepalese, Bhutanese, Muslim, Chinese and Tibetan cuisines and this recipe is a wonderful example of that blending.

Serves 6

½ cup vegetable oil
1 teaspoon cumin seeds
300g cauliflower florets, about 2.5cm in size
1 teaspoon ground coriander
1 teaspoon ground cumin
¼ teaspoon ground turmeric
2 fresh chillies, chopped
1 teaspoon salt
1 teaspoon black pepper
200g frozen peas
200g boiled potatoes, diced
2 teaspoons chopped fresh coriander
2 teaspoons chopped fresh mint

▣ Heat the oil in a large non-stick frying pan over medium heat. When hot, add the cumin seeds which will sizzle. Add the cauliflower and stir over heat for about 3 minutes. Cover for a minute, stirring a few times.
▣ Add the ground cumin, coriander, turmeric, chillies, salt and pepper and stir.
▣ Add the peas and potatoes and mix in. Cook uncovered for about 3 to 4 minutes.

▣ Add the chopped fresh coriander and mint. Stir and serve with boiled rice or wholemeal grilled bread.

Succotash
(Four Vegetables Southern-Style)

Succotash is a mixture of corn and beans that was originally made by the American Indians and fast became and stayed a staple dish in the Deep South. Most succotash-eating southern folk grow their own vegies and are used to having up to six different vegetables each meal. A dash of tabasco gives this dish real kick. Succotash can be made in advance and reheated. This recipe from Alabama-born chef Forrest Moebes.

Serves 4

2 cups fresh broadbeans (or soaked overnight and cooked until tender)
2 cups freshly cooked corn, removed from cob
1 large ripe tomato, skinned, seeded and cubed

Forrest Moebes

1 cup okra, cut into bite-sized pieces
1 teaspoon salt
1 teaspoon pepper
1 teaspoon sugar
2 tablespoons butter
½ cup water
¼ cup cream (optional)

■ Combine all ingredients (except the cream) in a large saucepan and cook over low heat for 10 minutes. If you want to use cream, add and heat through but do not boil.

Spanish Vegetable Terrine

Here's a Spanish recipe with not a hint of garlic — a vegetable dish that can be served as an entree or as an accompaniment to a main course. With its layers of orange, white, green and red vegetables, it's also a very beautiful dish to serve. The recipe is from Seb Bosch, chef at Sisco's restaurant, Hobart, a family-run business that serves beautiful traditional food from the Iberian Peninsula.

Serves 6
½ cup olive oil
1 cup breadcrumbs
4 large potatoes, sliced into 2–3cm thin strips
5 ripe tomatoes, sliced
1 quarter medium-sized pumpkin, sliced into 2–3cm thin strips
1 zucchini, sliced into 2–3cm thin strips
200g baby spinach, washed
salt and pepper to taste

■ Drizzle enough olive oil to just coat the bottom of a baking tray. Sprinkle half the breadcrumbs evenly over surface.

■ Lay the potato slices evenly, overlapping if necessary to avoid any gaps. Lay alternate layers of the vegetables, making sure you can finish with a potato layer. Drizzle olive oil and sprinkle salt and pepper over each layer.

■ To finish, sprinkle the remaining breadcrumbs over the last layer and bake in a medium 180°C oven for 1 to 1½ hours until all vegetables are tender when tested with a wooden skewer. Serve in slices as entree or accompaniment to main course.

Palu Sami (Baked Taro Leaves with Coconut Cream)

The food of the Pacific remains something of a mystery to many Australians, despite the proximity to our shores of the Polynesian and Melanesian islands. What's more, thousands of Islanders have made their homes in Australia — and continue to enjoy all their traditional foods and feasts in their kitchens and backyards. When it comes to larger gatherings, there is always someone who directs proceedings — 'the main man' as Samoan-born Leo Tanoi calls him.

At Tanoi family parties, family friend Moise Failagi is called upon to supervise the preparation, cooking and serving of authentically Samoan fare — baked fish, sides of mutton, pigs' heads, green bananas, whole taro and palu sami (also known as Lu Pulu in Polynesia), a delicacy worth sharing with the broader community. (It's a little like the Central European creamed spinach! Delicious.)

You will need taro leaves — which are relatively easy to come by these days at Asian or Pacific grocery stores. The other ingredient, coconut cream, can be extracted fresh from coconut pulp or poured from a can. Use the Samoan brands of coconut cream — they are thicker and richer than some of the South-East Asian products.

We also give a recipe using corned beef and onion — the most common way to serve this dish. Both are delicious. You can make individual parcels, or one big one. Just vary the cooking time as below.

Version one:

about 3 taro leaves per person (in varying sizes)

about 100ml of coconut cream per person

aluminium foil for baking (or banana leaves)

▓ Place the largest of the leaves across the palm of your hand, then arrange two or three smaller ones across it, overlapping. Cup your hand to form a small bowl, lined with the leaves. Pour in the coconut cream, close the leaves over the liquid and fold. Place parcel on a piece of foil and wrap, twisting the top to seal the contents carefully. Cook in a steamer for around 30 to 40 minutes, or bake in a covered container in a moderate 180°C oven. Of course, you can always bury it in the embers of a fire and cover it with damp newspaper and palm leaves.

▓ The finished dish is great with a baked green banana to dip into the thick, sweet cream.

Version two:

1 can corned beef (New Zealand's Hellaby brand is good or Tongan 'Ikuna')

1 onion, sliced in rings

1 400ml can coconut cream

banana leaves, if available

Polynesian hungi

▓ Lay out several taro leaves on top of each other, the larger ones on the bottom. Place the contents of a can of corned beef in the centre and top it with onion rings and coconut cream. Fold the lot into a square package, secure it with a little twine and wrap again in a banana leaf, or failing that, aluminium foil. Bake for 1 to 1½ hours, preferably in a ground oven! If not, an electric or gas substitute will have to do, on a low 150°C setting.

Water Spinach with Sambal

Jimmy Shu is a Melbourne-based restaurant wizard. An accomplished chef, he is behind some of the more innovative Asian restaurants to have opened in Australia. One of his establishments is the stylish Hanuman Thai restaurant in Darwin, which serves a blend of Asian dishes with a fair emphasis on Thai and Nonya-style food. (Nonya is a blend of Chinese, and indigenous Malay styles).

This is a fiery vegetable accompaniment to almost any Asian dish — the freshness of the water spinach combining well with the hot salty flavour of the sambal. Allow 30 minutes preparation time.

Water spinach, also known as water convolvulus, can be found in most Asian grocery stores. Other Asian greens can be substituted.

Serves 6

400g water spinach, washed and drained
130g dried shrimp
1½ tablespoons vegetable oil
1 tablespoon onion, finely chopped
1 teaspoon ginger, finely chopped
1 teaspoon garlic, finely chopped
½ tablespoon salted soya beans, coarsely chopped
½ tablespoon oyster sauce
sugar to taste
black pepper to taste

■ Cut spinach into 2.5cm lengths. Quickly wash, rinse and soak dried prawns in hot water for about 15 minutes. Drain and chop finely. Heat oil and saute onions, ginger and garlic until they turn light brown. Add the salted soya beans, followed by the dried prawn mince. Cook for a further 3 minutes and add all the remaining ingredients, except sugar and pepper. Finally add the sugar and pepper to taste.

Feijao a Brasileira (Brazilian Beans)

Rice and beans are as Brazilian as the samba. 'Actually, it's our national dish,' says Sao Paulo-born Paulo Weinberger. Popular all over South America, even Cuba, the beans are nonetheless prepared differently from one country to the next. And even within Brazil itself you can get slightly different versions. Here are two simple,

nourishing and very flavoursome bean stews — one from broadcaster/actor Renato Brandao, the other from musician and SBS employee Paulo Weinberger.

Renato Brandao's version
Serves 6

3 cups borlotti beans
1 small onion, chopped
2 cloves garlic, crushed
olive oil
oregano
salt and pepper to taste
4 bay leaves
4 dessertspoons olive oil

■ Soak beans overnight, then cook in pressure cooker for 30 to 35 minutes or in saucepan for 1 hour or until they are soft but not slushy. Fry onions and garlic in olive oil until transparent. Add 1 ladle of the cooked beans to onion and garlic mixture along with a little water. Mash beans with onion and garlic and season with oregano, salt and pepper.
■ Add the rest of the whole beans, 6 cups of water and the bay leaves and simmer until the beans dissolve.
■ The final result should be a thick dark-brown broth that is served with rice.

Paulo Weinberger's version
Serves 4

375g red kidney beans
1 tablespoon ground cumin
4 large bay leaves
1 tablespoon crushed garlic
1 tablespoon salt to taste
1 big onion (thinly sliced)
4 tablespoons olive oil

Zulma Otero and Diana Pinon

Serves 4

500g small white beans

1.5 litres water

¼ cup olive oil

chopped onions

½ teaspoon chopped garlic

6 tomatoes, peeled and chopped

2 teaspoons chopped basil

ground pepper

500g cubed pumpkin

fresh corn kernels

salt

■ Leave beans soaking overnight (in plastic or wooden container — not in a metal saucepan) in double the amount of water. Place beans and water in a saucepan, add cumin, garlic, bay leaves and salt. Cook on a high heat until water boils, then simmer for 30 minutes, checking every 10 minutes. Add more boiling water if necessary.
■ When soft and cooked, turn off the heat. The dish should be quite liquid but with a thick gravy. Fry onion in olive oil until golden brown. Pour the mixture into the cooked beans. Mix well and cook for another 10 minutes. Serve.

■ Rinse the beans and put them with water in a large casserole. Bring to the boil and cook for 2 minutes. Turn off the heat and let them soak for an hour. Heat the oil in a heavy-based frying pan and add onions and garlic and cook until soft and transparent.
■ Stir in tomatoes, basil and ground pepper and boil briskly until it becomes a puree. Add this together with pumpkin to the beans. Cover and cook over low heat for 1½ hours. When the beans are tender, stir in the corn and simmer for 5 minutes. Season with salt and if you like, serve Chilean pebre sauce with it.

Porotos Granados (South American Beans with Pumpkin and Corn)

Beans are big in South, Central and Latin America — nutritious and filling and rather irresistible. The wonder of this dish is the juxtaposition of several very indigenous ingredients — including of course, corn, an Indio staple. Try this with Chilean pebre sauce (see p. 175). This recipe comes from Uruguayans Zulma Otero and Diana Pinon of Sydney's Casa Pueblo restaurant.

Tavce Gravce (Macedonian White Beans)

The white beans dish with the bouncy name is the national dish of Macedonia, so we could hardly go without it. We're grateful to Macedonian broadcaster Zaga Dobrosavlev for her tasty recipe.

Serves 4

250g white beans

1 onion, chopped

2 long green chillies, whole but without stem

2 tablespoons sunflower oil

1 tablespoon plain white flour

salt to taste

red paprika to taste

Meatballs: (optional)

500g beef mince

1 onion, chopped finely

1 egg

chopped parsley

salt

black pepper

oil

▓ Place beans in a saucepan, cover with cold water and bring to the boil. Allow to cook for approximately 5 minutes, then drain, discard the water and replace with fresh hot water. Add chopped onion and whole green chillies and leave to simmer for 1 to 1½ hours, depending on the freshness of the beans. They should be nearly tender.

▓ Heat oil in a separate dish and fry plain flour in it. Remove the chillies from the bean broth when beans are nearly tender, mash and salt the chillies and return to the beans. Add the oil and flour to make gravy, more salt, if needed, and red paprika. Place the lot in an oven dish and cook in a low 150°C oven for another 30 minutes to finish off.

▓ If serving with meatballs, fry small balls made by mixing the beef, onion, egg, parsley, salt and pepper in a little oil for a few minutes only, until half-cooked. Then place the meatballs in the bean stew before the last stage (when beans are placed in oven dish) in the oven.

Moroccan Chickpeas

This recipe gives the chickpeas a lovely sweet taste that blends beautifully with lamb couscous with vegetables pp. 73–4. The dish can be stored in a refrigerator for up to a week; heat prior to serving.

Serves 4 as a side dish

250g chickpeas, soaked in water overnight

100g sultanas

4 tablespoons honey

1 tablespoon cinnamon

juice of 1 orange

500ml water

salt

▓ Boil the chickpeas in the water they soaked in until the water just covers the chickpeas. Add sultanas, honey, cinnamon, orange juice and salt to taste and cook a further 10 minutes. Serve hot.

Mary's Chickpeas

'I just adore this dish,' says SBS newsreader Mary Kostakidis. 'And it's so cheap and easy to make!'

Serves 4

350g chickpeas

2 medium onions, finely chopped

2 tablespoons olive oil

parsley

1 lemon

▓ Soak chickpeas overnight. Drain, then cover with cold water again and bring to the boil. Once it is boiling add onion and oil. Simmer until quite soft. Cool and leave until the following day. Enjoy it chilled with plenty of parsley and lemon juice to taste. 'Divine with crusty bread,' sighs Mary.

David's Dhal

In the spirit of multiculturalism, a recipe for the Indian staple, dhal, from SBS's David Mar (of Chinese parents) using a kosher ingredient. Dhal can be eaten on its own, as an accompaniment to curry or as a soup.

Serves 4

1 cup mung dhal (red lentils)
1 teaspoon ground turmeric
1cm piece root ginger
1 kosher chicken stock cube (Ossem brand, which is not as salty as the Oxo type — David says it gives the dish 'a sort of lift')
1 teaspoon black mustard seeds
1 teaspoon cumin seeds
1 onion
sambal oelek to taste (red chilli paste in vinegar or tamarind — can be bought ready-made)

▨ Wash lentils in as many changes of water as necessary to rinse clear. Add to saucepan with turmeric and scraped and bruised ginger and bring slowly to the boil. Scrape off scum as it occurs.

▨ Continue to boil lentils on a low to moderate heat, until they break easily between the fingers, adding only enough water to stop the mixture burning. Take the saucepan off the stove and remove the ginger. Add the crushed stock cube and combine well. Allow a little time for the flavour to permeate.

▨ In a non-stick pan, toast the mustard seeds and cumin seeds until they become fragrant and start popping. Add to dhal mixture.

▨ The onion should be sliced and slowly fried until dark brown, even crisp, then added to dhal at the end.

▨ Add enough water to saucepan to give desired consistency — some (like David) prefer it runny, others thick. Heat gently. Just before serving add as much sambal oelek as you can stand (he adds about 1 teaspoon). Remove from heat. Ladle into bowls and serve with garnish — perhaps sour cream, yoghurt, chopped coriander or mint.

▨ Notice that you basically cook the dhal then flavour it. So all the ingredients go in at the end. You can add tomato, garlic, ground cumin or coriander, washed and finely minced basil leaves, mint leaves or coriander leaves, salt, roasted salt, roasted black or white pepper.

Ashok's Aloo Tikki Plate (Potato Balls with Tamarind Sauce)

Like many professional Indian chefs in Australia, Ashok Sharma trained with the Taj Mahal group of hotels in India. Now most of his time is spent making the most heavenly, rich Indian sweets for the Maya Sweets chain — saffron-coloured jelabis in rich sugar syrup, reduced milk slices called burfi that come in all flavours, golden ladoo balls, milky rosewater-flavoured rasmalai, the list goes on. At weekends, savoury smells emanate from the kitchen as Ashok prepares the delicious treats that Indians call 'chat'. This is one of the most popular dishes at this Indian-style brunch, consisting of a selection of savoury snacks. The tamarind sauce keeps for ages and is delicious with a range of vegetable dishes. You could also experiment and see how it works with your next Aussie barbie!

The Taj Boys Club

While many restaurants are at loggerheads, vying to be the best, to have the most customers or the highest turnover, there is a group of restaurateurs and food professionals who go against that trend. In fact, they operate like a gentlemen's club of yesteryear with regular meetings and certain unwritten codes of practice that are adhered to meticulously.

This group call themselves the 'Taj Boys' and they are found in most capitals of Australia — owning and running the best Indian restaurants. A 'Taj Boy' is someone who has graduated from the rigorous five-year training course offered by the Taj group of hotels in India.

Most start with a three-year diploma course in hotel management, then the best and brightest are chosen for an apprenticeship in the Taj kitchens. After 18 months, they can then choose a speciality. Many of those who chose Indian cooking are now running their own restaurants in Australia while some are the power behind the scenes at big hotels and convention centres around the country. With all that training, it's not surprising to find that 'Taj Boys' establishments are head and shoulders above the crowd of Indian eateries.

Not only that, the 'boys' have something of a gentlemen's agreement between them. 'We try not to move into someone else's area,' explains restaurateur Wilson Varghese, who specialises in South Indian regional dishes.

While Wilson was one of the first arrivals in 1985, chef Ajoy Joshi's visit to Australia in 1988 had a significant impact on a number of Taj boys back home in India. 'I came for six months and then went home to work at the Taj again and to get married — to a Taj girl, in fact. I was so excited about the possibilities in Australia that some of the others from the class of 83 also applied for visas.'

That class is still going strong, many of the Sydney-based members meeting regularly and the Taj connection in Melbourne providing work for a number of chefs. For instance, owner and chef of the Haveli Indian Restaurant in East Doncaster, Baby Thomas, has two other 'Taj Boys' working with him in the kitchen. Together the boys at Haveli cook up a storm, especially with their South Indian buffet breakfasts on Sundays, complete with rawa dosai (paper-thin semolina pancakes with chopped coriander and grated coconut), rasam (lentil soup mixed with tomatoes, garlic and spices) and sambar, a sour vegetable soup made with okra and eggplant and served with coconut chutney.

Meanwhile 'Taj Boy' Ashok Sharma is hard at work using his skills to create the most heavenly concoctions for Maya Sweets — the

The Taj Boys clockwise from front: Rathnavelu Nagalingam, Binny K. Phillip, Kumar Mahadevan, Wilson Varghese and Sandeep Chatterjee.

biggest Indian sweetmaker in Australia. In fact, every day he makes up to 30 different sweets using milk, ghee, flour, nuts and spices and says that because Australian produce is so good, his sweets taste even better here than in India!

For Taj Boys' recipes see Ajoy Joshi's chicken chettinad, malai kofta, samosa and Indian lemon pickle recipes and Ashok Sharma's aloo tikki plate.

Ashok Sharma with Maya Sweets owner Mr Biloo

Makes 12 portions — each serve is 2 pieces
Potato balls:
2kg old potatoes
200g washed yellow lentils (moongdal in Hindi)
¼ cup salt
150g breadcrumbs
1 bunch fresh coriander, chopped

Tamarind sauce:
lkg tamarind paste (any Asian grocery will carry this black viscous mixture)
1.5kg sugar (brown or rock sugar is best)
2 litres water
100g salt
50g red chilli
50g ground coriander
50g garam masala
100g ground ginger
1 dessertspoon saffron colour

To make potato balls:
■ Boil potato and mash. Boil lentils until cooked. Add all ingredients to a large bowl and mix well.

■ Form into balls the size of a small tennis ball and flatten top slightly so ball is about 2cm high.
■ Deep-fry in vegetable oil or shallow-fry on hotplate. While hot, serve with tamarind sauce.

To make tamarind sauce:
■ Soak the tamarind in boiling water and mix to a thick paste consistency. Add the sugar and 2 litres of water and stir well. Add the salt and remainder of ingredients. Bring to boil, reduce heat and simmer for 30 minutes.

Chickpea Curry

This simple curry comes from Ashok Sharma.

Serves 4
250g white dried chickpeas
1 tablespoon chana masala (a commercial mixed spice of coriander, cumin, pomegranate seeds, cinnamon — Mangal brand for preference)
vegetable oil for frying
1 tablespoon salt
1 tablespoon cumin seeds
garlic paste (or 2 cloves, crushed)
ginger paste (or small knob finely chopped)
3 large tomatoes, chopped
1 large onion, finely chopped
1 bunch fresh coriander, chopped

■ Soak chickpeas overnight and then boil until soft. Mix with the chana masala mix and salt. Heat oil in pan and when it's hot, add cumin seed, garlic and ginger and brown slightly before adding the chickpea mixture. Garnish with slices of fresh ginger and serve with tomato, onion and coriander.

Fijian Indian Potato and Spinach

A quick and easy accompaniment to curries or a simple dish to enjoy with boiled rice. From Fijian–Indian chef Barbara Brewer.

Serves 4
¼ cup or less vegetable oil
½ teaspoon each mustard and fenugreek seeds
1 small onion, sliced
2 medium-sized potatoes, diced small
½ teaspoon ground cumin
½ teaspoon ground turmeric
a little salt
1 clove garlic, crushed
250g packet of frozen spinach
a few red chillies
a little water

■ Heat oil in a wok. When it's hot, add the seeds, being careful they don't spit at you. Add onion and cook until they start to brown, add potatoes, cumin and turmeric, salt and garlic. Sprinkle liberally with water.
■ Cook over a gentle heat until the potatoes are almost done and all the liquid is gone. Add spinach and chillies. Cook for a further 10 minutes with the lid on. As soon as the spinach is cooked, take off the lid (to retain colour).

Rakottkrumpli (Hungarian Potato Bake)

If anyone ever told you potatoes were fattening, wait until you try this decadent Hungarian dish. The recipe was inspired by two Hungarian friends of ours — the debonair culinary whiz, Gabriel Carr and the musical culinary whiz, Agnes Oltvay.

Serves 6
100g smoked speck
1kg parboiled potatoes, skinned and sliced ¾cm thick
1 big red capsicum, sliced into thin rings
salt to taste
freshly ground pepper to taste
1 level tablespoon paprika mixed with a carton of light sour cream
1 teaspoon caraway seeds
1 stick of csabai sausage (or the very garlicky clobessi), sliced
6 hard-boiled eggs, sliced
breadcrumbs
1 dessertspoon chives
1 dessertspoon chopped parsley

■ Dice smoked speck and fry until crisp, retaining fat. Rub the inside of an earthenware dish liberally with butter. Place onc layer of potatoes on bottom, add a few capsicum rings, salt, pepper, a little of the paprika and sour cream mixture and a sprinkling of caraway. Top this with the csabai sausage and one layer of hard-boiled eggs, then start the next layer the same way.
■ The top layer must be potatoes. Sprinkle with smoked speck crackling, douse it with the retained fat, pour over more sour cream and paprika and sprinkle liberally with breadcrumbs.
■ Bake in preheated 175°C oven, covered, for 30 to 35 minutes. Then remove cover and bake for another 10 minutes or until top is crisp. Done in a glass ovenware dish the colours are a blast, says Gabriel Carr.

Hutspot (Dutch Potato Mash)

Once a year Dutch-Australian Mia van Loo gives in to her heritage and cooks 'something Dutch'. There are more complicated and refined items in the Netherlands' culinary repertoire, she hastens to add, but says this is super simple, super cheap and really, really delicious. Make tonnes, is her advice, then you can eat it again the next day, when it tastes even better.

Serves 6
1kg potatoes, chopped into chunks
1kg onions, chopped roughly
1kg carrots, sliced
spek (Dutch smoked bacon) or rookworst (a Dutch smoked sausage available from delis all over and even some supermarket chains), as preferred (optional)
salt and pepper to taste

■ Boil the lot in a covered pot for 30 minutes, with water about halfway up. If you're adding meat, put it on top. Mash it all up when cooked. (You can leave the sausages out of the mashing if you like.) Salt and pepper go in at the end to taste. Some people even like it with butter.

Jansson's Frestelse (Swedish Potatoes)

This potato and cream bake makes no apologies for being high-cal. It's luscious. And the name just adds to its charm — it means 'Jansson's Temptation'. Several versions of this incredibly popular Swedish dish have come to us over the years — most notably from cherished (former) colleagues like Louise Hammarstrom and Lillan Wall.

Serves 4
500g potatoes, sliced very thinly
1 small can anchovies
1 onion, sliced thinly
300ml thick or normal cream or half milk/half cream
breadcrumbs

■ Layer alternately potatoes, anchovies and onion in a buttered oven dish and finish with thick cream. Bake for around 45 minutes in a medium 180°C oven. Breadcrumbs can be sprinkled on top. 'I suppose it's a bit fattening,' Louise Hammarstrom says, 'but it's lovely'.
■ You may find you cannot add all the liquid at once. Try baking it for around 35 minutes with 200ml of cream or milk and cream, then add the rest for another 10 to 15 minutes' baking. Some people brown the onions and potatoes first but this does make the dish just an extra bit richer (too much so, perhaps!).

Colcannon (Creamy Irish Potatoes and Cabbage)

A vegetable dish traditionally eaten at Halloween, the Irish Eve of All Hallows, when dead relatives are remembered and family and personal wishes are prayed for. Irish-born Jean Tongs remembers being told as a little girl that the sparks that shot up the chimney when the bellows were used on Halloween were souls going up to heaven. This is Jean's family recipe for colcannon.

Serves 6
500g old potatoes, peeled and chopped
500g green cabbage, shredded
onion, chopped
100g butter

1 cup full-cream milk

pepper

chopped fresh parsley

■ Boil potatoes, strain and mash. Set aside. Boil cabbage until cooked but not soft. Cook chopped onion in butter until soft. Add milk and warm through, then add the mashed potato and cabbage and mix well. Season to taste with pepper and serve with a dollop of butter on top and a sprinkling of parsley.

Irish Potato Pancake (or Boxty Bread)

After all the jokes about the Irish and potatoes, here's a recipe that uses that fine vegetable to great advantage. As you can see, it's more potato than bread but is just delicious. You may want to add a teaspoon of caraway seeds to the dough for extra flavour.

Serves 4

2 large raw potatoes

2 cups mashed potatoes

1 teaspoon salt

1 teaspoon baking powder

½ cup plain flour

1 teaspoon caraway seeds

■ Grate the raw potatoes. Add to the mashed potatoes and salt. Mix the baking powder with the flour and add to the potatoes. Add caraway seeds. Roll out on a floured board to a circle of 1cm thickness. Cut into 4 quarters and put on an ungreased pan over a gentle heat for 30 to 40 minutes, turning the bread over halfway through. The 'farls' or quarters should be well-browned on both sides.

Scheherazade Latkes

Scheherazade Coffee Lounge in Melbourne was named after a wartime nightclub in Paris, where owners Masha and Avram Zelesnikov celebrated a very special New Year's Eve together — just after the horrors of war were over. When they opened their simple cafe close on forty years ago, it was to serve the sort of simple Eastern European/Jewish fare that they knew from home. The dishes they cooked then — gefilte fish (see p. 103), boiled brisket, cold borscht (see pp. 20–1) and latkes, to name a few — are still being prepared there now and despite the fact that Masha is no longer at the stove, the precision of her recipes and training technique has ensured that the quality and taste have remained unchanged. Latkes just have to be the most delicious way to consume fried potatoes.

Serves 2

2 medium-sized potatoes

1 egg

1 tablespoon self-raising flour

pinch of salt

safflower oil for frying

■ Peel and grate the potatoes by hand. Add the egg, flour and salt and mix thoroughly. Heat the oil in a frying pan. When it is ready, drop a heaped tablespoon of the mixture into the hot oil. Flatten and cook each side until brown.

Malai Kofta
(Indian Cottage Cheese Dumplings)

A sensational dish from the north of India which consists of delicious cottage cheese dumplings (the kofta) wallowing in a spicy sauce, fragrant with coriander, cinnamon, cardamom and cloves. Allow about an hour to prepare the dish and a further hour's cooking time. This recipe from chef Ajoy Joshi is a great hit at his annual Indian cooking classes in the salubrious resort of Noosa on Queensland's Sunshine Coast.

Serves 4–6
Cottage cheese:
2l milk
10ml white vinegar
muslin cloth

Dumplings:
3 medium-sized potatoes
10-15g cumin seeds, roasted
1 small knob fresh ginger, finely chopped
2 fresh green chillies, finely chopped
salt to taste
cornflour to dust the dumplings before frying
oil to fry

Malai sauce:
30ml vegetable oil
5g cumin seeds, roasted
5g cinnamon sticks
5g whole cardamom pods
5g whole cloves
3 large onions, chopped
10g ginger paste
10g garlic paste
salt to taste
10g ground turmeric powder
10g ground chilli powder
10g ground coriander powder
100g cashew nuts, soaked in milk for 30 minutes and then ground to form a thick paste
2 large tomatoes, cut, de-seeded and pureed
20ml fresh cream
half a bunch of coriander leaves, chopped
4 fresh chillies, slit lengthwise
15g almonds and cashew nuts, toasted

To prepare homemade cottage cheese:
Boil milk and keep aside in a jug to cool slightly. Add vinegar and stir until the milk curdles. Pass through a muslin cloth and keep the cheese pressed until the whey drains out completely. Keep refrigerated and grate finely before using in the dumplings (kofta).

To prepare the kofta:
■ Boil potatoes, then peel and grate them. Add grated cheese along with roasted cumin, chopped ginger and chillies and add salt to taste.
■ Mix together and roll into dumplings. Lightly dust in cornflour and fry in vegetable oil until light golden brown.

To prepare the malai sauce:
■ Heat oil in pan. Crackle cumin seeds, then the whole cinnamon, cardamom and cloves. Add the chopped onions and saute until golden brown, then add the ginger and garlic pastes and cook for a few minutes.
■ Add salt, then the ground turmeric, chilli and coriander powders and stir for a few moments. Add the cashew paste and cook on a low heat until the oil leaves the sides of the pan. Stir in the pureed tomatoes and simmer until cooked. Add the fresh cream and keep the sauce aside.

To serve:

■ Place the warm dumplings in a bowl and pour the hot malai sauce on top, until the dumplings are fully covered. Garnish with fresh coriander leaves, slit green chillies and the toasted nuts.

Spicy Sri Lankan Potatoes

A popular side dish for curry in Sri Lanka, this is very easy to make, according to Marita Forbes, restaurant owner and chef extraordinaire. Curry leaves are available in most good fruit and vegie shops while Maldive fish (tiny dried fish from Sri Lanka) can be found in Sri Lankan/Indian spice shops.

Serves 4

½ onion, chopped finely
1 sprig fresh curry leaves
oil or ghee for frying
6 potatoes, peeled and cubed
¼ teaspoon saffron
salt to taste
5cm stick cinnamon
½ teaspoon Maldive fish
¼ teaspoon fenugreek
1 tin coconut milk

■ Fry onions with curry leaves in a little oil or ghee. When onions are transparent, add the potatoes, saffron, salt, cinnamon, Maldive fish and fenugreek and cover with water. Bring to boil and when potatoes are almost cooked, lower heat, add coconut milk and simmer gently for 5 minutes.

Sauces, relishes and marinades

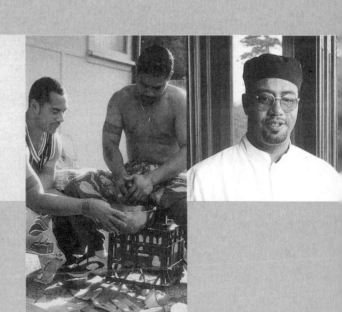

Layering Flavours

This chapter contains the essence of our book. Here are the spices, the layers of flavours that can turn fairly ordinary dishes into truly wonderful meals.

Many of the recipes go wonderfully with plain grilled meats.

Try the tomato chermoula with whole or filleted fish, Moroccan harissa with sausages or chicken and Portuguese piri piri is a natural (and traditional) accompaniment to charcoal chicken. Barka's preserved lemons are great with any sort of fish and are one of the essentials for Hassan's chicken tajine (see p. 53).

Korean dipping sauces are lovely with thin slices of grilled meat — and of course Korean kimchi is the ideal side dish.

Some true Australian salsas are perfect for barbecues — bush tomato and chilli salsa, for example, or lemon aspen salsa with its fresh flavours of mango, capsicum and bush lemon sauce. For a taste of the Levant try zhug — a rich green blend of fresh coriander and cashews with cardamom and caraway flavours, popular in Lebanon, Syria and Palestine. Chilean pebre sauce is another coriander-based recipe with a hint of chilli and garlic.

If you're serving curry, try the two coconut side dishes — coconut chutney and coconut sambol.

Finally, if you're planning one of those long lunches or dinners with a sumptuous spread laid out in advance, try crunching up walnuts, chilli and paprika with a drizzle of pomegranate syrup to make muhammara, a wonderful paste that teams perfectly with salads, bread and yoghurt dips and adds a uniquely Middle Eastern touch to the table.

Muhammara

Passing on recipes is a really special family thing. We will never cook anything quite the same way as our parents did, and while our versions may not be better, they will be ours. Former restaurateur George Haddad talks a great deal about the classic Lebanese dishes his mother taught him and which he has varied at whim! This magical nutty paste is now sometimes made by his daughter Eloise, using George's instructions written neatly on a recipe card and often under George's supervision.

Muhammara is used as a side dish — little tastes of it broken off from the ball served on a central plate can be just the thing to snack on between dishes at a Lebanese banquet. It is great served as an accompaniment to any sort of mezze-style feast, with salads, pickles, bread and yoghurt dips.

Makes one heaped platter
300g finely ground walnuts
50g roughly chopped walnuts
130ml olive oil
¼ cup pomegranate syrup (available from Middle Eastern grocers)
a pinch of harissa (Tunisian chilli relish sold in most good delicatessens or see recipe on pp. 175–6)
50ml water
100g toasted breadcrumbs
2 teaspoons allspice
2 teaspoons ground cumin
4 tablespoons ground sweet paprika
ground black pepper
½ teaspoon salt

▨ Mix all the ingredients together until a paste forms. Don't forget to add a little extra oil or water if it is at all dry and crumbly, as it should be moist. Shape with your hands into a mound and serve in a shallow bowl or dish.

Three Korean Dipping Sauces

Here are three sauces that are perfect with any sort of grilled meat. They're based on the shabu shabu sauces used by Korean friend Doo-Young Lee, a photographer, food lover and restaurateur. These are generally served with Korean shabu shabu — a meat and vegetable steamboat, where you cook your own tidbits in a pot of steaming broth. Increase quantities as you see fit.

Chilli sauce:
Makes 1 small dipping bowl
1 tablespoon chilli powder
1 tablespoon soy sauce
1 teaspoon crushed garlic
1 tablespoon water
1 tablespoon Hot sauce

▨ Mix ingredients together and cook gently over low heat for a couple of minutes. Serve in a dipping bowl.

Sesame sauce:
Makes 1 small dipping bowl
4 tablespoons sesame seeds, crushed
1½ tablespoons peanut butter
½ teaspoon chilli powder
½ teaspoon tomato sauce
½ tablespoon soy sauce
½ tablespoon sugar
½ teaspoon crushed garlic
1 tablespoon sake

▨ Mix all ingredients together other than sake and cook gently over low heat for a couple of

The Flavours of the Bush

Bush tomato gatherers at Utopia, Northern Territory

It's not often in this day and age that a completely new flavour comes onto the food scene. Most of what we may discover in the course of culinary adventuring is usually a spice, a seasoning, a combination or a technique that comes from a long and respected gastronomic tradition — new on our horizons but well-known in other parts of the world. The same could be said for the flavours of the Australian bush, for many thousands of years known only to the Aboriginal people but now emerging as something truly undiscovered by the vast majority of the population.

The best way to use 'bush foods' like lemon aspen, wattleseed, native pepper and mint, bush tomatoes and kakadu plums, is not to consume them in their native, undiluted state but to use them as new and exciting flavours. Their bite, their pungency, their quintessentially Australian aromas and perfumes, are as revolutionary in their own way as the highly developed, market-tested and multi-processed food products large companies keep trying to launch on an increasingly jaded public. Small quantities go a long way, the flavours are unique and will add a whole new dimension to everything from salad dressings to desserts, sauces to stews.

minutes. Add sake just before moving sauce to serving bowl.

Lemon sauce:
Makes 1 small dipping bowl
1 tablespoon soy sauce
1 tablespoon vinegar
1 tablespoon lemon juice
2 tablespoons water
1 tablespoon sake

■ Mix all ingredients together other than sake and cook gently over low heat for a couple of minutes. Add sake just before moving sauce to serving bowl.

Bush Tomato and Chilli Salsa

The flavours of the Australian desert contribute to this tangy salsa, perfect for accompanying grilled meats or chicken, even char-grilled vegetables. It comes courtesy of Juleigh and Ian Robins, of Robins Bush Foods and was originally published in their book *Wild Lime: cooking from the bushfood garden* (Allen & Unwin 1996).

Makes 2 cups
¼ cup white vinegar
1 teaspoon salt
1 tablespoon castor sugar
3 small red chillies, finely chopped
2 teaspoons ground bush tomatoes
10 large ripe tomatoes, finely chopped (skinned if preferred)
2 onions, finely chopped
2 cloves garlic, chopped
2 tablespoons good-quality olive oil

■ In a medium-sized stainless steel saucepan, bring the vinegar, salt, sugar and chillies to the boil. Add the ground bush tomatoes and cook for 10 minutes on a low heat. Remove from the heat.

■ Combine the tomatoes, onions and garlic in a large bowl. Add the saucepan ingredients to the bowl.

■ Let the salsa sit for an hour for the flavours to infuse before serving. Just before use, drain off any excess liquid that has collected and stir through the olive oil.

Chilean Pebre Sauce

A spicy coriander-based sauce that goes well with porotos granados (South American beans with pumpkin and corn) in the Vegetables chapter.

Makes 1 cup
5 teaspoons olive oil
2½ teaspoons vinegar
½ cup water
½ cup chopped coriander
½ cup chopped onions
fresh chopped chilli
chopped garlic
salt to taste

■ Mix the oil, vinegar and water in a bowl. Stir in the coriander, onions, chilli, garlic and salt. Let the mixture stand for 2 to 3 hours before serving.

Moroccan Harissa (Chilli Sauce)

This recipe is from Sydney restaurateur Hassan M'Souli. If you make it according to the recipe and are careful to leave a fine film of oil over it when you're not using it, this harissa can be stored in the refrigerator indefinitely. It can be added to marinades and sauces and substituted in any recipe that calls for chilli. Be warned: Wear double gloves when chopping the chillies if you want to keep your hands and fingerprints!

Makes 1 large jar

1kg hot red chillies, stalks removed (you don't have to remove the seeds)

4 large red capsicums, grilled or roasted and peeled

2 preserved lemons

6 cloves garlic

1 bunch coriander, chopped

¼ cup ground cumin

2 tablespoons salt

olive oil to cover

Mince or process the chillies, capsicum, preserved lemons and garlic, then mix together with cumin, coriander and salt.
Let the mixture breathe for an hour, then transfer to a sterilised preserving jar and cover with olive oil.

Piri Piri Sauce

We are very proud to have a recipe for this Portuguese staple — a legacy of Portugal's African colonisation. Piri piri is a hot chilli sauce, used especially on barbecued chicken or even meats. Thanks to Fatima Barroso, Portuguese caterer-about-town, who shared her tips with us. (Getting the secrets of piri piri is quite a task!)

Makes about 500ml

5 medium-sized red chillies, sliced with seeds left in

2 cloves garlic, chopped

350ml good olive oil

350ml good whiskey

Fill the jar with chillies (they should come about ⅓ of the way up a 500ml jar). Drop in the garlic. Warm the olive oil but don't let it boil. Pour on top of the chillies and garlic. Top up the jar with whiskey. 'The better quality the whiskey, the better the result,' says Fatima. Shake the mixture every now and then to allow to brew. 'You can use it straightaway if you must,' Fatima concedes, 'but it's better if you leave it for at least a few days, better longer. It will keep for a month.'

Lemon Aspen Salsa

This recipe is from bush food chef, Danni Murray, who makes it to go with her rack of crocodile (see p. 90). It is perfect too with any firm-fleshed fish, or grilled chicken breasts. Lemon aspen can be bought from any good deli and some supermarkets are now carrying a range of bush flavourings.

Makes enough for 8 serves

20-25 lemon aspen berries, cut into quarters

20g fresh ginger, finely chopped

2 red birdseye chillies, seeded and finely chopped

250ml rice wine vinegar

½ stalk lemongrass, finely chopped

200g white sugar

250ml macadamia oil

250ml vegetable oil

½ red capsicum, julienned

2 mangoes, chopped into small squares

handful Italian flat-leaf parsley

sprigs of coriander to decorate

■ Mix together lemon aspen, ginger, chilli, rice wine vinegar, lemongrass and sugar together in a large saucepan and bring to the boil. Simmer for 5 minutes over low heat. Let cool and strain well, pressing down hard to extract all the liquid from the lemon aspen. Mix in the macadamia and vegetable oils. Add the capsicum, mango and parsley and season well.

Tomato Chermoula Sauce

This is an all-purpose sauce that can be used with any sort of grilled meat, its Moroccan flavours working especially well with lamb. It follows the basic recipe for chermoula marinade (see p. 188) with a few small changes.

Makes 2 jars (5–6 cups)

2 large onions, diced
¼ cup olive oil
1 tablespoon crushed chilli
1 tablespoon sweet paprika
1 teaspoon grated fresh ginger
1 tablespoon ground cumin
2 cloves garlic, chopped
1 tablespoon freshly chopped flat-leaf parsley
½ preserved lemon, thinly sliced
juice 1/2 fresh lemon
2kg canned peeled tomatoes
½ teaspoon saffron strands
½ tablespoon thinly sliced fresh coriander

■ Fry diced onions in olive oil until softened, then add chilli, paprika, ginger, cumin, garlic, parsley, preserved lemon and lemon juice and simmer for 1 to 2 minutes. Add the peeled tomatoes, crushed saffron and coriander and simmer for 20 minutes, stirring occasionally.

Zhug (Mediterranean Sweet Coriander and Cashew Sauce)

This bright-green puree of herbs, spices, nuts and chilli is ideal as a salsa over baked fish, grilled meats or even plain steamed vegetables. The Haddad family of Hobart gave us this treasured recipe — part of George Haddad's amazing collection of ideas from all over the Mediterranean and Middle East.

Makes 1½ cups

3 cardomom pods
1 teaspoon caraway seeds
1 tablespoon black peppercorns
4-6 hot chillies
1½ cups fresh coriander leaves and stems
6 cloves garlic
½ teaspoon salt
100g cashew nuts
250ml olive oil

■ Place cardomom pods, caraway seeds and peppercorns in a food processor and blend to a coarse powder. Trim stems from chillies leaving rest of chilli intact. Add to food processor with the remaining ingredients and blend to a coarse puree.

Three Thai Curry Pastes

From renowned Thai chef Prasit Prateeprasen who says some of his earliest memories are helping the other great cook in his family, his grandmother, peel garlic cloves and watching her pound these delicious pastes. They can be frozen — place what you don't use immediately into ice-cube trays, freeze and keep in small plastic freezer bags.

Basic curry paste:

Makes 1 cup

2 stalks lemongrass (use the soft white sections only)

2 tablespoons kaffir lime zest

¼ cup chopped red onions

1 teaspoon cumin seeds

1 bunch coriander root

4 large dried red chillies

2 dessertspoons galangal

6 cloves garlic

1 teaspoon coriander seeds

1 teaspoon shrimp paste

kaffir lime leaves

▧ Pound all ingredients together in a mortar and pestle or blender.

Yellow curry paste:

Makes 1 cup

▧ To the above ingredients add 1 tablespoon cumin seeds or brown caraway seeds, half a bunch of coriander and 1 fresh root turmeric, about the size of a thumb.

Red curry paste:

Makes 1 cup

10 fresh or dried hot red chillies

½ cup red onion or 2 small brown onions, chopped

1 tablespoon chopped garlic

¼ cup finely sliced lemongrass, or thinly peeled rind of 1 lemon

1 tablespoon galangal, fresh or frozen, or 3 teaspoons powdered galangal

1 tablespoon chopped fresh coriander root

1 tablespoon fresh coriander stems, chopped

1 teaspoon finely grated kaffir lime rind

4 kaffir lime leaves, mid ribs removed

2 tablespoons oil

2 teaspoons dried shrimp paste

1 tablespoon coriander seeds

2 teaspoons cumin seeds

1 teaspoon black peppercorns

2 teaspoons paprika

1 teaspoon ground turmeric

▧ Put the chillies, onions, garlic, lemongrass, galangal, coriander roots and stems, lime rind and lime leaves into a blender. Add the oil and blend to a smooth puree.

▧ Wrap the shrimp paste closely in foil, flattening to make a small packet. Place under a hot griller and cook 2 to 3 minutes on each side.

▧ At separate times, toast coriander seeds, cumin seeds and peppercorns until fragrant. Pound all three ingredients to a powder in a mortar and pestle. Add to the blender with the paprika, ground turmeric and shrimp paste. Blend once more.

Satay Sauce

You'll never buy a commercial satay sauce once you've made this thick peanut sauce with garlic, ginger, lemongrass and tamarind flavours. A blender is essential. This recipe comes from Malaysian chef Alvin Tan (and his satay beef and chicken marinades can be found on pp. 188–9).

Serves 6

3 cloves garlic

2 slices galangal

2 slices ginger

100g onion

½ cup oil

1 stalk lemongrass, smashed slightly

¼ cup chilli powder

½ teaspoon ground turmeric

2 cups water

5 teaspoons salt
300g roasted peanuts, ground coarse
¼ cup tamarind juice (1 tablespoon tamarind paste with ¼ cup water)
150g sugar

■ Blend garlic, galangal, ginger and onion with a little water to help make a smooth paste.
■ Using ½ cup of oil, fry blended ingredients along with lemongrass stalk, chilli and turmeric for 10 minutes or until it's fragrant and the oil seeps through the paste. Then add the water, salt and peanuts and simmer for 25 minutes. Stir constantly to avoid burning.
■ Add the tamarind juice and sugar and simmer for another 20 minutes until the sauce has a nice thick consistency. Check the seasoning.

Cha Son Hi's Kimchi

This recipe for a traditional Chinese cabbage and spinach kimchi comes from Cha Son Hi who runs a small barbecue and noodle restaurant in the very Korean suburb of Campsie in Sydney with her husband Lee Tae Back. She trained as a cook before coming to Australia from her home town of Inchon and the restaurant is named after her — probably because she is such a good cook!

Serves 6
1 head Chinese cabbage
salt
1 bunch pak choy or other green 'spinach' like vegetable
2 teaspoons sugar
20g piece ginger
good splash fish sauce

½ cup Korean chilli powder
2 cloves garlic, finely sliced

■ Slice the cabbage finely, wash and sprinkle with salt. Mix sugar, ginger, garlic, fish sauce, chilli powder to a paste and add to washed pak choy.
■ Layer cabbage with chilli and pak choy mix in a stoneware or earthenware crock. Stand in a cool place to ferment for a couple of days.

Cucumber Kimchi

No Korean meal is complete without kimchi — an all-purpose word that covers pickled vegetable side dishes. The vegies should have a crunch to them and a fair bit of bite, thanks to the liberal use of chilli powder. Melbourne Korean broadcaster Jaesun Woo's recipe is not for the traditional cabbage version but a more exotic, cucumber-based kimchi. As a teacher of Korean, he often cooks at home with his students and they have all declared his recipe 'fabulous'.

Serves 6
8 Lebanese cucumbers
2 tablespoons sesame seeds
2 tablespoons sesame oil
6 cloves garlic, crushed
3 teaspoons finely chopped fresh ginger
2 teaspoons chilli sauce
sprinkling of chilli powder
2 carrots, cut into long very thin slivers
6 spring onions, cut into very fine rounds
1 small onion, sliced very finely

■ Cut cucumbers in half lengthways. Blend sesame seeds, sesame oil, crushed garlic and ginger, chilli sauce and powder into a drizzly

Traditional Kimchi

Kimchi is the classic accompaniment to any Korean meal. It goes beautifully with grilled, marinated meats and steamed short grain rice but can also add an interesting tang to noodle soup or a hot pot. Most Koreans, in fact, would rather starve than dine without it! Considered healthy and nutritious, kimchi even has whole museums dedicated to it — focussing on everything from its history to the hundreds of ways it can be prepared. While kimchi can be made with a variety of vegetables, including radish and cucumber, the best-known uses long, curly Chinese cabbage and comes flavoured with all sorts of vegetables and seafood — anchovies, shrimp, even fresh oysters. One important ingredient is the powerful ground red chilli powder available in all Korean grocery stores. You just can't substitute anything else!

paste and pour over cucumbers. Add fine strips of carrots, onions and spring onions.

▨ Place in airtight container, give a good shake to mix it all in and leave in the refrigerator for two days.

▨ Jaesun says it makes a refreshing spicy mixture to accompany rice, grilled fish and other Korean food.

Ukrainian Beetroot Relish

Marika Freeman grew up in Adelaide eating a fairly solid diet of Ukrainian food, care of her mother Anastasia, who's from Western Ukraine. This recipe, based on a Ukrainian staple — beetroot — is a family favourite stretching back generations but it has found a niche in modern Australia. Marika sells her beetroot relish through markets and delicatessens in South Australia. It would normally be made in springtime when the ingredients are at their best and be served at Easter with ham or suckling pig. Do be wary when you're grating the horseradish — it's a real tear-jerker.

Makes 5–6 cups
1.5kg beetroot
½ cup freshly grated horseradish
2 cups cider vinegar
1 tablespoon mixed spice (optional)
½ cup sugar
3 teaspoons salt (sea salt is best)
sterilised jars

▨ Remove the leaves from the beetroot, leaving 2cm of stem and roots intact. This prevents the beetroot from bleeding during the cooking and losing a lot of the colour.

Marika Freeman

▨ Wash the beetroot and cover with cold water. Bring to the boil, then simmer until tender. Cooking time will depend on the size of the beetroot. Drain the cooked beetroot and immerse in cold water.

▨ Remove skin, stems and roots. Grate beetroot on a fine grater and mix with the prepared horseradish. Place the vinegar, spice, sugar and salt in a saucepan and bring to the boil then strain into the beetroot mixture. Mix well and spoon into sterilised jars and seal. Store the relish in a cool dark place. Allow at least 24 hours before using.

Barka's Preserved Lemons

If Barka M'Souli ever sees this recipe in print, her eyes will grow wide with surprise. She lives in Casablanca, Morocco, looking after her large family of children and grandchildren but one of her children is here in Australia — her son Hassan who came ten years ago to open a restaurant. While he's a professional chef, there were a few things he found he hadn't perfected in his repertoire, particularly some of the traditional recipes from home. He just couldn't match his mother's preserved lemon recipe — until she sent him her secrets.

Makes 8 preserved lemons — 2 jars full
8 thin-skinned juicy lemons
cold water
rock salt
large glass screw-top jar
6 cardomom pods
3 bay leaves
3 birdseye chillies
boiling water

■ Break the pores of the lemon by scraping gently against the medium setting of a grater. Place in large bowl and cover completely with cold water. Put aside in cool place.

■ Next day, pour the water off the lemons and cover with fresh water. This removes any bitterness.

Hassan M'Souli with his preserved lemons

■ On the third day, pour off the water. Using a sharp knife and chopping board, make 4 deep slits in each lemon (they should go about halfway to the centre). Pack each incision with a good heaped teaspoon of rock salt.

■ Place stuffed lemons in a glass jar, add cardamom pods, bay leaves and chillies. Pour boiling water over contents and screw on lid while the water is still hot. Leave for 40 days in a cool dark place.

■ Serve by themselves as an accompaniment to a cold beer; use in tajine and couscous dishes.

Indian Lemon Pickle

Did you know that lemon pickle is one of the most popular pickles in Northern India? It's certainly up there alongside the famous mango pickle. In a country that takes its condiments and side dishes extremely seriously, the divide between north and south is seen in many ingredients including those for pickles. Lemons give a sharper, tangier taste than limes which are more popular in the south. This is an old family recipe from chef Ajoy Joshi.

Makes about 1kg
12 big lemons
1½ cups salt
juice of 4 lemons
½ cup chilli powder
1 heaped teaspoon fenugreek seeds, roasted in oil and powdered
1 level teaspoon asafoetida powder
2 teaspoons ground turmeric

■ Cut the lemons into quarters or smaller pieces as required. Add salt and lemon juice and store in an airtight container for 1 week.

After a week, mix the chilli powder, fenugreek, asafoetida and turmeric and add to the lemons. Keep aside for another 2 weeks for the lemons to pickle. Do not use a wet spoon or wet container for any of the above.

Vietnamese Pickled Vegetables

The ideal life for a chef is to be situated somewhere beautiful with enough time off to enjoy the wider world and with a magnificent showcase for his or her food. Vincent Rae has found that perfect life and he's still under 30! He lives in a Moorish-style palace on one of the most spectacular beaches in Australia, Watego's at Byron Bay — perfect for surfing year round with great whale-watching through the winter from the nearby lighthouse. Vincent's food blends a number of influences. This works as a great side dish.

Serves 4

250ml Thai rice wine vinegar

150g castor sugar

salt

1 whole red chilli

1 daikon radish

4 cucumbers

½ lemon

■ In a saucepan mix the vinegar and sugar together, bring to boil, add a pinch of salt and let cool. Slice the chilli very finely and add to the mixture. Julienne the radish. Remove the seeds from the cucumber and julienne. Cut the lemon half into halves again. Seed and cut into thin slices.

■ Mix the vegetables together, tossing lightly. (For more colour, you may want to add some red cabbage, julienned.)

■ Pour vinegar over mix and leave to marinate for no more than half an hour before serving. Serve cold as a side dish with chopsticks.

Byron Bay Nectarine Chutney

This is a perfect chutney to make in the summer months when stone fruit is plentiful. It's from that idyllic part of Australia — the far north coast of New South Wales where growers in the hinterland are stretching the geographical boundaries of where stone fruit can be grown. Normally found in areas where it gets chilly overnight, new varieties now make it possible to grow nectarines and peaches in warmer areas. This chutney is lovely with sausages, pork and, of course, Indian-style curry.

Makes 2 large jars

1kg nectarines

2 onions, finely chopped

500g muscatel raisins

150g glace ginger, sliced

1kg sugar

3 small hot chillies, chopped finely, including the seeds

700ml white wine vinegar

1 teaspoon salt

■ Wash, dry, then chop the nectarines into chunky pieces. Combine with all other ingredients and cook in heavy-based pan, stirring frequently to prevent sticking. The mixture will normally thicken in about 1½ hours.

Fresh Coconut Cream and Freshly Scraped Coconut

If you really want the taste of the Pacific (Fiji, Tonga, Samoa, Cook Islands et al!), you need coconuts. Better still, you need fresh coconut cream, which those in the know make themselves using a clever little gadget called a coconut scraper. 'My non-Fijian husband got a shock when we were married,' remembers prolific Indo-Fijian cook and caterer Barbara Brewer. 'He thought my coconut scraper was some kind of exotic back scratcher!' Back scratcher or not, it's a kind of serrated disc that can be attached to a table or benchtop. Its real use of course is as a device to scrape out the sweet white coconut flesh. (Always choose a firm, brown, heavy fruit and save the coconut juice!) The flesh can also be processed in a blender if removed from the husk. Soak the white, grated mix in a little warm water and knead it a little, place in a piece of muslin, cheesecloth or even a coconut-fibre mesh and squeeze the liquid out into a bowl. You can make more by adding a little water — using no water makes a very dense cream.

Coconut is used in sauces, sweets, baking taro leaves or even for marinating fish (along with a good dash of lemon juice and a handful of chillies). And Indo-Fijian food makes good use of coconut milk in a selection of light, fragrant curries. Try using your own freshly scraped coconut in Barbara Brewer's coconut chutney or Marita Forbes's coconut sambol.

Barbara's Coconut Chutney

Fijian-Indian chef Barbara Brewer was sadly missed when she left her homeland for Australia — after all, her canteen-style eatery in Nadi catered for everyone, with Indian and plenty of island food as well. See the Noodles, Dumplings and Rice chapter for tamarind rice and the Meat chapter for pork malabar so you can put together a full meal.

It's amusing to note the evolution of this old recipe — it now requires the use of microwaves and blenders! Do try and get hold of fresh curry leaves, advises Barbara, as they really add such a lovely flavour. Green-thumb Barbara always has a few bushes growing just outside the back door.

Note: Fresh coconut chatni or chutney bears little resemblance to the sweet pickled bottled sauces sold as chutneys.

Serves 6 as an accompaniment

1½ cups fine dessicated coconut

sufficient coconut milk to moisten coconut

1 small onion, finely chopped

2–3 red hot fresh chillies or dried variety

2–3 cloves garlic

2.5cm piece of ginger

a walnut-sized piece of tamarind soaked in 1/4 cup hot water

1½ teaspoons salt or to taste

mint, fresh coriander or fresh curry leaves

▪ Cover the moistened coconut with plastic wrap and microwave on medium for 1 to 2 minutes or until all the moisture is absorbed by the coconut. Alternatively, bake in a covered pot in a moderate 180°C oven for about 15 minutes.

▪ Squeeze the tamarind and strain. Add all the ingredients to the coconut, mix and blend together in a blender for 1 minute or until thoroughly mixed. Taste and adjust salt. Add mint, coriander or curry leaves to give an extra-special flavour.

Sri Lankan Coconut Sambol

This fiery yet marvellously tasty side dish accompanies many curries in Sri Lanka. The recipe is from restaurateur Marita Forbes who has been making it for over thirty years. If you live in Sydney, Aum's Spice Shop in Strathfield grates coconuts with a special grater imported from Sri Lanka. Otherwise, the taste is worth the hard work involved in cracking and grating the nut (see the box on coconut scraping opposite).

Serves 8–10

1 fresh coconut, grated

3 teaspoons dried and crushed chillies

2 teaspoons Maldive fish (small dried fish available from spice stores)

1 small onion sliced

salt to taste

juice of 1 lime or lemon

2 teaspoons paprika

▪ Using a blender or mortar and pestle, blend together the chillies, Maldive fish, onion, salt and paprika. (To moisten blender ingredients, use a little water or even better, coconut milk.) Add coconut and moisten with the lime or lemon juice and mix well together.

▪ Use within a couple of days.

RIchard Nichols

Brazilian Marinade (Chicken)

Brazilians love to barbecue and a typical
Brazilian churrascaria (barbecue feast) will
feature any number of cuts of meat, from beef
to pork and chicken. Sydney restaurateur
Richard Nichols knows all about these things,
running a popular Brazilian barbecue and
samba venue which features a genuine
churrasqueira, or rotisserie. He and chef Gary
Scigliano offer us this combination for
marinating chicken drumsticks.

Serves 6 (for 12 plump chicken drumsticks)
good pinch of ground cumin
good pinch of ground sage
good pinch of paprika
pinch of salt
freshly ground black pepper

3 cloves garlic, crushed
500ml dry white wine

■ Mix all the marinade ingredients in a large
sealable bowl. Add the chicken and mix well,
seal bowl and leave in fridge overnight.
Richard suggests grilling the drumsticks on a
relatively high heat for 20 minutes, then
reducing to low for a further 20 to allow the
meat to cook through. Remember to turn
them constantly for the full rotisserie effect.

Iranian Chicken Marinade

This recipe is from a third-generation expert on
the subject of kebabs. Jimmy Ghafari grew up in
Teheran and remembers spending a lot of time
with his grandfather who ran a popular kebab
cafe in the heart of town. 'Kebabs are such a
healthy and delicious food,' says Jimmy. What he
really misses is the special flat, stone-baked
Persian bread called sangkak that kebabs are
sandwiched in — a bread cooked on hot stones
and sprinkled with poppy seeds.

Serves 2 (4 as an entree)
1kg chicken thigh fillets
½ cup lemon juice
½ cup white vinegar
2 teaspoons salt
½ teaspoon saffron strands, crushed

■ Slice chicken thigh fillets into halves and
place in a bowl. Add lemon juice, vinegar, salt
and saffron and mix well. Leave for 9 hours or
overnight. Thread onto skewers and grill or
barbecue until golden outside.
■ Serve with Iranian rice (see recipe in
Noodles, Pasta, Dumplings and Rice)

Portuguese Charcoal Chicken Marinade

Celina and Americo Stantos manufacture a range of Portuguese delicacies in Sydney. They were also among the first people to introduce Portuguese charcoal chicken (marinated and butterflied) to Australia.
Remember to serve your barbecued chicken with piri piri sauce (see Sauces p. 176).

For one chicken

1 cup vinegar, preferably wine vinegar
¼ cup dry white wine
2 tablespoons lemon juice
1 dessertspoon paprika
2 cloves garlic
bay leaves
oregano

▨ Mix all ingredients together and taste. If it's too tart with vinegar, add a little more wine and lemon juice or temper with a little water. Place chicken in a dish, pour in the marinade and make sure it covers chicken. Leave for no longer than 2 hours — otherwise the vinegar will start to cook the meat.
▨ You can use the marinade again if you make sure it's refrigerated when not in use.

Moroccan Barbecue Chicken Marinade

This is adapted from a recipe for chicken tajine given to us by chef Hassan M'Souli. While he recommends marinating overnight, the result is even more fabulous over a longer time as Maeve discovered by accident,

completely forgetting the chicken immersed in spices for four days! If you have preserved your own lemons (according to Hassan's mother's recipe on pp. 181–2), do remember to wash the rock salt out of the slits in the lemon first — it's way too salty if you don't!

Serves 4
1 whole chicken

Marinade:
2 cloves garlic, chopped
1 soup spoon-sized knob of fresh ginger, chopped
1 bay leaf
1 large onion, chopped
1 pinch ground saffron
1 soup spoon ground cumin
salt and pepper to taste
½ bunch fresh coriander
1 preserved lemon, cut into fine wedges
½ cup extra virgin olive oil

Garnish:
½ bunch shallots, finely chopped
15 marinated green olives
1 preserved lemon cut into fine wedges

▨ Cut the whole chicken into large serving pieces. Wash chicken pieces and dry with paper towel.

For the marinade:
▨ Use a blender or mortar and pestle to combine garlic, ginger, bay leaf, onion, saffron, cumin, salt, pepper, coriander, preserved lemon and olive oil.
▨ With a sharp knife, make small slits along chicken flesh, especially the breast area and rub in the marinade. Cover with plastic and refrigerate overnight.
▨ Cook over hot barbecue coals and garnish

with preserved lemon wedges, olives, shallots and freshly chopped coriander.

Chermoula Marinade (Lamb, Chicken or Fish)

This is a great marinade for grilled, barbecued or pan-fried lamb. If you want to use it for chicken or fish, add a little more cumin and paprika. Don't confuse this recipe with that for our tomato-based chermoula (see p. 177). Chermoula is a generic Moroccan word for a spicy sauce.

For 1kg meat
1 tablespoon crushed chilli
1 tablespoon sweet paprika
1 teaspoon grated fresh ginger
½ teaspoon saffron strands
2 onions, diced
1 tablespoon ground cumin
2 cloves garlic, chopped
1 tablespoon freshly chopped flat-leaf parsley
½ tablespoon thinly sliced fresh coriander
½ preserved lemon, thinly sliced
½ cup olive oil
juice ½ fresh lemon

▪ Mix all the ingredients together thoroughly. Leave for 30 minutes before you add the meat. Marinate for 2–3 hours. This can be refrigerated and stored for up to seven days.

Satay Marinade (Beef and Chicken)

Fragrant with spices, ginger, garlic and lemongrass, satay has easily jumped the culinary divide between the exotic and the mainstream. These simple instructions for marinating meat come from Malaysian chef Alvin Tan. Remember to soak the satay sticks before use and to cover the pointed ends with meat when threading them. And for tasty satay sauce, see Alvin's recipe on pp. 178–9.

Beef marinade:
For 600g topside, rump or round
50g onion
1 stalk lemongrass
3 cloves garlic
2 slices ginger
2 slices galangal
2 teaspoons ground turmeric
1 teaspoon ground cumin
100g sugar
2 teaspoons salt
a little oil

▪ Blend the onion, lemongrass, garlic, ginger and galangal together, using a little oil to make it into a paste. Mix in the turmeric, cumin, sugar and salt.
▪ Remove any excess fat and sinews from beef. Cut the meat across the grain and slice into 5mm slices.
▪ Rub the marinade mixture into the meat thoroughly. Marinate for 2 to 3 hours tossing from time to time to marinate evenly before threading onto skewers.

Chicken marinade:
For 600g chicken, cubed
3 cloves garlic
50g onion
1 stalk lemongrass
½ tablespoon ground turmeric
½ tablespoon ground coriander
½ tablespoon ground fennel

1 teaspoon ground cumin

100g sugar

1½ teaspoons salt

a little peanut oil

■ Process all the marinade ingredients in a blender until smooth, adding a little water to help make a paste.

■ Marinate the cubed chicken in the mixture for 2 hours.

■ Note: the chicken can be served with 1 cubed cucumber, 1 cubed red onion, and 1 quantity nasi empit (compressed rice), cubed (see p. 121).

Maeve's Chicken Marinade

This is perfect on a warm summer's evening, the scent of rosemary grilling over hot coals is quite heavenly.

For 2kg chicken

1 bunch fresh rosemary, stalks removed

juice of 3 limes

¼ cup honey

dash of olive oil

pinch salt

ground black pepper

■ Mix marinade ingredients together and cover chicken fillets. Marinate for minimum 2 hours or overnight is even better.

Indian Marinade (Lamb, Beef, Pork, Chicken)

Perfect for diced lamb, beef or pork pieces, or even chicken on the bone, this delicious

tandoori marinade is very similar to the other one given to us by Inder Mehandiratta for his chicken tikka (see pp. 48–9) — the addition is the vinegar.

If using meat on the bone, score the meat to the bone and rub the marinade into the incisions to better distribute the flavour.

For 1kg of meat

¼ cup natural set yoghurt

50ml vegetable oil

2½ teaspoons minced fresh ginger

2½ teaspoons crushed fresh garlic

2½ teaspoons salt

1½ teaspoons ground cumin

3 teaspoons garam masala

½ teaspoon hot chilli powder (optional)

1 tablespoon lemon juice

1 tablespoon vinegar

2–3 pinches of tandoori colour or ground turmeric or 5 teaspoons sweet paprika powder (for that unmistakable brick-red colour)

■ Blend the yoghurt with a whisk then add all the other marinade ingredients. Mix well. Add the meat and ensure that it is well covered with the marinade. (Score chicken legs or chops to the bone and fill incision with marinade). Cover the bowl and refrigerate overnight (or for at least 8 hours). Cook on a relatively low barbecue setting for about 20 minutes.

Iranian Beef or Lamb Marinade

This lemon, peppery marinade is from Asie Kodeiri from Teheran, who is justifiably proud of the dishes from her part of the Middle East, notably, of course, the famous marinated kebabs. So here's the secret. Nothing could be simpler.

Ideally, Asie says, the kebabs should be cooked slowly over a charcoal or coal barbecue.

Serves 8

1.5kg beef or lamb fillet, sliced
2 onions, grated
1 cup olive oil
salt, pepper and butter to taste
sumac to taste (this is a purple-brown Middle Eastern spice with an acid, lemon-peppery taste)

■ Slice the meat into 5mm thick pieces and leave in the marinade of grated onions and olive oil for at least 24 hours.
■ Slide onto skewers and cook over a grill plate. When done, place in a dish and add salt and butter. Serve with Persian rice and sprinkle with sumac.

Korean Barbecue Marinade (Beef and Pork)

One cuisine that specialises in marinating meats for grilling is Korean. Barbecue restaurants are a major feature of Korean dining, and have certainly begun springing up around Australian cities as more and more Korean migrants make their home here. The ingredients in this marinade are the quintessential flavours of Korea — listed for us by Cha Son Hi, a Korean-trained cook who runs her own very successful barbecue restaurant with her husband Lee Tae Back.

For 500g meat

1½ tablespoons of soy sauce
1 tablespoon minced spring onions
½ tablespoon minced garlic
¾ tablespoon sugar
½ tablespoon sesame oil

■ Slice beef fillet into thin strips about 5cm long. Dip each strip in the seasoning sauce then lay them in a bowl. Pour the remaining marinade over the top and leave for at least 30 minutes. You can add a little ginger, especially for pork, and a little fresh pear juice, made by grating a pear and passing it through a sieve.

Kailis Fish Marinade

Freshly grilled seafood is a perfect barbecue feast. Often all you need to do is finish your fillets, prawns, squid, baby octopus or even whole fish with a drizzle of olive oil dressing. But you can also marinate and baste any kind of seafood prior to grilling in this simple combination of Mediterranean flavours used by Theo Kailis, third generation Australian-Greek and part of the mighty Kailis fishing empire in Western Australia. 'Be careful never to overcook your seafood,' Theo warns. Most fish fillets, prawns or octopus only need a couple of minutes on each side and they are done.

For 1kg seafood

4 cloves garlic, crushed
⅓ cup lemon juice or white wine
½ cup olive oil
2 tablespoons French mustard
½ teaspoon chilli powder or freshly ground black pepper
1 teaspoon salt
¼ cup finely chopped parsley

■ Combine all the ingredients in a large bowl. Add your prawns or other seafood and allow to marinate for at least 2 hours. Baste the fish with the marinade during cooking.

Desserts

Bartolillos (Spanish Custard Puffs)

Kate Johnson is a translator of Spanish and French who was born and raised in England but always had an interest in and love of languages. She spent many summer holidays in Spain and France during her school years. Her mother was an excellent cook 'but very English', says Kate. 'I came back from my stays abroad enthralled at the different things you could do with food and dying to try for myself.' One of these taste sensations was bartolillos, decadent deep-fried custard puffs. She remembers the time ('don't ask me how many years ago!') she came back from her annual holiday in Miraflores de la Sierra with her Spanish 'family', Dona Maria and her daughters, clutching the precious recipe for bartolillos — 'like a talisman'. Bartolillos are not all that difficult to make, Kate assures us, just take care the pastry casing doesn't split. Every bite is guaranteed to transport you to sun-drenched summer afternoons in Spain!

Serves 4
400g plain flour
teacup of white wine
teacup of light olive oil
1 cup of créme patissiére, not too sweet
light olive oil for frying
castor sugar

■ Sift flour onto a board or into a large bowl and make a well in the centre. Pour in the white wine and the olive oil. Work the flour into the liquid with your fingers until you have a rather firm dough. Flour varies in absorbency so you may need to add a little oil and wine: the dough should be soft and springy.

■ Roll it out, a portion at a time, about 2.5mm thick. Use a small saucer as a guide to cut out circles, which you will then fill with a dollop of custard, fold into half-moons and seal firmly by dampening and crimping the edges.

■ Have ready a deep-frying pan with hot oil. Fry the bartolillos until golden, turning carefully once. Drain on paper towel and sprinkle with castor sugar. Serve warm if possible. They don't keep well but are delicious when fresh.

Ovocne Knedliky (Strawberry or Other Fruit Dumplings)

At the heart of Czech and Slovak cooking are knedliky — made with bread, with potatoes, with yeasty bread dough or with cottage cheese. They are sweet, they are savoury, they adorn roast pork dishes, they sit in soups. If you've ever tried the sweet version you'll be back wanting more (when your cholesterol count has subsided that is).
Marie Spacek, wife of former radio broadcaster Vladmir Spacek, let us in on the secret of fruit knedliky with yeast dough.

This version makes 50 dumplings, so divide accordingly!
20g fresh yeast
30g granulated sugar
250ml milk, warmed
500g continental flour (any delicatessen will have it, otherwise use half normal flour with half fine semolina flour)
pinch of salt
1 egg yolk
any kind of relatively hard fruit — strawberries, apricots, blueberries, plums (raspberries are an extra-special treat).

Whatever you choose, one per dumpling.

50g cottage or farm cheese

50g icing sugar

50g butter, melted

◼ Mix yeast and sugar and a little of the warm milk. Leave to rise. Sieve flour and add to it the rest of the milk, salt and egg yolk. Add yeast mixture, knead dough and leave for 1 hour in a warm place. Make a long roll of the dough and then cut into pieces the size of a walnut. Press a piece of fruit into each piece of dough. Leave for a further 15 minutes to prove.

◼ Drop into boiling water and cook for approximately 2 minutes, then turn. Cook for another 3 minutes or so. Use a really large saucepan but only put in a few at a time. They need room to move.

◼ Remove from the water, and prick them with a fork to let the steam out. Sprinkle them with the cottage or farm cheese (grated if hard), icing sugar and butter.

Moshe's Blintzes (The Ultimate Comfort Food)

Israel-born TV producer Moshe Rosenzweig knows that when you are feeling sick or miserable there is no better cure than the blintz cure. 'They may take a little time to prepare, but they are easy to eat and very nutritious. Of course, they should be enjoyed with proper hot chocolate.' Once, when Moshe was feeling particularly low, his father rang him all the way from home in Israel to prescribe a hearty dose of blintzes. Luckily Moshe was in Melbourne, near the famed Scheherazade Restaurant in Acland Street and was able to enjoy a huge schnitzel, followed by an hour-long walk, then a plate of these pancakes filled with sweet cheese. It worked.

Makes 12 pancakes

1 cup plain flour

2 large eggs

a teaspoon of melted butter

a pinch of salt

approximately $\frac{2}{3}$ cup milk added to $\frac{1}{3}$ cup water (added until the egg and flour mixture has a runny consistency)

Filling:

1½ cups of curd cheese, ricotta or kosher white cheese

2 handfuls of raisins

sugar to taste

cinnamon (about 1 teaspoon)

1 egg extra, separated

light sour cream to achieve consistency

To prepare the pancakes:

◼ Beat the flour, eggs, melted butter, salt, water and milk until smooth. Heat your frying pan with a little oil. Pour in a small puddle of mixture and turn to coat the pan, pouring off the excess. 'You always throw the first one away,' says Moshe. 'It's just a warm-up.' Fry both sides, one side a little longer than the other, and set aside.

To prepare the filling:

◼ Beat the eggwhite separately. Combine the yolk, cheese, raisins, sugar, cinnamon and fold into the eggwhite. Add a couple of tablespoons of sour cream to bring the mixture to an easy spreading consistency. Fill each pancake, on the well-done side, roll them up and fold in the sides. Return to pan and fry quickly in butter to firm them up.

Colleen's Orange Liqueur

We never thought we'd get this one! In fact its 'Australian importer' (it came originally from France, but more on that in a moment) warns us that she is planning to produce this on a commercial scale, 'so readers beware — I have the rights to this in Australia!' says Colleen Coghlan.

After seventeen years' jealously guarding the secret to 'Colleen's Christmas liqueur', all is finally revealed. The source of *SBS Eating Guide to Melbourne* co-author Colleen Coghlan's little tipple — lovingly presented to friends at Christmas time — is Francoise Fontaine, head of a family Colleen met while living in France back in 1980. Visiting them regularly in their huge home alongside the Seine, in the tiny village of Gommecourt, south-west of Paris, Colleen would be greeted with a glass of their family brew, an aperitif redolent of sweet oranges. Its name is important: *Recette peu couteuse pour la preparation d'un aperitif pas trop degueu*★

Makes 1 litre

the skins of 4 oranges dried and lightly browned in the oven
30 heads of dried camomile
30 sugar cubes (170g)
1 litre dry white wine
1 glass of white spirit (fruit alcohol, 40–45% proof)

Leave all ingredients to macerate for 4 or 5 days in a large jar, then filter and decant into attractive bottles!

'Long after my own supply has run out,' says Colleen who makes this once a year (at Christmas) 'I sometimes discover one of my beribboned bottles tucked away in a friend's cupboard — a lovely surprise.'

★Cheap recipe for a reasonably drinkable aperitif

Barbara Zagar

Barbara's Kasha

Barbara Zagar is one of Slovenia's more exotic exports. She has worked in a number of places around the world as an interpreter and translator, beautician, aromatherapist and homeopath. In Australia she also throws mad, wonderful parties. This dish, served to the great delight of her guests, is from the Alpine regions of her home country where, she says, the millet is cooked in milk and served at weddings as a symbol of fertility. She does warn though that eating kasha 'causes great winds' but it's so delicious that no-one really minds.

Serves 6
1 full cup millet, washed in hot water (buy in health food stores — labelled organic millet seed, hulled)
1 litre milk, boiled and still hot
2 eggs, beaten
5g butter
10g sugar
3 large Granny Smith apples, peeled and chopped
a handful of sultanas
250ml litre cream
good sprinkling vanilla sugar
pinch salt
cinnamon

■ Put washed millet into boiled milk, add salt and let it boil until it starts to thicken but keep stirring as it burns easily. Remove from heat, add butter, well-beaten eggs, apples, sultanas, cream, vanilla sugar, salt and cinnamon, mixing well. Transfer to a buttered baking dish.
■ Place in a preheated 150°C oven and cook until golden brown. When almost ready, lower the heat and cover the dish. Barbara says extravagant people can use foil, she uses newspaper. Serve with cooked fruit — traditionally pitted prunes softened in boiling water.

Malakoff

Another divine, and very simple recipe from Daniela Thorsch — well, actually from her Czech-born mother Mimi. No cooking!

Serves 8–10
equal parts brandy and milk, as required
4 packets Italian sponge biscuits (Savoiardi or Pishkoten)

Chocolate cream:
250g melted cooking chocolate
250g unsalted butter
1 egg yolk
a splash of cherry brandy
a splash of coffee
sugar to taste

■ Combine brandy and milk and dip the biscuits quickly into mixture but avoid getting them soggy. You may find it easier to sprinkle mixture over biscuits.

■ Beat together ingredients for chocolate cream until light and fluffy. On a flat tray put one layer of biscuits and cover with chocolate cream and continue to make about three layers. Refrigerate and serve with whipped cream sprinkled with chocolate.

Falooda (Iranian Frozen Noodles)

This rosewater-flavoured frozen noodle dessert is what homesick Iranians hanker for when the weather is warm and balmy. It's served throughout Iran though our recipe is from the capital Teheran, courtesy of chef Jimmy Ghafari.

Serves 6
2 litres hot water
300g icing sugar
250ml rosewater
1 packet rice noodles
lemon juice

■ Put the water in a large pan to boil and add the icing sugar and rosewater. Stir well and boil for 30 minutes. Allow the mixture to cool before putting it into the freezer.

■ Cook the rice noodles and store them in cold water in the fridge.

■ Before the rosewater mixture becomes icy, add the noodles and then allow the lot to freeze completely.

■ To serve, scratch a spoon across the icy surface so you get a granita-like substance. Keep shaving the ice and place in glasses.

Add a teaspoon of fresh lemon juice to each glass just before serving.

Icelandic Ice-cream

Even in cold icy countries, ice-cream is still a favourite. This family recipe comes from salmon expert, Iceland-born Sofia Oddsson.

Serves 6
2 eggs
2 egg yolks
75g sugar
2½ cups thick cream
1 tablespoon dessicated coconut
2 tablespoons crushed nuts
1 tablespoon grated chocolate
juice from 1 lemon

■ With an electric mixer, whisk together eggs, egg yolks and sugar until light and frothy. Carefully add the cream to the mixture and stir in gently.

■ Heat the coconut slightly in a dry pan, being careful not to burn it. Set aside and cool before adding to the mixture. Add the nuts, chocolate and lemon juice and stir well. Put into freezer trays and chill overnight .

Iranian Rosewater Ice-cream

This recipe had to be prised from Iranian chef Jimmy Ghafari — it was passed on to him by his grandfather who was also a professional in the kitchen. He has given us a short-cut (using pre-bought vanilla ice-cream). Starting from scratch, he says, would be too time-consuming. The result is a creamy, delicately flavoured ice-cream with a warm butterscotch colour. The extra-creamy version (which takes two days to prepare) is much-prized by Iranians though Jimmy says the Australian palate seems to prefer the basic recipe.

Serves 1 large tub (about 12)
4 litres good-quality vanilla ice-cream
250ml rosewater
300g icing sugar
5g saffron strands
2 tablespoons hot water

■ Take the ice-cream from its container and put into a large mixing bowl. With a large wooden spoon, stir the ice-cream for 30 minutes until it becomes thick and viscous.
■ Use a mortar and pestle to crush the saffron strands until they form a powder. Put a teaspoon of rosewater and a teaspoon of icing sugar into a glass then add two tablespoons of hot water. Mix well and add to powdered saffron. Then pour the liquid into the ice-cream. Stir again with a large spoon so it's well mixed in. Pour into freezer trays and allow to set for a few hours before serving.

To make a creamier version, add this next step, but you need to do this a day earlier.

250ml cream
10 tablespoons rosewater
100g icing sugar

■ Mix these together well and freeze. The next day, chop the frozen cream mixture into small squares and stir through the ice-cream. Pour into freezer trays as before.

Baked Crumble Cheesecake

Elizabeth Marchand has spent her life surrounded by cows. She grew up in Switzerland in a small village and learnt to milk from an early age. Later she married and emigrated to Tasmania where her cheesemaker husband Frank spent a couple of years working for a large factory before the pair decided to buy a farm and set up their own cheesemaking factory — Heidi Farm Cheese. It's no surprise that all Elizabeth's recipes require cheese of some sort. With this recipe make sure you use the right sized pan, otherwise ingredients spill over the top as it cooks.

Serves 12
Pastry:
250g butter
125g sugar
1 teaspoon vanilla essence
2 egg yolks
375g plain flour
1 tablespoon baking powder

Filling
2 cooking apples
1kg cottage cheese (if skim milk cheese, add 100ml cream)
250g sugar
2 teaspoons vanilla sugar
grated peel and juice of one lemon
2 eggs
2 eggwhites (beaten separately to form peaks)
50g cornflour

To prepare the pastry:
■ Cream butter and sugar, then add vanilla essence and egg yolks, and beat well. Sift dry ingredients into butter mix and combine to

make a soft pastry. Cool in fridge for 1 hour. Reserve a quarter of the pastry for the crumble. With the rest, line a 26cm springform pan.

▦ Peel and slice the apples, arrange on the pastry and keep in the fridge while preparing the filling.

To prepare the filling:

▦ Combine all the ingredients for filling and gently beat until smooth. Pour into the pastry-lined tin, crumble the remaining dough on top. Bake at 180°C for 90 minutes. Let the cake cool in the tin completely. Dust with icing sugar.

Mrs Anne Oates

Mrs Anne Oates's Pavlova

Mrs Anne Oates is one of the stalwarts of that great Australian institution, the Country Women's Association. Not only has it united women isolated in the bush, whether in country towns or on farms, but the association has also set standards for excellence in cooking, including updating a recipe book, first published in 1937, which covers everything from good plain bush fare to the rather more exotic and even unusual hints such as a 'Method for Tanning Sheepskins'. Each rural region has a president and other office-bearers, including a Group Cookery Officer who will judge bake-offs and is often able to adjudicate on cooking matters. In the Central West region of New South Wales, Mrs Anne Oates is the Group Cookery Officer. Asked for a recipe, she chose pavlova — the light meringue dessert developed in Australia.

Serves 6

4 eggwhites
pinch salt
1¼ cups castor sugar
1 level tablespoon cornflour
1 dessertspoon vinegar
1 teaspoon vanilla

▦ Place eggwhites in a clean, dry, warm basin, add a good pinch of salt. Beat eggwhites until mixture stands in peaks, add half the sugar, one dessertspoonful at a time. It should be thick and glossy. Fold in remainder of sugar, then cornflour. Quickly add vinegar and vanilla. Put onto well-greased baking paper, dusted with equal amounts of icing sugar and cornflour and bake in a slow 150°C oven for approximately 1¼ hours. Serve topped with whipped cream and fruit salad, passionfruit or bananas.

Sweet Potato Pecan Pie

This recipe, adapted from Louisiana chef Paul Prudhomme by Sydney-based Alabama-born chef Forrest Moebes, looks long but it's dead easy to assemble and so impressive — the sweet potato giving a lighter filling than the traditional caramel. Note that you need to rest the dough for at least one hour. The pie keeps for a week in the fridge — if you have the willpower to wait that long!

Pastry:

3 tablespoons unsalted butter, softened

2 tablespoons sugar

pinch salt

1 egg, beaten

1 cup plain flour

Sweet potato filling:

2–3 sweet potatoes, baked (1 cup cooked pulp)

¼ cup brown sugar

1 egg, beaten

2 tablespoons sugar

1 tablespoon cream

1 tablespoon butter

1 tablespoon vanilla extract

pinch of salt

½ tablespoon cinnamon

pinch allspice

pinch nutmeg

Pecan filling:

¾ cup sugar

¾ cup dark corn syrup

2 eggs

2 tablespoons unsalted butter,

pinch salt

pinch cinnamon

2 teaspoons vanilla extract

¾ cup pecan halves

To prepare the pastry:

▪ With an electric mixer, beat butter, sugar and salt on high speed until creamy. Add egg and beat 30 seconds. Add milk and beat on high speed for 2 minutes. Add flour and mix until just blended.

▪ Wrap the dough in plastic wrap and rest in the refrigerator for at least an hour (overnight is even better).

▪ On a floured surface, roll out to about 5mm thickness. Place in a greased 20cm cake pan and press firmly out to the edges. Refrigerate for 15 minutes.

To prepare the sweet potato filling:

▪ Combine all ingredients in a mixing bowl, beat on high speed until batter is smooth — about 2 minutes. Do not overbeat.

To prepare the pecan mixture:

▪ In a mixing bowl, combine all ingredients except pecans. Mix on low speed till syrup is opaque (about 1 minute). Gently stir in pecans.

To assemble:

▪ Spoon sweet potato filling into pie shell, pour pecan mixture on top and bake in 160°C oven for 1¾ hours until a knife inserted in the centre comes out clean. Serve with fresh whipped cream.

Victor's Pudina Tal-Hobz (Maltese Bread Pudding)

Pudina Tal-Hobz is one of the national dishes of Malta and according to Melbourne-based broadcaster Victor Aquilina, it's easy to make and doesn't require any special ingredients. The taste, he says proudly, is out of this world.

Serves 8

1 loaf stale white bread

sugar — ⅓ the weight of the bread

220g margarine
2 tablespoons cocoa or drinking chocolate powder
dried fruit (the more the better)
mixed nuts (the more the tastier)
fresh orange, lemon and mandarin peel (chopped)
½ cup fresh or evaporated milk
1 teaspoon vanilla essence
tot of brandy
1 teaspoon baking powder
2 eggs

■ Soak bread in water, then drain completely. Add sugar and mash, then add margarine and mix thoroughly. Add cocoa, dried fruit, mixed nuts, peel, milk, vanilla essence and brandy, then mix. Add baking powder and mix, then finally blend the two eggs into mixture. Pour into a deep-greased dish and bake in medium–hot 200°C oven for approximately 2 hours or until sides begin to contract and brown. Serve by itself. Kulu bl-aptit! (bon appetit in Maltese).

Sticky Rice and Thai Custard

Thanks to Thai chef Anne Sanpasiri — a recipe for one of Thailand's most famous sweets. Remember to leave time for the rice to soak.

Serves 12
1kg sticky rice, soaked in water overnight
6 eggs
2 cans coconut milk (in total)
500g palm sugar
1 tablespoon salt
3½ teaspoons sugar

■ Drain the rice and steam in a large steamer for 25 minutes. Place in a large mixing bowl and set aside.

Custard:
■ Beat eggs in blender, add coconut milk and mix. (Anne says to measure the egg mixture and to use an equal amount of coconut milk.) Add the palm sugar and blend mixture well. Put the bowl in a steamer and steam for 25 to 30 minutes.
■ Heat one can of coconut milk in a saucepan — do not boil. Add salt and sugar and simmer until sugar has dissolved. Pour the mixture onto the rice a little at a time, gradually mixing it through until it has all been absorbed.

To serve:
■ Put the sticky rice on a plate, cut the Thai custard into thin slices and place on top of sticky rice.

Mango Lassi

As any traveller to India will tell you, lassi is the drink to follow a spicy meal. This Queensland version features that magic fruit, mango. 'Very refreshing drink in summer,' says Inder Mehandiratta of the Magic of India restaurant in Noosaville, Queensland. He's certainly in the right part of the world to enjoy this almost all year round.

Serves 2
¼ cup natural yoghurt
50ml mango pulp
1 tablespoon sugar (or to taste)
100ml milk
dash of rosewater

■ Blend all the ingredients together for a few minutes and serve in a glass on ice.

Biscuits and slices

Swiss Hazelnut Horseshoes

Chocolatiers Paul and Beatrice Haefliger are perfectionists and two of the most dedicated craftspeople you'd ever meet. Not only do they specialise in chocolate, they also bake the finest pastry and biscuits. While there is no doubt their smooth Swiss chocolate truffles are utter heaven, it's not all that simple to reproduce them in a domestic kitchen without years of training in the chocolatier's craft. But delicate little hazelnut horseshoe biscuits we can handle. Beatrice learned to bake biscuits during her apprenticeship in her native Switzerland. 'Since then I have changed the recipes a bit,' she admits, 'but sometimes something will just give you an idea'.
You will need a piping bag for this recipe.

Makes 15
80g butter
50g icing sugar
25g beaten egg
60g ground hazelnuts
lemon
cinnamon
80g plain flour
seedless jam of your choice
dark chocolate

▨ Cream the butter and sugar, add the egg, ground hazelnuts, spices and flour, mix well. Using a piping bag with a medium-sized star nozzle squeeze out long snakes of dough. Cut them every 7cm and shape into a horseshoe with your thumb and forefingers. Dust a baking tray with flour taking care NOT to grease it and bake for about 15 minutes in a 200°C oven. (Flour is all you need as the oil from the nuts will come out with the heat.)

When they are cool, stick two horseshoes together with a very thin layer of seedless jam and dip the ends in melted dark chocolate.

Wiener Waffles

These delicate squares are known as 'Viennese waffles' but are actually like a sweet almond shortbread. Another recipe from Paul and Beatrice Haefliger.

Makes about 24
150g butter
150g almond paste (not marzipan)
150g flour
thick apricot jam flavoured with a little rum
icing sugar for dredging

▨ Mix the butter, almond paste and flour to a smooth dough, then roll out into two even squares about 2.5mm thick. Bake at 180°C for about 10 to 15 minutes on two 21cm x 24cm trays. When cold, turn one out and cover the one in the pan with a thick layer of apricot jam. Place the other square on top. Leave the cake overnight and the following day cut into squares, 3cm x 3cm, with a very good, thin, sharp knife. Dredge with icing sugar.

Persian New Year's Biscuits

New Year (Noruz) in Iran is a time for eating sweets. In fact, any time that families get together there will be sweets, candied fruits and jams, fresh fruit, nuts and plenty of tea to enjoy together. Sepi Zanganeh is an accomplished home-baker (she says that as a teenager she preferred baking to going out

Sepi Zanganeh and her daughters

Cream the butter and icing sugar with the cardamom. Add the chickpea flour and beat until it forms a ball. Take a piece the size of a hazelnut and roll between your hands until it forms a ball. Place on a greased baking tray, make a small round incision in the top of each biscuit (using one side of a piping bag nozzle for example), decorate each one with a pistachio sliver and bake in a moderate 180°C oven for about 20 minutes.

Gerdouee (Walnut Drops)

6 egg yolks
6 heaped tablespoons sifted icing sugar
2 teaspoons vanilla essence
300g walnut pieces
pistachio slivers for decoration

Beat the egg yolks with the sugar and vanilla for 5 minutes on a high setting. Add the walnut pieces and mix very gently by hand. Line a baking tray with baking paper and carefully drop teaspoonfuls of the mixture onto the tray. Decorate with pistachio slivers. Bake in a slow 150°C oven (130°C in a fan-forced oven) for 10 to 12 minutes.

disco dancing!). These days she supplies many Persian-Australian families with exquisitely delicate biscuits for all their tea parties and celebrations. She generously parted with these recipes. They seem simple, and they are, but do not overwork the dough.

Nokhodchi (Yellow Flour Shortbread)

125g clarified butter or ghee
125g sifted icing sugar
1 teaspoon ground cardamom
250g yellow roasted chickpea flour (available in some Middle Eastern grocery stores although Sepi makes her own by roasting yellow chickpeas and grinding them)
pistachio slivers for decoration

Granny Erskine's Shortbread

'It's not real shortbread', Granny Erskine used to say in her lilting Scots burr (meaning that it's not the 'authentic' butter, flour and sugar recipe). 'But it's divine,' says her granddaughter Lindsay Cullens, whose mother and godmother still bake Granny's recipe regularly. Granny Erskine lived in the town of Bridge-of-Allen near Stirling, in Scotland (William Wallace country), and as a child Lindsay would spend every school holiday there.

The Perfect Cup of Tea — Indian-style

Your views on the perfect cup of tea depend on where you've been brought up, and what you're used to. Darjeeling-born Mary Dorjee is from the heart of Indian tea country.

'Our Dad makes the perfect cup of tea —' she says, 'the main ingredients of which are a lot of love and kindness. With the same admiration, as a little girl, I watched this wondrous, yet so humble achiever as he carried out the simple ritual of brewing his "champagne" of all teas.'

Makes 6 cups
(You may alter the quantity of the tea and milk to suit your taste)
6 cups water
2 tablespoons loose Darjeeling tea
¾ cup of milk
sugar to your taste

■ In a deep pan, boil 6 cups of water. When it reaches a rolling boil, add the tea. Turn to simmer, cover and let it brew for about 2 minutes.

■ In a separate pan boil the milk. Strain the tea into the milk. Take a cup and dip it into the tea, lifting it about 1.5cm above the pan, then pouring it back in. Repeat this about 4 or 5 times until the tea is frothy. Pour into individual cups. Add sugar as required and serve with a 'cheer'.

Moroccan Mint Tea

It's known as the 'gift of Allah' and it's considered polite for guests to drink not one but three glasses with their host. Mint tea is an absolute staple right through North Africa, a real thirst-quencher in the hot arid countries bordering the great Sahara. It's served during business negotiations in all the souks or marketplaces — in fact we're sure it's impossible to buy a carpet without the requisite three cups!

Moroccan mint tea is served with great ceremony, usually from a brass tray with small, ornate glasses instead of cups. One glass of tea is poured, then poured back into the pot to distribute the sugar evenly, this process is repeated. The pot is held high while pouring to aerate the tea.

These instructions come from Sydney restaurateur Hassan M'Souli.

Serves 4

2–3 teaspoons green tea (Formosa Gunpowder green tea is relatively easy to find)
1 bunch fresh short mint
boiling water
sugar to taste

Measure 2–3 teaspoons green tea into the pot. Pour in boiling water then immediately strain well to clean the tea. Pour on more boiling water and place the pot back on the stove or fire and allow to steep for 1 minute. Wash the mint well and pack tightly into the pot. Place the pot back onto the heat for a few minutes more.

Remove from the heat and add sugar to the pot to taste. Pour out one glass of tea, then return it to the pot. Repeat this process. It is now ready to enjoy. When serving, serve in glasses and pour with pot held high to aerate the tea.

Granny baked every day: scones, pancakes, baps with jam, kipper and boiled eggs for high tea and for lunch, a three-course meal, complete with such delicacies as haggis and tongue and stodgy veg like 'bashed neeps' (mashed turnips, in translation). Lindsay and her family migrated to Australia in 1969 and Granny Erskine died many years ago, but all those lovely memories remain.

Lindsay's mother always brings a batch of shortbread when she comes to visit and the minute her visit is announced Lindsay's friends are all on the doorstep begging for a slice. It's real melt-in-the-mouth stuff and very fattening.

Makes about 20 slices
250g butter
60g lard
60g margarine
125g cornflour
250g plain flour
60g self-raising flour
125g castor sugar

▪ Beat it all together in mixer until creamy. Place in three round tins about 1.25cm high. Put in 150°C oven for an hour, 95°C for 20 minutes, then turn oven off and leave in for 20 minutes. Dredge with castor sugar. Cut, serve and enjoy.

Mira's Ricotta Slice

Mira Valcich is a great baker and pastry cook — the perfect complement to her husband Dennis who prefers to tackle the savoury dishes at home. Dennis is a proud Croatian-born Australian who has written the first English-language Croatian cookbook —

featuring heaps of recipes from his and Mira's combined repertoires. This is one of our favourites.

Makes about 24 slices
Sponge:
3 eggs, separated
180g castor sugar
4 soup spoons boiling water
180g flour
½ teaspoon baking powder
icing sugar for dusting

Filling:
600g fresh ricotta
grated lemon rind
1 cup whipped cream
4 teaspoons castor sugar

▪ Preheat oven to 200°C. Beat egg yolks with sugar until they start to foam, gently add water and sifted flour and baking powder, alternating between the two, until it has all been incorporated.
▪ Beat the eggwhites to stiff peaks, fold into the mix. Spread on a shallow, greased 30cm x 20cm tray and bake for 15 to 20 minutes. When cool, slice lengthways into two halves.
▪ Strain the ricotta, mix with lemon rind, cream and sugar and spread on sponge. Cover with second layer and refrigerate for a few hours. Cut into small slices and dust with icing sugar.

Annetta Giuliani's Biscuits

While SBS videotape maintenance whiz Michael Dwyer sounds like he should be imparting Irish gems, his background is

Swiss/Italian and this recipe is from his grandmother Annetta Giuliani, who's from the southern Swiss town of Poschiavo. Michael swears they're fairly easy and says they're great with coffee.

Makes 36
170g butter
1kg self-raising flour
pinch of salt
5 large eggs
500g castor sugar

Rub the butter into the flour and salt and work the mixture until it is the consistency of fine breadcrumbs.

Beat the eggs and gradually add the sugar until mixture is thick and creamy. Add the flour mixture and mix together to a stiff dough. Roll into long snake shapes on a lightly floured board, working a little of the flour into the dough.

Shape small biscuits into knots and twists and rings. Bake in a moderate oven at 180°C for 15 minutes or until golden.

Dates in Alice Springs

Swiss-born Jim and Trudi Leudi have lived in Alice Springs since the late 1960s. He worked as an electrician for eighteen years before buying the Mecca Date Farm on the outskirts of town. The cool green shade of the small oasis set against the red desert sand conjured visions of a gentle retirement, says Trudi, but nothing could be further from the truth. The bunches of orange dates bewitched Jim who started planting new varieties of trees and even began a new plantation 70 kilometres south-east of

Alice Springs. And with tourists from around the world wanting a closer look at their gentle part of the world, Trudi started baking cakes and biscuits using some of the many varieties of dates grown.

The following Swiss recipes are traditional fare at Christmas when dates are one of the treats of the season. Date biscuits are popular, especially as the Swiss don't have Christmas cake but spend many days making beautiful seasonal biscuits.

Trudi always uses fresh dates for her recipes (well, wouldn't you if you had a plantation?). For those using the dried variety she recommends softening them in a little hot water and stand them aside for an hour or so before using.

Date Macaroons
Makes about 50
3 eggwhites
75g sugar
75g sugar
150g dates, chopped
150g almonds, slivered

Beat eggwhites until stiff, add first 75g sugar and keep beating until the mixture is shiny. Add second 75g sugar, dates and almonds and gently mix in.

With 2 teaspoons, place small amounts of the mixture on greased slide.

Bake at 180°C in the middle of the oven until lightly browned.

Cool biscuits and store in airtight container.

Date Crispies
Makes 32
100g margarine
65g brown sugar

280g dates, seeded and chopped into quarters
120g Rice Bubbles

■ Melt the margarine and brown sugar in a saucepan over low heat. Add the dates and stir until soft. Remove from heat and add Rice Bubbles.

■ Spread mixture into greased square or rectangular tin to a height of 2cm. Press down and smooth mixture. Cool then cut into fingers.

Date Confection
Makes 30

250g fresh dates (Medjool variety the best)
80g pink marzipan
80g green marzipan (use a tiny drop of food colouring)
almonds, halved

■ Remove seed from dates. Roll marzipan in your hands into thin snakes. Fill opening with marzipan and decorate with half an almond.

Otto's Coconut Macaroons

Otto Kuhn was a renowned Viennese pastry chef who set up one of the first 'Continental' cake shops in Bondi after he'd emigrated in 1939. His granddaughter Vivian remembers a delicious spread greeting the visiting extended family every Sunday afternoon. 'They hated not having enough to feed people twice over, so Opa (grandfather) and Oma (grandmother) would bake for the next Ice Age,' she laughs. One of the staples were these light macaroons.

Makes about 30
4 eggwhites
250g castor sugar
180g desiccated coconut

1 tablespoon plain flour (or matzo meal)
1 tablespoon cocoa (optional)

■ Beat eggwhites in large saucepan over a very low heat and gradually add the sugar — this should take about 5 minutes. Remove from stove.

■ Add the coconut, flour and cocoa and stir gently to combine the ingredients. Let stand for a few minutes.

■ With a spoon, drop small amounts onto greased, floured baking trays. Bake in a very slow 90°C oven until cooked, about 12 minutes.

Frappe/Crostoli/Chiacchiere

It's deep-fried, sweet pasta and it has all sorts of names, depending on where you find it in Italy. In Parma it's known as 'chiacchiere croccanti', meaning 'crunchy chatter' which probably refers to the sound it makes when you eat it. Rod Webb who gave us this recipe is a well-travelled TV exec who learned how to make chiacchiere as the result of a romance with a Parma girl he met in Germany. (He didn't learn much German but he did learn about Italian cooking!)

This delicacy is enjoyed during Lent. Each region has its own recipe and shape for the dish. His *amore's* mother was responsible for this recipe and says Rod, 'for changing the way I prepare and enjoy food'.

Makes 50
200g hard wheat flour ('continental' flour)
50g rice flour
20g unsalted butter
20g castor sugar

a pinch of salt
1 egg plus 1 egg yolk
a little warmed rum or grappa
icing sugar

■ Combine the above, except the alcohol, in a food processor. Add warmed rum or grappa to bring the dough to the right consistency for rolling, either through a pasta roller or with a rolling pin. Roll the dough to the thinnest setting on the pasta roller and cut it into rectangles about 10cm x 7cm. Make three parallel scores about 4cm long in the centre of the rectangle, in the direction of the longest dimension. Take one corner of the rectangle and draw it through the nearest score and repeat the process with the diametrically opposite corner, drawing it through its nearest score. Deep-fry in hot peanut oil until the shapes puff up considerably and turn a golden colour. Remove excess oil with kitchen paper and dust with icing sugar when dry and cool.

Tarte de Amendoa
(Portuguese Almond Tart)

'Simple and yummy,' says Fatima Barroso, who knows a fair bit about simple and yummy Portuguese sweets. (She shares her catering kitchen with a brilliant Portuguese pastrycook whose custard tarts are a dream. But that's another story.) Fatima chose this very typical tart as an uncomplicated way for others to enjoy the joys of Portuguese baking.

Serves 6
Pastry:
175g flour
90g softened butter

1 egg
90g castor sugar
pinch of salt

Filling:
350g sugar
150ml water
150g ground almonds
3 eggs
3 extra egg yolks

■ Mix the flour rapidly with the other pastry ingredients and spread over the bottom of a buttered tart tin. Bake blind for about 15 minutes at 200°C.
■ Boil the sugar with water for 5 minutes. Whisk the eggs and the yolks in a bowl. Pour in the cooled sugar syrup. Mix the almonds into the filling and pour over pastry base. Bake for about 20 minutes at 180°C or until the almond mix is set.

The Schenker Family Cookbook

Emma Schenker has cooked all her life. She remembers preparing the family meals from the age of about ten, as both her parents, Mitzi and Otto Kuhn, owned and worked in the Marie K, one of the first continental cake shops in the Sydney suburb of Bondi. The Kuhns had emigrated to Australia in 1939 from Vienna where they had run *konditoreien* — typically Viennese cafes dedicated to coffee and sumptuous cakes.

As a young man, Otto had travelled around Europe learning a different skill or technique in each town or city. In Australia he and his wife produced mainly cupcakes, lamingtons and jam tarts to begin with, gradually introducing more exotic European specialties as their customers became more adventurous and sophisticated.

At home, the pair were always prepared to entertain any unexpected visitor ('or army,' laughs granddaughter Vivian, who well remembers groaning tables every Sunday afternoon) with a staggering variety of cakes, biscuits and yeast pastries filled with apples, walnuts, cream cheese and the dense plum concentrate called povidl.

Towards the end of her mother's life, Emma sat her down and went through the recipes of a lifetime. 'She had so very many recipes and I wanted to write them down to pass on to my own daughters Susie and Vivian', she recalls. Days later, Emma had amassed a huge number of recipes, intriguingly, most of them for cake and sweets and all very central European in flavour.

'The reason was simple,' she explains. 'My mother had also started to cook very young and just seemed to *know* recipes for meals without ever referring to a book. But she had one basic rule — whatever you do, don't muck around with cake. The proportions have to be exact and everything has to be weighed properly.'

Emma then bought two thick, bound address books and painstakingly wrote out her mother's recipes for her daughters. On the first page she inscribed: '20th August, 1988 … Long may you cook and enjoy, Love Ma' and then followed pages of family riches including Mitzi's chocolate parisier cream, used on or in cakes, a rich hazelnut torte, no-fuss gefilte fish, Auntie Edith's guglehuph and Cousin-Yael-in-Israel's poppyseed cake.

It's the little annotations and quirky lines that make the book special and titles that say it all such as 'Chocolate Cake — No Nuts — Mitzi'. There are also some recipes with no method at all — just the ingredients. Perhaps

Three generations of the Schenker family: from left Sophie, Vivian, Alice, Susie and Emma

Mitzi felt that any descendant of hers would know what to do instinctively!

But it wasn't all just sitting around the kitchen table and taking notes. Emma asked her mother to demonstrate some of her recipes again so she could see those important techniques that are never written down. Her labours run to well over a hundred closely written pages, the recipes much appreciated by her daughters.

'I'm making the same things my grandparents and even their grandparents did before them,' says Vivian. 'There's a nice sense of continuity.'

See recipes for: Mitzi's chocolate cake, Israeli poppyseed cake, Otto's coconut macaroons and gefilte fish.

Cakes and sweet breads

Bara Brith (Welsh Fruit Bread)

Here's a really easy and delicious speckled fruit bread, courtesy of Welsh-born Alice Rees.

Serves 10

500g mixed fruit
250g brown sugar
1½ cups cold tea
400g self-raising flour
1 egg
1½ teaspoons mixed spice

Place the mixed fruit and the sugar in a bowl and allow to stand overnight in cold tea. The following day mix in the flour, egg and mixed spice. Grease a couple of standard loaf tins and cook for 1 hour at 150°C. Eat buttered.

Ludmilla's Babka (Russian Easter Bread)

Australian-born Alex Seneta's mother Ludmilla is from Leningrad. Part of the family tradition is to eat babka (Easter bread) every year at Easter, by the old (orthodox) calendar — in fact, Alex has eaten it for the last 35 years. She remembers that, as a child, she used to creep around the house when the bread was being baked, as it falls very easily. 'We'd spend Easter Saturday on tiptoe in the kitchen, in case it caved in,' says Alex. It never has so far.

Serves 8

1 cup milk
1kg plain flour
2 teaspoons sugar
100g yeast (active yeast from blocks sold in delicatessens)
10 egg yolks

2 whole eggs (this and the yolks above from medium to small eggs)
½ teaspoon salt
1 scant cup sugar, extra
1 scant cup melted margarine
few drops vanilla essence
grated rind 1 lemon
few raisins

▪ Scald the milk. Remove from the stove and allow to cool to body temperature. Add ⅓ cup plain flour to the milk and beat thoroughly.

▪ Dissolve the 2 teaspoons of sugar in ½ cup lukewarm water. Add yeast and mash with fork. Combine this mixture with the milk-flour paste and leave to rise in a warm place until light and bubbly.

▪ Beat egg yolks, eggs and salt, adding 1 cup sugar gradually. Add melted margarine (slowly), vanilla and grated lemon rind. Combine this mixture with the sponge mixture.

▪ Stir in remaining flour to make a soft dough. (You may have some flour left over.) Let dough stand in a warm place to rise. To encourage this, the bowl containing the dough may be placed in another containing hot water. Once it has risen, add raisins and knead lightly in bowl. Cover and let it rise again.

▪ Divide into portions — probably two — and place into well-buttered deep round tins. Let rise again. Brush with milk, water or eggwhite or a combination of these. Allow to rise until double the size. Preheat oven to 180°C. Place babka in oven for about 15 minutes (depending on the size of the cake tins) and then finish off at 170°C.

▪ The moderately high temperature at first puffs up the babka and ensures a firm crust, then the lower temperature allows cooking through. Remember that sweet dough burns easily. Once the bread is in the oven, don't open the door, at least for the first part of the cooking time. Babka can be iced or left glazed.

Cloutie Dumpling

For a taste of the real Scotland, and nothing could be more Scottish, here's Mairi McIntosh's recipe for the kind of comfort food most of us only ever dream about. We've seen cloutie dumpling made at Havelock Meats, a tiny Scottish butchery in the Sydney seaside suburb of Coogee. They call it simply 'Cloutie dump'.

Serves 8–10

500g plain flour
500g suet (Mairi often uses suet mix and suggests using margarine or butter if suet is unavailable)
350g sugar
250g raisins
250g currants
2 level teaspoons cinnamon
2 level teaspoons ginger
2 level teaspoons mixed spice
2 dessertspoons marmalade
2 dessertspoons golden syrup
2 level teaspoons baking soda dissolved in a little milk (say 2 tablespoons)
buttermilk (or plain milk) to mix
1 large piece cotton or linen cloth

■ Mix all ingredients in basin with buttermilk or milk to a dryish consistency. Wet cloth in boiling water and leave for a few minutes. Lift out with some tongs and allow excess water to drain off. Lay cloth out and sprinkle with a thin layer of flour to form a seal.

■ Add the mixture, draw up the edges and tie up with some string, leaving a little room for expansion.

■ Bring a large saucepan of water to the boil and put a plate into the bottom of it. Add the dumpling. Bring to simmering point, cover and cook for 4 to 4½ hours, adding water as needed — it should be about halfway up the side.

■ To turn out the dumpling and serve, fill a basin with cold water and have ready a bowl that the dumpling will fit into neatly. First dip the dumpling into cold water for a second only — this prevents it sticking to the cloth. Place the dumpling in the bowl and loosen the string. Open out the cloth and hang it over the sides of the bowl. Place a heated serving dish over the bowl, invert it and remove the cloth carefully. Dry off in the oven or in front of a fire (a good winter thing to do and the wonderful aroma fills the house). Sprinkle with some castor sugar and eat hot with cream or custard.

Sour Cream Scones

This is translator Kate Johnson's variation on her Scots grandmother's original. 'They're good with all the usual things,' says Kate, 'butter, jams, marmalades etc, but a nice farm honey really does them proud.'

Makes 12

1 pound self-raising flour
a generous teaspoonful of cooking salt
1 300g tub of light sour cream
a little cold water

■ Stir the salt into the flour, then make a well in it and pour in the sour cream and half a cup of water. Stir, working in the flour and adding a little more water if you need it, until you have a sticky-looking dough, which has come away from the sides of the bowl. Don't overwork it. Flour it over so you can handle it comfortably and divide into three portions. Pat these out into circles, don't hit them with a rolling pin but use your hands — and cut the circles into quarters. Place on a greased baking sheet and bake in a fairly brisk oven (about 200–220°C) until very lightly browned on the top and deliciously fluffy inside.

Irish Barmbrack (Matchmaking Bread)

And it works! Where else but in Ireland would you find such a charming story attached to this delicious sweet loaf studded with sultanas, currants and mixed peel and fragrant with cinnamon and nutmeg? If it's served as part of Halloween celebrations, barmbrack is baked with a gold ring in the mixture. Legend has it that the person who finds the ring will be married before the year is out. Maeve discovered the truth to the tale during a year living in Ireland — with some engineering on the part of friends Monica and John, she found a ring in her slice of Barmbrack … and married handsome Ben just over a year later!

Serves 6–8

500g flour
2 teaspoons ground cinnamon
2 teaspoons ground nutmeg
pinch salt
60g butter
20g yeast
2 tablespoons sugar
300ml milk, warmed
2 eggs
250g sultanas
250g currants
120g mixed peel
beaten egg for glaze
1 gold ring

■ Stir the flour together with spices and salt, then rub in the butter until mixture resembles breadcrumbs. Cream yeast with half the sugar and a little of the milk. Mix the rest of the sugar into the flour and add the remainder of the milk, the eggs and yeast mixture. Mix well. Knead in the sultanas, currants and mixed peel, then add gold ring to dough and place in a buttered loaf tin.

■ Cover with a damp tea towel and leave in a warm place until it has doubled in size (about 1 hour). Brush top with beaten egg and bake in the top of 200°C oven for 1 hour. Test with a skewer — the bread is cooked if it comes out dry. Good luck!

Mrs Joy Press's Scones

Joy Press is an amazing woman. Like many country women, she's a whizz in the kitchen and can also wield a chainsaw, drive a tractor, dip sheep, ride horses and motorbikes and class wool. She's a mother and grandmother, president of the local Country Women's Association and on top of that, makes fabulous scones. Scones are essential in the bush, she says, as you always seem to run out of bread and the nearest shop is a 100 kilometres away. She learned to cook at the age of twelve and

Mrs Joy Press

minutes until scones are golden brown. Serve with cream and jam — homemade blackberry jam is Mrs Press's choice.

◼ Tip: Mrs Press likes her tray to be hot so the scones start rising even before you put them into the oven.

reckons she's turned out thousands of scones over the years — her record is 65 dozen over three days.

Marilena's Savarin (Yeast Cake)

Marilena Coutinho is second-generation Italian, married to Jose (of Portuguese background). They both work with her father, the King of Prosciutto in Adelaide — Tony Marino — so a love of food is really in her genes! 'We love eating and I've grown up knowing what makes good food and how to put it together,' she explains. 'It's an absolute passion but with three children it's hard to find the time.' From Northern Italy, this recipe is quick and easy to make.

Makes 1 dozen
2 cups self-raising flour
30g butter
a sprinkling of castor sugar
¾ cup of milk (you can use half cream/half milk; half buttermilk/half milk for a richer flavour and denser texture or you can beat an egg and add the remainder of milk to make ¾ of a cup)

◼ Rub the butter into the flour until it resembles fine breadcrumbs. Add the milk and with your hands, mix through until mixture is soft but not sticky — add more flour if necessary. Turn onto a floured board or table and knead until smooth then cut into rounds with a scone cutter. Mrs Press says you can cut the mixture into rectangles if desired. Place on greased tray.

◼ Glaze top with milk and cook in a very hot oven (over 200°C – 220°C) for 12 to 15

Serves 8–10
Cake:
15g dry yeast
8 tablespoons warm milk
300g plain flour
4 eggs, beaten
½ teaspoon salt
1 tablespoon sugar
150g soft butter/ margarine

Syrup:
500ml water
200g sugar
5 tablespoons Galliano

To prepare cake:
◼ Dissolve yeast in milk, stirring gently. Sieve flour in bowl then add yeast mixture. Add

Caramel!

When it comes to the gentle art of coffee and cake, Ian Bersten is an authority. As a coffee importer and the author of *Coffee Sinks, Tea Floats*, the definitive book on those indispensable beverages, he has definite views on which cake works best with coffee. 'Take any cake baked with nuts,' he says, 'especially fresh crunchy walnuts or roasted hazelnuts, finely ground. The most important part is the icing. It should be made caramel in flavour with a dash of dark rum and a couple of teaspoons of strong espresso coffee, then topped with a couple of tablespoons of roasted hazelnut or walnut pieces to match the nuts in the cake. If using a plain nut cake, add a dash of dark rum, hazelnut or walnut liqueur to your coffee — the perfect complement to the flavour of freshly roasted beans.'

As for the caramel icing, try melting 60g butter with ½ cup brown sugar, stirring for a couple of minutes over heat before stirring in 2 tablespoons of milk and 1½ cups of icing sugar. Take off the heat while stirring in the icing sugar, you don't want it to get too dry. You can also buy ready-made South American caramel, known as dulce de leche or manjar blanco. It's a very rich and rather decadent blend of milk and sugar, a little like that condensed milk caramel some of us made as children. Chileans and Argentinians use it like we use butter or cream — as a cake filling, on toast, in profiteroles and even in sandwiches. Mixed into whipped cream it makes a perfect caramel cream frosting. Very naughty.

beaten eggs and mix well with hands, letting air through mixture. Cover with a tea towel and set aside in a warm place until the dough doubles in size — about an hour.

■ Add salt, sugar and butter and work through again with your hands, letting air into the mixture. Place mixture in greased 20cm ring tin. Let mixture double in size again then place in hot 200°C oven for 10 minutes. Lower heat to 180°C and bake for a further 30 minutes.

To prepare syrup:

■ Bring water to the boil in a large saucepan and add sugar, stirring continually. When at full boil, add Galliano. Let syrup cool and pour over cake.

■ Tip: Cake should be eaten within 48 hours. You may wish to glaze cake with a couple of tablespoons of warmed apricot jam brushed over the top while still warm. Whipped cream in the centre of the cake is another serving suggestion.

Black Bun

This rich fruit cake used to be eaten on Twelfth Night, but nowadays, according to Scots-born Mairi McIntosh, it is more commonly served at Hogmanay (New Year's Eve). It should be made several weeks in advance, like a Christmas cake, so it can mature.

Serves a hungry family (8–10)
Casing:
125g butter
250g plain flour
½ teaspoon baking powder
1 beaten egg for finishing

Filling:
1kg seedless raisins
1.5kg currants
250g chopped almonds
350g plain flour
250g sugar
2 teaspoons allspice
1 teaspoon ground ginger
1 teaspoon ground cinnamon
½ teaspoon black pepper
1 level teaspoon cream of tartar
1 level teaspoon baking powder
1 tablespoon brandy
150ml milk

To prepare casing:

■ Rub the butter into the flour, add baking powder and mix to a stiff paste with water (about 4 tablespoons). Place on a floured board, and roll out to a thin sheet. Grease a large tin — traditional shape is rectangular (roughly 20cm x 10cm x 8cm) — and line with the pastry, keeping back enough for the lid.

To prepare filling:

■ Mix all the ingredients together except the milk, then add just enough milk to moisten the mixture. Place into pastry casing and smooth top. Cover with the remaining rolled pastry, dampening the edges to make it stick. Prick pastry all over with a fork and with a thin skewer make four holes right down to the bottom of the cake. Brush with beaten egg and cook in a slow 120°C oven for 3 hours.

■ Black Bun will keep in an airtight container for up to twelve months.

Kugelhopf

It's very hard to get anyone to part with their kugelhopf recipe. For some reason it is one of those cakes that is a measure of personal achievement and skill and no-one seems willing to let anyone else in on the secret. In fact, one friend who wheedled the recipe from her mother swears she has not been told the whole story — that some vital ingredient is missing from the version given her — as it never quite turns out as well as mum's.

One of the best we have ever tried comes from the Monarch Cake Shop in Acland Street, St Kilda (Melbourne's legendary coffee shop strip). Unfortunately that recipe is off-limits! Owner Judy Chaberman declined most graciously to contribute it to this book. Thank goodness for Daniela Thorsch and this recipe from her Czech-born mother Mimi!

250g butter
2 cups sugar
4 eggs
4 cups self-raising flour
1½ cups milk
1 teaspoon vanilla essence
125g melted cooking chocolate

■ Cream butter and sugar. Add eggs and continue beating.
■ Add self-raising flour then the milk with the vanilla essence. Mix together well. To a quarter of the mixture add the melted cooking chocolate.
■ Pour half the plain mixture into a buttered Kugelhopf (ring mould) tin, then the chocolate mixture, then the remaining plain mixture. Run a knife through the mix once or twice to create a swirling effect.
■ Cook 1 hour in a 180°C oven.

Welsh Griddle Cakes

An afternoon tea treat from Welsh-born broadcaster Alice Rees. In Alice's days at SBS Radio in Sydney, she would often bring in a batch of griddle cakes to feed her starving colleagues. A great recipe for kids and best eaten while still warm.

Makes about 24
250g margarine
500g self-raising flour
200g sugar
250g currants
3 eggs
a little milk

■ Rub the margarine into the flour until the mixture resembles breadcrumbs. Add the sugar and currants and mix. Make a well in the middle of the mix and drop in the eggs. Mix them in, with a little milk if necessary, to form a stiff dough. Roll out dough to a thickness of about 1cm, cut into rounds with a glass. Brown on a griddle plate (Alice Rees suggests an electric frypan set at about 150°C). They should brown fast and furiously.

Peter Ipper's Strudel

Apple strudel is often considered an Austrian or Hungarian specialty, but it is also well-known as a Jewish dish — especially in Eastern Europe. Whatever its origin, it's definitely recommended by Peter Ipper, a seasoned broadcaster and journalist originally from Hungary. He has a family of cake lovers so we can definitely trust his recipe. A little warning though: strudel dough takes practice and patience. Your first few tries may not be successful 'but try again', Peter says, 'it's worth it!'.

Makes about 10 slices

3 cups plain flour, sifted

¼ teaspoon salt

2 eggs

¼ cup salad oil

¼ cup lukewarm water

Filling:

4 cups chopped apple

2 tablespoons grated lemon rind

2 tablespoons lemon juice

1 cup seedless raisins

1 cup fine breadcrumbs

1½ cups ground nuts

½ cup sugar

2 teaspoons cinnamon

■ Sift the flour and salt into a bowl. Make a well in the centre and drop the eggs, oil and water into it. Work into flour, mixing until the dough leaves the sides of the bowl. Knead the dough for 10 minutes or until very smooth and elastic. Place a warm bowl over it and leave it to rest for 20 minutes.

■ In the meantime, mix the apples, lemon rind, lemon juice and raisins together.

■ For the next step you will need a large working surface, preferably one you can walk around! A kitchen table is best. Cover it with a cloth and sprinkle with flour. Roll out the dough as thin as you can. Now you must begin stretching it. Flour the knuckles of your hands and gently pull the dough toward you from underneath, using the back of your hands. Change your position as the dough stretches so as not to put too much strain on any one part. Stretch until the dough is

transparent, then brush with oil or melted butter. Cut away any thick edges.

■ Spread breadcrumbs over half the oiled, stretched dough. Sprinkle nuts over it and spread evenly with your hand. Spread the apple mixture over the top, sprinkle with the sugar mixed with the cinnamon. When the filling covers half the dough, raise the cloth and roll up the strudel from the filled side, guiding it with the other hand. Place on a heavily greased baking pan. Brush with oil or melted butter. Bake at 200°C for 35 minutes or until browned and crisp. Cut into 4–5cm slices immediately. If you like a smaller strudel, divide dough in two before rolling and make two.

Schnecken (Czech Snails)

Daniela Thorsch remembers many home-baked aromas from her youth – her mother Mimi came to Australia from Czechoslovakia in the late 1940s. 'I loved it when she'd cook schnecken,' Daniela remembers, 'The whole kitchen would be warm and full of the smells of yeast and then these lovely little baked "snails" would appear.'

Makes 30

50g block yeast

½ cup milk

¼ cup castor sugar

500g plain flour

200g unsalted butter

1 egg, beaten

cinnamon, sugar, melted butter, sultanas mixed together

or melted cooking chocolate and sultanas mixed together

lemon juice for glaze

1 teaspoon lemon peel

icing sugar

■ Prepare yeast by crumbling it and adding to the warm milk with 1 tablespoon of castor sugar. Sprinkle a little flour on top and set aside in a warm place. Melt butter and into it stir remaining castor sugar. Put warm plain flour into the middle of a big bowl. Make a well in the flour and add butter mixture. Stir well and add yeast mixture. Add the beaten egg and enough milk to make a smooth dough, stirring with a wooden spoon.

■ Put mixture in a warm place and let it rise until it has doubled in size, about 1 hour.

■ Later roll the dough out with a rolling pin.

■ Sprinkle with either mixture of cinnamon, sugar, butter and sultanas or cooking chocolate and sultanas. Roll it up like a strudel and cut into pieces to make the schnecken.

■ Place on well-buttered tray and bake in hot 220°C oven until golden (about 40 minutes).

■ While still hot, glaze the schnecken with lemon juice and peel mixed with icing sugar. Serve cool.

The CWA women, Mrs Joy Press, Mrs Anne Oates and Mrs Joyce Pascoe

CWA Lamingtons

The CWA is, of course, the Country Women's Association — one of the great bastions of Australian country life, its members so adept in the kitchen, they've put out a best-selling cookbook full of tried and true recipes. Lamingtons are perhaps the definitive Australian cake, possibly developed as a means to use up stale cake. Mrs Joyce Pascoe's recipe is legendary across the central western area of New South Wales amongst the local country women gathering for afternoon tea and the shearers stopping for a 'smoko' on her husband's 400 hectare property 'Loloma'. She's thrown away the heavy buttercake recipe that's normally the basis for lamingtons and opted for a much lighter sponge. Lamingtons freeze beautifully.

Makes 12 lamingtons

3 eggs
4 tablespoons castor sugar
½ teaspoon vanilla essence
125g Fielders cornflour (wheaten cornflour)
1 teaspoon baking powder
125g butter

Coating:

200g icing sugar
1 tablespoon cocoa
1 teaspoon butter
½ teaspoon vanilla essence
boiling water
fresh dessiccated coconut

■ Beat eggs until frothy — this recipe is much easier if you use an electric mixer. Add the sugar slowly, continuing to beat the mixture. Add vanilla essence.

■ Sift flour and baking powder three times. Add to egg mixture then add the butter which has been melted and just brought to the boil.
■ Pour the mixture into a greased, lined lamington tray (27cm x 20cm). Bake in a moderate 180°C oven for 20 to 25 minutes.
■ Turn out and cool on a wire rack.

Coating:

■ Combine icing sugar, cocoa and butter in an enamel bowl, adding a little boiling water to make mixture runny. Stand over bowl of boiling water to keep icing mixture liquid. Cut cake into 5cm squares, skewer each with a fork and with a knife coat with icing mixture. Roll in coconut, coating evenly. Sit on waxed paper to dry. Serve on large platters on paper doilies.
■ Tip: A tea towel over the rack stops marking. Also put cooled cake into freezer for 10 to 15 minutes before cutting — it makes slicing so much easier.

David Mar's Coconut and Lime Cake

'A fairly common marriage of flavours,' says Chinese-Australian and multiculinary food lover David Mar, who loves being creative in the kitchen. So he invented this divine cake and hasn't stopped having to give out the recipe ever since. We joined the queue.

Serves 6

125g unsalted butter
½ cup castor sugar
2 egg yolks
zest and juice of 1 lime
¼ cup plain flour, sifted
¼ cup coconut macaroons, crushed with a rolling pin
2 eggwhites
icing sugar for dusting

David Mar

■ Cream butter and sugar until white and fluffy. Add the egg yolks, one at a time. Add the lime zest, then the flour and the crushed macaroons. Beat the eggwhites to stiff peaks, add about a third to the mixture to soften it, then fold in the remainder.
Butter and flour a 20cm round cake tin. Preheat oven to 190°C.
■ Spread mixture in cake tin evenly, taking care as it's now quite thick. Bake for 30 minutes or until a skewer comes out of the cake clean. Tip out upside down onto a plate. Pour the lime juice over the upside-down cake and allow to soak through.
■ Turn the cake right-side up onto another plate and dust with icing sugar. This is excellent served with vanilla bean ice-cream.

Macadamias (the 'boomerang' nut)

The round, crunchy, pale honey-coloured macadamia nut is Australia's most widely known 'bush food' but its history in this country has evolved more by accident than design.

Before white settlement, Aborigines would congregate on the eastern slopes of the Great Dividing Range to feast on the seeds of an evergreen tree which they called 'kindal kindal'.

Later, macadamias were discovered by the 'white fellas' in the early 1800s but weren't seriously cultivated until much later in the century. Visiting American horticulturalists saw the potential of our native nut and took many seeds to Hawaii where they really built up the industry.

Finally in the 1960s, Australia came to appreciate that we'd missed a significant opportunity and started importing trees grafted from successful Hawaiian varieties. They were planted in the rolling hills of north-eastern New South Wales and south-eastern Queensland and a new industry was born.

The nuts are marvellous in salads, cakes and slices; fabulous dipped in chocolate and when crushed make a lovely crunchy coating for pan-fried fish.

Dianne Kailis's Grecian Fig Cake

From the West Australian fishing dynasty, the Kailis family, comes this luscious cake. Its creator, Dianne, is a Kailis by marriage — also of Greek heritage like her husband Theo, who runs the Kailis Bros. seafood business (with his brothers, as the name suggests!) In the recently published 'Kailis Cookbook', a private collection of recipes from three generations of the now very extended family, Dianne's recipes feature prominently. Her fig cake is moist and rich in dried fruit and spices.

Serves 10

½ cup butter

1 cup sugar

2 eggs

1½ cups sifted plain flour

1 teaspoon baking powder

1 teaspoon salt

½ teaspoon ground cinnamon

½ teaspoon ground cloves

½ teaspoon baking soda

½ cup milk

500g diced dried figs, stewed in water

½ cup liquid from stewed figs

1 teaspoon vanilla

½ cup chopped walnuts

½ cup raisins

icing sugar to serve

■ Cream butter and sugar until light and fluffy. Beat in eggs.

■ Sift together dry ingredients and add to egg mix along with the milk and liquid from figs.

■ Add the figs, vanilla, walnuts and raisins.

■ Bake in a preheated 190°C oven for 1 hour in your favourite shaped tin. Allow to cool and sprinkle with icing sugar to serve.

Irish Whiskey Cake

This recipe comes from our Irish friend Rita Fenelon who, with husband Bill, runs Sydney's home away from home for Celts — Emerald Meats in Sydney's beachside suburb, Harbord. Rita, who spends most of her days in the shop, knows how to relax in the little time she has off — and wouldn't be caught dead spending hours in the kitchen. The only time-consuming thing about this cake is soaking the rind and sultanas for several hours, so factor that in to your preparations.

Serves 8

rind from 1 orange or lemon

2 tablespoons Irish whiskey

1¼ cups sultanas

¾ cup butter

¾ cup sugar

3 eggs

2½ cups plain flour, sifted

¾ teaspoon baking powder

pinch of salt

■ Peel the rind from orange or lemon using a sharp knife and soak in whiskey for a few hours to draw out the flavour.

■ Remove the rind and put the sultanas in whiskey to soak for as long as possible.

■ Cream the butter and sugar and add the eggs, one at a time with a teaspoonful of flour and beat well. Sift remaining flour, baking powder and salt and fold into egg mixture. Then fold in sultanas and whiskey and pour into a greased 18cm cake tin, lined with baking paper. Bake at 180°C for 1¼ to 1½ hours. Reduce heat by about half towards end of baking time, say the final 30 minutes.

Cakeland Street

The beachside suburb of St Kilda in Melbourne's south-east has long been the heart of cafe society — cosmopolitan, artistic and bohemian. It's also the home of cakes. Acland Street. Seriously. Although stories of its origins differ from bakery to bakery (there are about eight of them lined up next to one another, each trying to outdo the other in variety, colour, lusciousness and sometimes downright eccentricity).

One version of Cakeland Street's history comes from the son of pastrycook Peter Siapantas. As his son Leon tells us, Peter arrived in Australia in 1955 from Istanbul (he was of Greek origin but trained in Turkey as a pastry chef during the Second World War). During the war years many European food specialists had moved south to Istanbul and their styles and culinary origins created something of a melting pot — even in the cake and pastry baking industry. So it was quite normal for Peter Siapantas to make anything from Greek baklava to sacher torte or French fruit flan. In 1958 he opened his own shop on Acland Street. Almost 40 years later

Peter still owns a shop on the strip, part of which has since become a sightseeing attraction thanks to the gradual arrival of other masters of cakery. ('But Dad started it all,' says Peter's son Leon). Known as Le Bon, the family's shop at no. 93 sits in a row of pastry palaces lining one side of the street — window upon window of decadence.

Israeli Poppyseed Cake

A marvellous seed cake that stores well for up to a week. This recipe is from the Schenker Family Cookbook (see pp. 210–11) and is labelled simply: 'From Yael in Israel'.

Serves 8
150g butter
½ cup sugar
4 egg yolks
½ cup self-raising flour
1 heaped teaspoon baking powder
grated zest of 1 lemon
½ cup brandy
½ cup milk
150g ground poppy seed
4 eggwhites
½ cup sugar

■ Cream the butter and sugar well, then add the egg yolks and continue to beat. Sift the flour and baking powder together and add to mixture along with lemon zest, brandy, milk and poppy seeds. Stir well.
■ In a separate bowl, beat the eggwhites until stiff, gradually adding the sugar. Fold into cake mixture. Bake in well-greased and floured loaf or sandwich tin at 190°C until top is golden brown and springs back lightly when pressed with a finger (roughly 30 to 40 minutes, depending on the size of the tin you use).

Jan's Macadamia and Date Roll

A delicious, easy recipe that is a little slice of old Australia — the call for baked beans tins is rather unusual but they are the perfect size. And, as you make 5 small rolls, you're able to eat one or two and freeze the remainder for later. This recipe is from Jan Fuller, who was born and raised in Alstonville on the NSW north coast and who works in the Macadamia Magic Tourist Centre, cooking beautiful recipes using Australia's native nut.

Serves 8–10
2 cups All-Bran
2 cups milk
1 tablespoon golden syrup
1 cup sugar
1 cup chopped dates
2 teaspoons bicarbonate of soda
½ cup chopped macadamia nuts
2 cups plain flour

■ Soak the All-Bran in milk for 1½ hours. Add golden syrup, sugar, chopped dates, soda and macadamia nuts. Add flour and mix well.
■ Grease 5 baked beans tins or those of equivalent size (425 grams each). Spoon mixture equally into tins, cover with foil and hold in place with rubber bands. Place in a saucepan one-third full of hot water and simmer for 1½ hours. Remove from tins immediately and cool.
■ Note: You can also add/substitute other kinds of mixed fruit. A mashed banana in the mix makes the rolls even more moist.

Mitzi's Chocolate Cake

A special recipe from the Schenker Family Cookbook (see pp. 210–11). It was hard to choose from the extensive section covering chocolate but this recipe is a tried and true family favourite from grandmother Mitzi.

Serves 6

180g butter, softened

180g sugar

4 egg yolks

125g chocolate, melted

125g self-raising flour, sifted

4 eggwhites, beaten stiff

dash vanilla essence

Glaze:

125g cooking chocolate

60g (or less) unsalted butter

■ Cream the butter and sugar. Add the egg yolks and then stir in the melted chocolate, then the flour. Fold in the stiffly beaten egg-whites and add a few drops of vanilla essence. Bake in a 23cm cake tin at 180°C for about 1 hour. When shrinks from sides and has a golden top, it's done. Turn onto a wire cooling rack and when cold, cover with warm glaze.

Glaze:

■ Melt the chocolate together with the butter and cool. When barely warm, use to cover the cake. Leave to set before serving.

Nili Palti's Matzo Cake

A delicious chocolate layer cake with a difference. This is very popular to make around Pesach or Passover and calls for matzo and potato flour. This recipe was passed on to Nili Palti (wife of our Melbourne-based broadcaster colleague, Uri) by her mother, Mrs Shoshana Ben Dov.

Serves 6

½ litre milk

125g margarine

¾ cup sugar

2 tablespoons potato flour

2 heaped teaspoons cocoa

½ teaspoon instant coffee

½ teaspoon vanilla essence

6–7 sheets matzo (available Jewish grocery stores)

hundreds and thousands or chocolate sprinkles

■ Warm, but do not boil, the milk, margarine and sugar in a medium-sized saucepan. Mix the potato flour, cocoa, coffee, vanilla essence and half a glass of water in a bowl and then add to mixture in the saucepan. Bring to the boil and remove from heat. (This makes cream mixture for the next step.)

■ Cover each piece of matzo with the cream mixture, one sheet on top of the other, ending with cream, and then cover all the sides with the remaining mixture. Decorate with hundreds and thousands or chocolate sprinkles as you wish and refrigerate (easier to cut after one day in the fridge).

Happy Pesach!

Acland Street Chocolate Brandy Cake

Amid the fruit flans, giant tortes and brightly coloured novelty confections at no. 93 Acland Street in Melbourne's St Kilda, you'll spot this very decadent pure chocolate and brandy cake. The recipe comes to us courtesy of pastrycooks Peter Siapantas and his proud son Leon. 'We've had it forever,' says Leon.

Serves 8

50g dark chocolate

50g butter

6 eggs

Peter Siapantas

Melt the chocolate over boiling water then stir into a mix of milk, butter and brandy. Allow to cool. Slice the cake across into three pieces and soak each section in the chocolate and brandy mix. Set the slices on top of each other, sprinkle with sugar syrup. Allow to set in the fridge. You can decorate the cake if you wish with icing or fill with cream, or simply dust the top with chocolate sprinkles.

¾ cup icing sugar
¼ cup water
1 cup plain flour
¾ cup self-raising flour

Filling:
250g dark bitter chocolate
1 cup boiled milk
60g butter
60ml brandy (or whiskey or rum if you prefer)
sugar syrup (sugar boiled in water)

Preheat the oven to 190°C and grease and line a deep 20cm round pan. Melt the chocolate and butter in a Pyrex dish over boiling water. Beat the eggs with the icing sugar and water until light and fluffy. Stir in gently the sifted flour. Pour in the melted chocolate and butter mix. Stir and pour into baking pan. Bake for about 20 minutes or until the cake springs back to the touch. Turn out and allow to cool.

Conversions

The recipes in this book use the Australian measures.

Oven temperatures

	Fahrenheit	Celsius
Very slow	250°F	120°C
Slow	275–300°F	140-150°C
Moderately slow	325°F	160°C
Moderate	350°F	180°C
Moderately hot	375°F	190°C
Hot	400–450°F	200–230°C
Very hot	475–500°F	250–260°C

Mass (Weight)

Imperial	Metric
½oz	15g
1oz	30g
2oz	60g
3oz	90g
4oz	125g
5oz	155g
6oz	180g
7oz	220g
8oz	250g
9oz	280g
10oz	315g
11oz	345g
12oz (¾lb)	375g
13oz	410g
14oz	440g
15oz	470g
16oz	750g
24oz (1½lb)	750g
32oz (2lb)	1000g
3lb	1500g

Liquid

Imperial	Cup	Metric
5floz (¼ pint)	⅔ cup	150ml
6floz	¾ cup	200ml
8floz	1 cup	250ml
10floz (½ pint)	1¼ cups	300ml
12floz	1½ cups	375ml
14floz	1¾ cups	425ml
16floz	2 cups	500ml
20floz (1 pint)	2½ cups	600ml

Standards

Cup	Spoon
¼ cup = 60ml	¼ teaspoon = 1.25ml
⅓ cup = 80ml	½ teaspoon = 2.5ml
½ cup = 125ml	1 teaspoon = 5ml
1 cup = 250ml	1 tablespoon = 20ml

Different countries use different tablespoon sizes
In Australia: 1 tablespoon = 20ml or 4 teaspoons
In New Zealand: 1 tablespoon = 15ml or 3 teaspoons
In the United Kingdom and the United States:
1 tablespoon = 15ml or 3 teaspoons

Index

D

Dany chouet's cleopatra cassoulet 85–6
date confection 208
date crispies 207–8
date macaroons 207
dates in Alice Springs 207–8
David Mar's coconut and lime cake 223
David and Rosie's eggier than egg mayonnaise 143
David White's seafood salad 111–12
DESSERTS 191–211
    baked crumble cheesecake 197–8
    Barbara's kasha 194
    bartolillo's (spanish custard puffs) 192
    falooda (iranian frozen noodles) 196
    Icelandic ice-cream 196
    Iranian rosewater ice-cream 196–7
    malakoff 194, 196
    mango lassi 200
    Moshe's blintzes 193
    Mrs Anne Oates's pavlova 198
    ovocne knedliky (strawberry or other fruit dumplings) 192–3
    sticky rice and Thai custard 200
    sweet potato pecan pie 198–9
    Victor's pudina tal-hobz (Maltese bread pudding) 199–200
dhal, David's 161
Dianne Kailis's Grecian fig cake 225
dip
    baba ghannouj (eggplant) 3–4
    black bean and roasted garlic 5–6
    cheese 6–7
    eggplant and mint 4–5
    eggplant and peanut 8
    fish roe 7–8
    garlic and potato 6
    lebanese fresh cheese 7
    Persian yoghurt and cucumber 4
    pumpkin and sesame 8–9
    Turkish carrot 3
    yoghurt and cucumber 4, 5
duck soup, Thai 25–6
dumplings
    cloutie 215
    fruit 192–3
    Indian cottage cheese (malai kofta) 168–9
    pierogi (Polish ravioli) 130
    Ukrainian (varenyky) 132

E

Edytta's israeli cholent 65, 67
egg fettuccine, tomato and basil sauce for 139
eggplant
    dip (baba ghannouj) 3–4
    and mint dip 4–5
    and peanut dip 8
    marinated 9
EGGS 29–35
    beid hamine (Moroccan-style eggs) 30
    Elizabeth's tilsit 34
    huevos motulenos (Rattlesnake eggs) 33–4
    Hungarian scrambled 31
    kai yang nam pla wan (eggs with sweet fish sauce) 30
    Katrina Karon's jajka z pieczarkami (Polish stuffed eggs) 33
    potato and scrambled 31
    preserved 35
    shakshooka (Israeli eggs) 31–2
    Victoria's frittata 32–3
eight treasures chicken 59–61
Elizabeth Marchand's cheese dip 6–7
Elizabeth's quiche lorraine 43–4
Elizabeth's tilsit eggs 34
emu fillet with yoghurt 90

J

Jan's macadamia and date roll 227
Jansson's frestelse (Swedish potoatoes) 166
Japanese wakame salad 147–8
Jewish stuffed chicken legs 55–6
Joanna's pizza dough 45

K

kai yang nam pla wan (eggs with sweet fish
    sauce) 30
Kailis fillets in herb and vinegar sauce 99
Kailis fish marinade 190
Kailis whole fish 113
kangaroo à la Ghan with a bush tomato
    barquette and kumara wedges 88–9
kangaroo fillets with beetroot puree 89–90
Katrina Karon's jajka z pieczarkami (Polish
    stuffed eggs) 33
kefta/kufta/koefte/keftedes 70
khasi ko tarkari (Nepalese goat curry) 78
khoreshe ghormeh sabzi (tangy Persian lamb) 76
kimchi 178, 180–1
Kim's baby barramundi and Nonya-style sauce
    112–13
kokoda (marinated fish) 96
kolyva (Greek whole wheat salad) 148–9
Korean barbecue marinade (beef and pork) 190
Korean dipping sauces 173, 175
Korean mung bean pancake 38
kufta 70
kugelhopf 220
Kylie Kwong's steamed whole fish with ginger
    and shallots 114
Kylie's hot and sour szechuan noodles 136–7

L

labneh (Lebanese fresh cheese dip) 7
lakror (Albanian pizza) 45
laksa lemak 16–17
latkes 167
lentils (David's dahl) 161
LAMB AND GOAT 72–8
    abbacchio alla Romana (Roman spring
        lamb) 74–5
    fasule me pasterma (Albanian lamb and
        beans) 75
    Fijian lamb curry 75–6
    khasi ko tarkari (Nepalese goat curry) 78
    khoreshe ghormeh sabzi (tangy Persian
        lamb) 76
    lamb couscous with vegetables 73–4
    Mrs Vatsikopoulos's Greek leg of lamb in the
        oven 73
    racks of lamb in massaman curry 77
    Rita Fenelon's Irish stew 77–8
    Uncle Tony's lamb on the spit 72
lamingtons, CWA 222–3
lassi, mango 200
lechon (Filipino suckling pig) 80
lemon aspen salsa 176–7
lemon consomme 15
lemon pickle, Indian 182–3
lemons, preserved 181–2
lentil soup 24
liqueur, Colleen's Christmas 195
Ludmilla's babka (Russian Easter bread) 214–5

M

macadamias (the 'boomerang' nut) 224
macadamia and date roll, jan's 227
macaroons, Otto's coconut 208
Maeve's chicken marinade 189

venison with swede and sweet potato puree
   served on a red currant jus 93–4
Victoria's frittata 32–3
Victor's pudina tal-hobz (Maltese bread
   pudding) 199–200
Vietnamese pickled vegetables 183
vinaigrette, classic 143
vinaigrette, Susie's raspberry 143–4
Virginia's chicken la-oya (chicken with ginger
   and lemongrass) 51
Vivien's potato salad 150

W

waffles, Wiener 202
wakame salad, Japanese 147–8
walnut paste and chilli 173
water spinach with sambal 157–8
Welsh griddle cakes 220
West African groundnut soup 22–4
wok-fried four seasons beans 154

Y

yoghurt and cucumber dip 4, 5

Z

zap gum lo mai fan (Bea's savoury sticky rice)
   123
zganci (Slovenian buckwheat) 129
zhug (Mediterranean sweet coriander and
   cashew sauce) 177
zucchini soup 24